Australians and Globalisation
The Experience of Two Centuries

Is globalisation new? Are its effects inevitable? Are the concepts of national sovereignty and global markets incompatible? In this provocative book, the authors argue that Australia has always been a 'globalised' country. In terms of its economy, political sovereignty and sense of national identity, Australians have had to create for themselves a complex position between dependence and irrelevance. *Australians and Globalisation* tells how governance and citizenship developed in response to global forces, starting with colonial societies and moving through the federation period and the twentieth century to the present day with the accelerated impact of globalisation.

Brian Galligan is Head of the Department of Political Science at the University of Melbourne and is widely published in Australian politics, federalism and citizenship. He is the author of *A Federal Republic: Australia's Constitutional System of Government* (Cambridge University Press, 1995).

Winsome Roberts is a Research Fellow in the Department of Political Science, University of Melbourne, specialising in politics and civil society.

Gabriella Trifiletti is a lawyer and a graduate of the Centre for Public Policy at the University of Melbourne.

Australians and Globalisation

The Experience of Two Centuries

Brian Galligan

Winsome Roberts

Gabriella Trifiletti

University of Melbourne

CAMBRIDGE
UNIVERSITY PRESS

PUBLISHED BY THE PRESS SYNDICATE OF THE UNIVERSITY OF CAMBRIDGE
The Pitt Building, Trumpington Street, Cambridge, United Kingdom

CAMBRIDGE UNIVERSITY PRESS
The Edinburgh Building, Cambridge CB2 2RU, UK
40 West 20th Street, New York, NY 10011–4211, USA
10 Stamford Road, Oakleigh, VIC 3166, Australia
Ruiz de Alarcón 13, 28014 Madrid, Spain
Dock House, The Waterfront, Cape Town 8001, South Africa

http://www.cambridge.org

First published 2001

Printed in Australia by Ligare Pty Ltd

Typeface Adobe New Aster 9/12 pt.   *System* QuarkXPress® [BC]

A catalogue record for this book is available from the British Library

National Library of Australia Cataloguing in Publication data
Galligan, Brian.
Australians and globalisation: the experience of two centuries.
Bibliography.
Includes index.
ISBN 0 521 81199 6.
ISBN 0 521 01089 6 (pbk.).
1. Globalisation. 2. Australia – Foreign economic relations.
I. Roberts, Winsome. II. Trifiletti, Gabriella.
III. Title.
337.94

ISBN 0 521 81199 6 hardback
ISBN 0 521 01089 6 paperback

Contents

Acknowledgments

This book is the product of four years of research at the Centre for Public Policy and the Department of Political Science at the University of Melbourne. We thank all our colleagues who have contributed to the collegial environment at the university, and all who have been supportive on the home front.

Research for the book was generously funded by the Australian Research Council's Large Grants Scheme during 1997–1999 for the project 'The Impact of Globalisation on Australian Citizenship and Governance'. Needless to say, without it the project could not have gone ahead.

We are also indebted to the team at Cambridge University Press, and in particular Peter Debus, for turning the manuscript into a book, and to Cambridge's readers for their suggestions for improving the manuscript.

Introduction

The Challenge of Globalisation

Globalisation is widely considered to be the major challenge facing nation-states and democratic polities at the beginning of the twenty-first century. Although a much contested concept, globalisation means essentially an intensification of multinational, international and transnational linkages in all spheres of human activity, including trade and commerce, governance and non-government lobbying, as a consequence of new communications technology. As a result some argue that the nation-state is becoming increasingly obsolete as its power to govern domestic affairs is undermined by international forces and supplanted by transnational regulatory regimes. Globalists emphasise that governmental powers are passing upwards from the nation-state to international bodies that set rules and standards for an increasing range of public policy matters. On the other hand, communitarians claim that power is moving downwards through locally based social movements. The communication technology that is driving globalisation can also facilitate localism. These twin forces of 'glocalisation',[1] although pulling in different directions, are said to be eroding the sovereignty of the nation-state. Those who believe that the nation-state is the foundation of modern democratic governance view this process as detrimental, while others argue that cosmopolitan citizenship is enhanced by globalism. Those who favour greater citizenship participation may also see advantages in glocalisation.

Many Australians are anxious about the impact of globalisation on the nation's relatively small economy that is dependent on international trade and investment. This concern is heightened because Australia cannot readily join a congenial regional association of states such as the European Union as Britain has done, or the North American Free Trade Association as Canada has done. Despite increased orientation towards Asia since the Second World War, Australia remains apart in its cultural and social institutions that derive mainly from British settlement and are more akin to Europe's and America's. Australia's exposure and relative isolation heighten anxieties about globalisation that have been exacerbated by the deliberate exposure of our economy to global market forces. Australia's 'protective state' (Capling & Galligan 1992) that was established following Federation has been rolled back and the national economy opened up to competition from world markets. The 'settled policies' of Australian political economy, tariff protection for manufacturing industries, wage fixing to ensure a basic wage and reasonable work conditions, and state provision of infrastructure, have been demolished or curtailed. Australia's people and industries have been exposed to the buffeting, as well as the opportunities, of world markets, as they were in the colonial era of the nineteenth century. As a consequence of our exposure and the intensification of global forces, globalisation has become something of a fearful bogey.

Add to this current uncertainty about Australian identity and citizenship and we have a troubled nation. Economic deregulation has occurred in advance of renewal in Australian civic culture and articulation of Australian citizenship. Old certainties about national identity have been eroding without a new consensus emerging. Questions and contestations dominate contemporary civic discourse. Who are we as Australians and how do we fit into the Asia-Pacific region? Is multiculturalism appropriate and does it capture our strong Anglo-Irish heritage? How do indigenous Australians fit into the identity mosaic of modern nationhood and why were they dispossessed and excluded for so long?

What happens to democratic rule when egalitarianism is being eroded by structural inequality? When did we become an independent sovereign nation? Or do we still need to break the last ties of formal monarchism and republicanise the head of state in order to be truly independent? Can we cope as a nation-state with strong forces of globalisation that are undermining national sovereignty? Our national mood at the beginning of the twenty-first century is tinged with anxiety, confusion and lack of confidence. This is evident in populist movements like Pauline Hanson's One Nation party that has tapped grass roots disaffection in depressed areas of rural, regional and urban Australia. It is also reflected in leading public documents such as the Australian Citizenship Council's report on *Australian Citizenship for a New Century* that found 'no particular answer' to the question of what was distinctive about Australian political life (Australian Citizenship Council 2000, p. 6).

Current anxieties about globalisation and national identity are in sharp contrast to the confidence and political creativity of Australians a century earlier. Secure within the British Empire that was the dominant global organisation of the day, Australians then constituted a new nation-state to enhance their collective identity within the world and expand domestic governance in a way that would preserve what was seen as a distinctive way of life. Federation was a significant feat of political architecture that enabled nation building through subsequent legislation and public policy making. It created a new national citizenship that extended the colonial citizenships already enjoyed in self-governing colonies, while at the same time retaining the political identity of British subjects. At federation, Australians fashioned a nation-state that expanded self-government but they did so within a global empire which, on balance, they were proud to remain part of. The nation-state was a vital instrument for mediating global forces in order to build a White Australia with a protected national economy, while at the same time remaining within Britain's protective global umbrella of diplomacy, defence and culture.

One hundred years on, Australia has moved beyond the close ties with Britain and the cultural traditions of White Australia, but without properly articulating its national identity and citizenship. Some have found this in multiculturalism and diversity, assuming that this is sufficient to ground national cohesion and a stable democratic process. Such a view, however, misses the deeper foundations of political unity upon which Australian citizenship is based. Despite cultural and ethnic differences, Australians do share membership of a particular federal system of government whose polities provide institutions and laws that govern individual behaviour and collective decision making. Australian citizenship is particular and distinct, blending political principles and values that are more universal with distinctive Australian features of territory, heritage, society and culture. It is a citizenship with a history that spans two centuries. The national polity that dates from the turn of the twentieth century has a distinctive political history in a changing world and the state polities each have a political heritage that dates back to nineteenth-century colonial self-government and British heritage.

Modern multiculturalism is an excellent cultural policy for giving special assistance to migrants from non-English-speaking backgrounds and facilitating their gradual integration into mainstream Australian life. It has also helped to enrich and diversify that mainstream, making Australia less of a British cultural clone. Multiculturalism is a product of changed national policies on immigration and support for immigrant groups, combined with a deeper commitment to pluralism and cosmopolitanism. It is a consequence of changed policies that affect the composition of the body of Australian citizens and help underpin greater diversity. Some enthusiasts want to make multiculturalism more substantial and serve as the basis of the Australian polity and citizenship; for them, many cultures are better than one. Such a view, however, overstates the character and significance of Australian multiculturalism. It ignores the unity of Australian political culture and the shared commonalities of its citizenship. It also underestimates the strength of mainstream Australian civil society based upon the English language and a shared understanding of the institutions of civic life and a liberal democratic regime. Thus multiculturalism provides a leavening rather than an explanation of Australian civil society and citizenship.

Citizenship is grounded in political unity rather than diversity, or at least in a unity that underpins or overrides diversity and makes possible dissent within consensus. A tolerant society will allow, even favour, diversity and contested opinions and interests but that is only possible if there is a common commitment to respect and tolerance of differences. A liberal democratic regime opens up a large public space for parliamentary deliberation and extra-parliamentary politics. However, if civic processes are not understood, political unity is jeopardised and Australian citizenship undermined. Our purpose in this book is to explore and articulate how Australian citizenship has been constituted and citizenship practices developed over two centuries. We examine what has underpinned and at times challenged the consensual unity around Australian citizenship, and explore how that unity has been forged and fostered.

Citizenship is essentially a political construct and not a cultural or ethnic one. Confusion arises because building a nation-state as a political community has often relied on blurring citizenship with cultural and ethnic factors that are then used to buttress or even define citizenship of a particular state, as in the German and French cases. Similarly, in Australia, citizenship for much of the century was restricted mainly to whites who were preferably of British origin. Nonetheless citizenship itself refers to political institutions and practices – to civil rights, legal rights, social and economic entitlements and associated duties. Of course, citizenship is only one part of a person's total life, or one association among many of which they are a member. But memberships in the political institutions that govern community life offer a stake in determining a way of life. Such rules can substantially affect how people live much of their lives in private, with family and friends, in clubs and churches, and in work places and businesses. At the same time multiple and diverse associations can support political life and citizenship, but they can also provide its challenges and problems. Civil society may reinforce racial and cultural prejudices that narrow public life and restrict citizenship, or reinforce trust and tolerance that expand and broaden them.

This book studies governance and citizenship from the perspective of the global. Its central argument is that Australian governance and citizenship have been continually shaped by or in response to global influences and forces. Globalisation has always been with us but in different forms, and has been significant in explaining why Australian government and citizenship have developed the way they have. At the same time Australian governments have been important mediators, at times and in part blocking and channelling global forces, and at times exploiting opportunities and ameliorating adverse consequences. A global perspective gives a different picture of Australian political history from that assumed in the dominant narrative. The dominant narrative starts in the twentieth century and focuses on the nation-state. It assumes a progressive march from British dominion to sovereign nation, and from British subject to Australian citizen. The past is depicted as an era of immature subservience and dependency, while the present is presented as an age of national sovereign independence. Such an account heightens concerns about the modern inroads of globalisation on sovereign nationhood, while at the same time deepening the confusion about Australian political identity. Our nation seems not to be sovereign and, many fear, is being undermined by globalisation. Our identity is poorly articulated in domestic citizenship policy while uncertainty about who we are hampers our attempts to find a place in the Asia-Pacific region of which we are part.

Fortunately, we can discard aspects of this contemporary account that demean our origins and unsettle our current state of mind. Once we focus on the global, over the longer time frame of two centuries, we can substitute the paradigm of multiple polities for sovereign nation, and the perspective of complex dependency and interdependency for national autonomy, so that the picture changes and some of the anxiety evaporates. While the forces of globalisation have changed radically over two centuries, the policies for mediating and moderating the effect of global forces have changed just as dramatically. Our current exposure is in part a consequence of changed policies that capture certain benefits of globalisation such as economic advantage and aspects of cosmopolitan citizenship. At the same time there are costs such as economic disadvantage to less robust industry sectors and regions, constraints upon domestic governments in leveraging economic forces and increasing structural inequality. Recognising that Australia has never been an autonomous sovereign nation-state, but has always been a collectivity of political communities that have shaped and been influenced by international forces, helps in putting current affairs into perspective. There are benefits as well as costs from globalisation and these can be mediated by governments. For this purpose, having a federal system of government is an advantage because it allows multiple spheres of adjustment and broadens the public space for citizen contributions.

National government in Australia was constituted largely to mediate Australia's position in a changing world. Through selective immigration policies and assisted passages, successive governments have shaped the Australian citizen body by determining who migrates and in what numbers. National and state governments have both contributed to the developing definition of citizenship and been the sites for contestation of political, civil and social rights. Many accounts of Australian citizenship have been both too ambitious and too superficial: too ambitious in wanting to reduce or encapsulate the variety of private lives and civil society into the political categories of citizenship; and too superficial in finding only variety and difference when they do so. The genius of citizenship in our sort of liberal democratic polity is that it does not crowd out variety and difference. Its strength is that it does have a common foundation of concrete political values and is buttressed by a political culture of shared experiences and beliefs. Difference is not sufficient grounding for a stable polity. But in any case the Australian polity and citizenship are not grounded on diversity and difference, as those who confound multicultural policy with citizenship proffer,[2] but on shared political values and a common political culture.

Australians, in making a new nation-state one hundred years ago, did not define themselves wholly in peculiarly Australian attributes or terms. While they talked extensively about the new category of Australian citizenship that they were creating, they defined it in terms of 'British subject' that was not specifically tied to the new nation-state. In adopting a federal constitution in which neither the national nor state governments were sovereign, and retaining membership of the British Empire that underwrote a broader political association for both dominion nation members and individual subjects, Australians put in place a complex citizenship of multiple dimensions. The nation-state they created was not sovereign, nor was their citizenship restricted to it. We should not assume that what they created was deficient; rather that the sovereign nation-state paradigm does not apply.

Approach and Method of Inquiry

While the subject area of the book is extensive, encompassing large topics of globalisation, citizenship and governance, its focus is more specific. It is concerned with the meaning Australian citizenship has had in the lives of its people and how citizenship has been defined and developed by governments in a changing world over two centuries. We are concerned with political, legal and constitutional arrangements, as well as the lived experience of citizenship.

The broad political history of Australia within a global context provides the framework for our analysis and structures the contents of the book. Our main purpose, however, is not so much to provide a narrative of events as to focus on the ways in which political communities in Australia have been shaped by global forces and in turn the ways in which they have also mediated those forces through government policies. In this way we endeavour to ground theoretical concerns about globalisation, governance and citizenship in Australian practice, adding the extended dimension of historical experience to current issues and challenges. History enables a broadening and deepening of political analysis and can provide a corrective to contemporary assumptions and generalisations. The case for such a contextual approach has recently been put by Joseph Carens:

> A contextual approach offers three interrelated advantages. First, it can clarify the meaning of abstract formulations. Secondly, it can provide access to normative insights that may be obscured by theoretical accounts that remain at the level of general principle. Thirdly, it can make us more conscious of the blinkers that constrain our theoretical visions when they are informed only by what is familiar.
> ... [W]e do not really understand what general principles and theoretical formulations mean until we see them interpreted and applied in a variety of specific contexts (Carens 2000, pp. 2–3).

Besides being historical, our study also pays considerable attention to political culture and civil society and the broader context of citizenship and governance. This is appropriate because political institutions exist in this broader landscape of society and political economy that they partly inform and partly reflect. There is a symbiotic relationship between the two: while government rules the political community, it also manifests the collective will of the people who are sovereign. Citizenship is one dimension, albeit the political or ruling one, of a community whose members have multiple dimensions of identity and membership in diverse associations of civil society. Using this wider lens of investigation that encompasses society as well as polity is appropriate because of the nature of the subject. Such an approach enables us to both broaden and refine our analysis in ways suggested by anthropologist Clifford Geertz.

> The politics of a community lie everywhere within it, not just in the institutions, this monarchy or that republic, by which, for the moment, they are more or less focused and somewhat organised. And though they change they do so at the speed the country changes, not that at which leaders, policies, or even regimes do ... it has to be learned if one is to understand what all the shouting is about; what sort of quarrel is going on (Geertz 1995, p. 41).

Australian citizenship is more complex than much contemporary scholarship allows. Examining Australian citizenship over time reveals a layering of memberships in multiple political communities from the imperial through to the local. The focus in contemporary studies has been primarily on citizenship that attaches to the nation-state, but this is by no means the only citizenship that Australians have enjoyed in the past or, for that matter, enjoy today. Multiple membership in global and local political communities has always been important for Australians. A federal system of government, that some have characterised as overgovernment, has allowed greater flexibility of political response. Global communities, whether the British Empire in the past or the various international associations under the United Nations umbrella in recent decades, have provided a reference and standard for national citizenship and something of a corrective against parochialism and xenophobic narrowness. Sub-national communities are also significant sites where citizenship rights and duties are contested and transacted in the day-to-day lives of people. Much of the lived experience of citizenship derives from the personal and the particular and, to reflect this, citizenship ceremonies are conducted in municipal communities. Nonetheless, given the significance attaching to the nation-state, we have organised our study according to the conventional understanding of Australian citizenship as a national institution with legal status and formal rights and duties. We have broadened this considerably in two dimensions: one is historically beginning our account of citizenship in nineteenth-century colonial Australia when Australians had citizenship without a nation-state; the other is by grounding citizenship in the experiences of Australians living in local communities and engaging in the associations of civil society.

The structure of the book reflects our overall method of inquiry. The first chapter outlines the theoretical framework of our study and explains how we use the key concepts of globalisation, sovereignty and citizenship that are central to the study and contested in the literature. Historically, we use three slices, or time frames, to order the sequencing of our analysis of Australian experience. The first is the early period of colonisation through self-government to the formation of Australia as a federal nation in 1901. The second and third time frames are shorter, and cover roughly the two fifty-year periods of the twentieth century. During the second period Australia developed as a federal nation-state, progressively becoming more independent of Great Britain. This period culminated in Australia's having to take a more independent stance and reorient its outlook towards America and the Asia Pacific in international affairs in order to survive the Japanese onslaught in the Second World War. Shortly afterwards in 1949 Australians defined themselves formally as Australian citizens for the first time but remained British subjects as well. The third period encompasses the second half-century of nationhood and the growth of international associations based around the United Nations up to the present time. This period ends with the centenary of nationhood that coincides with anxiety about national identity and coping with globalisation.

Within these time frames we examine how globalisation has affected Australian governance and citizenship, and how government has mediated those effects. Government has the dual role of constituting and advancing the good of the political community by ensuring order within and protection from outside. That entails responsibility for both domestic and international affairs which are linked in important ways. The political state has a primary responsibility for securing the safety and prosperity of persons within its realm, and so enters into transactions with foreign powers and adopts policies to help cushion the impact of world economic forces. The state also regulates domestic affairs and provides for orderly settlement of disputes among its own citizens. This bifurcated foreign and domestic role provides a further means of ordering our study of Australian governance and citizenship across the three time periods. We have pairs of chapters that deal alternatively with the mediation of globalisation by government and the effect on citizenship. Usually citizenship is defined only in terms of domestic issues but it is fundamental to our understanding of citizenship to look at global matters and how they impact on citizens.

Chapters Two and Three cover the period up to the formation of the federal nation-state at the turn of the century. Chapter Two focuses primarily on how Australian political communities were formed through global colonisation and had British-colonial citizenship without a nation-state. Chapter Three examines the political construction of Australia as a federal nation within the British Empire and the creation of a new sphere of national citizenship. Chapters Four and Five focus on Australian government and citizenships during the first fifty years of the twentieth century, up to the jubilee of federation. Chapter Four looks at how the fledgling nation-state attempted to define its place in the world and traces the reorientation of the Australian political community from imperial dominion to Pacific nation. Chapter Five shows how the new Australian citizenship added to, while encapsulating, the established core of colonial and British cultural homogeneity, with the formal title of British subject being appropriately retained. The final two chapters study the development of Australian nationhood and citizenship over the last fifty years. Chapter Six focuses on the new world orders established by international organizations regulating trade, government and civil society of which Australia is an interconnected part. The last chapter shows how citizenship in a global nation has witnessed both a waxing and waning of national identity and cohesion.

To summarise, the book focuses on how institutions of governance have mediated processes of globalisation and especially how this has affected citizenship in Australia over the last two hundred years. It draws on a wide range of primary and secondary sources in constructing and dissecting the nature of globalisation, governance and citizenship in Australia. It assumes that these abstract phenomena are best read and understood as embedded in the particular, concrete and local, and grounded in historical occurrence and development. Political questions are framed and answers sought in Australia's experience from British colonisation at the end of the eighteenth century to glocalisation at the beginning of the twenty-first century.

The book aims to fill a major gap in the literature of Australian politics and citizenship by giving an integrated account of the ways in which Australian governance and citizenship have developed in response to changing influences of globalisation. It is deeply historical and includes the colonial period and the formation of federation. It brings out the variety and complexity of Australian citizenship and the way it is exercised in civil society and in multiple political communities. By moving beyond an examination of the formalities of citizenship, it shows how the rich diversity of associations and groups has shaped political community life. Such a perspective helps correct the view that Australia has moved from an impoverished subjecthood at federation to full citizenship only in recent decades. Government is treated as the active intermediary between global influences and the citizen body, shaping and being shaped by both. Citizenship is understood as part of a collective paradigm rather than as the formalised public persona of atomised individuals. Moreover, citizenship is multi-dimensional with Australians being members of supra-national, national and sub-national polities.

Globalisation, citizenship and governance have all become subjects of extensive study in recent years. Globalisation has received the lion's share of attention, becoming the focus of a growing political economy literature.[3] This is hardly surprising, given Australia's dependence on international trade, investment and technology and its increasingly open domestic economy. Lawyers, too, are taking increasing notice of globalisation because it is affecting Australia's federal constitutional balance and its domestic law regime with the growing international regime of treaties, especially regarding human rights and the environment (Alston and Chiam 1995). Because of the primary concern with current issues in this burgeoning literature and the dearth of historical studies,[4] there is a tendency to assume that globalisation is a novel phenomenon. Our study corrects that by showing how extensively Australia has been a global country since first European settlement, becoming more introverted through the middle decades of high protection during the twentieth century but opening up to global opportunities and challenges in recent decades as it had done in the colonial era.

While citizenship has received less attention than globalisation from Australian scholars, it has also become the subject of increasing academic interest but little consensus. Hudson and Kane present a kaleidoscope of contemporary views about citizenship on the grounds that traditional discourses have been problematised and a 'confusing plurality of different perspectives prevail' (Hudson & Kane 2000, p. 4). While opening up the discourse on citizenship, this proves not to be a fruitful way of articulating Australian citizenship. What is ignored is the fact that citizenship relates to membership of a political community. If this is not recognised, 'no clear consensus emerges about exactly how to rethink Australian citizenship' (Hudson & Kane 2000, p. 3). Even when focused on the political, much of the theorising is ungrounded or selective in the current issues it appeals to, and Australia's citizenship heritage remains largely unexplored (Hudson & Kane 2000, p. 3). An example is Alastair Davidson who uses the formalised paradigm of 'subject to citizen' and various preferred European traditions to present critical views of Australian citizenship and governance (Davidson 1991). Our study is more positive in showing that early Australian citizenship was a robust blend of native Australian and transplanted British civic practice that is belied by the formal term 'subject' that critics have made so much of.

Our book gives an account that grounds the development of Australian citizenship historically in the civic practices and polities of colonial settlement and the founding and development of the nation-state at federation. It continues the historical exposition of Australian citizenship and governance used by Chesterman and Galligan in *Citizens Without Rights: Aborigines and Australian Citizenship* (1997). However, it goes further than the institutional focus of the earlier book and presents more of the political culture and life experiences of ordinary Australians. In so doing, it corrects the misunderstanding that some have mistakenly drawn from *Citizens Without Rights* that 'all this amounts to an Australian tradition of non-citizenship' (Hudson & Kane 2000, p. 3). While that was substantially the case for indigenous Australians for much of our history, it was not the case for others who shared a rich civic and political culture with multiple memberships in civic groups and political associations (some of whom championed the cause of indigenous Australians and other minorities). This book also provides a narrative complement to the documentary book by Chesterman and Galligan, *Defining Australian Citizenship*, from a global perspective.

The book is written for a general as well as a specialist audience. It seeks to respond to the widespread concern about globalisation and the interest in issues of citizenship and national identity because of the centenary and renewed concerns about regional instability on our doorstep. The book gives a sweeping reinterpretation of Australian citizenship and governance showing how both have been formed and developed as a consequence of, and in response to, global forces and challenges from the beginning. This enables us to give a more complete analysis of Australian citizenship that takes account of colonial governance and a more balanced treatment of the challenges of modern globalisation that Australia faces today. Our book puts globalisation in historical perspective and shows how it has always been a major formative force in Australian society, politics and economics. With such knowledge Australians should be more confident in enjoying the opportunities of modern globalisation and meeting its challenges. The federal system has allowed a complex layering of political mediation. While it has been said that Australia is overgoverned, multiple spheres of citizenship have allowed greater flexibility of response. Australia has a rich political heritage that comes from the experience of two centuries of citizenship that should be acknowledged. It is the intention of this book to give a full account of this heritage so that its positive outcomes can be celebrated and the lessons of its darker sides remembered and redressed.

Chapter 1

Globalisation, Sovereignty and Citizenship

Globalisation is widely seen as the great modern force reshaping contemporary politics through undermining the sovereign nation-state and affecting citizenship that is inextricably tied to national sovereignty. Globalisation is partly a perceptual phenomenon that feeds on the tendency of each generation to believe in its own uniqueness in confronting great challenges that it considers unprecedented in history. Yet globalisation is also a powerful force, or set of forces, combining new technologies in information and communication that are transforming the scope and speed of operation of capitalism on a global scale. The impact of globalisation on nation-states is especially significant because it entails global economic forces buffeting national and local societies, straining their political institutions and affecting citizenship practices.

If the world is 'on the edge: living with global capitalism' (as a recent book by Will Hutton and Anthony Giddens puts it), then countries like Australia with economies open to, and dependent upon, world markets must be especially precarious. Those who are most impressed by globalisation – 'gee-whizzers' as Giddens calls this group with whom he identifies – see the modern world as having 'turned on its axis' and 'breaking quite radically with its past' (Hutton & Giddens 2000, pp. x, 3). If that is the case for the world in general then we might expect it would be even more so for Australia's world and hence Australian citizenship and governance. The purpose of this book is to explore how globalisation is impacting upon Australia and whether it is affecting our institutions of citizenship and governance in ways that are radically different from the past. We argue that those who emphasise novelty overstate the case, partly because of a lack of historical perspective that we seek to redress in subsequent chapters.

In order to assess the impact of globalisation on governance and citizenship we need to examine critically the basic concepts of our analysis, all of which are contested. That is the purpose of this chapter. Our challenge is to articulate what citizenship, civil society and the nation-state mean and how these core elements of politics and political society are related to globalisation. Australia provides a marvellous case study for this purpose because it has been shaped by global forces since first European settlement. This historical perspective will help us put modern globalisation into context. The impact of globalisation is heightened if we assume that nation-states like Australia are essentially sovereign and independent. If we do not accept this formalist paradigm, then globalisation is less of a novelty or a threat. How globalisation has impacted upon Australian citizenship and been mediated by Australian governments during a century of nationhood since federation in 1901 and before that during a century of colonial settlement and self-government is the larger subject of the book. What globalisation means and how it relates to state sovereignty and citizenship is the concern of this chapter.

Globalisation

Globalisation is partly a phenomenon, partly an argument and partly a vision. Hence any discussion of globalisation needs to begin with critical examination of its contested meaning and the associated claims made on its behalf. So what does globalisation mean? As Higgott and Reich point out, globalisation 'is rapidly replacing the "Cold War" as the most overused and under-specified explanation for a variety of events in international relations'.[1]

Most would agree that globalisation is a complex phenomenon, or a mix of compounding forces. For example, one of its leading analysts, David Held, defines globalisation as a complex process made up of many facets:

> Globalization is neither a singular condition nor a linear process. Rather, it is best thought of as a multidimensional phenomenon involving diverse domains of activity and interaction, including the economic, political, technological, military, legal, cultural and environmental. Each of these spheres involves different patterns of relations and activity. ... It is important, therefore, to build a theory of globalization from an understanding of what is happening in each one of these areas (Held 1998, pp. 13–14).

Held's description of globalisation as a multi-dimensional phenomenon involving diverse domains of interaction with different patterns of relations and activity highlights the enormity of the challenge of understanding without actually telling us much. Narrowing the task to one country like Australia, as we do in this book, makes that challenge somewhat more manageable.

Besides complexity, heightened intensity of interactions is often given as the defining attribute of globalisation. Anthony Giddens takes this line in focusing on the intensification of global connections between actors as being the core element of globalisation. In his view:

> Globalisation refers essentially to that stretching process in so far as the modes of connection between different social contexts or regions become networked across the earth's surface as a whole.
>
> Globalisation can thus be defined as the intensification of worldwide social relations which link distant localities in such a way that local happenings are shaped by events occurring many miles away and vice versa (Giddens 1990, p. 54).

As with complexity, however, intensification of connections and social relations captures a significant aspect of globalisation but is hardly a defining attribute of modernity. The ancient Roman and early modern European empires were surely global in their day, even though large parts of the world were not affected by them. That is not so different from today when numerous less developed countries and their peoples are outside the web of intensifying inter-relations.

More precisely, the speed of intensification of worldwide social relations is considered to be the distinctive feature of modern globalisation. This is the view of Manuel Castells whose visionary perspective is grounded in the recent explosion of information technology and the consequent rise of what he calls 'network society'. According to Castells, globalisation should be distinguished from other international and world phenomena because of the modern conjuncture of capitalism and technological change that allows global functioning in 'instant time'. As Castells defines it: 'A global economy is something different: it is an economy with the capacity to work as a unit in real time on a planetary scale' (Castells 1996, p. 92). Castells is at pains to distinguish a global economy that he claims is historically quite new from a world economy that has been around for centuries. As the great French historian Fernand Braudel and his American disciple Immanuel Wallerstein have documented, capitalism has operated as a world system since the sixteenth century. Capitalist entrepreneurs ran the banking system on an international scale, financing princes and states, kings and countries, moving enormous sums of money around Europe (Braudel 1981, 1982, 1984).

Production and distribution linked core and peripheral nations in ways that shaped the political economies of both (Wallerstein 1974, 1980). What is new, according to Castells, is that information and communication technologies have transformed world financial markets to enable instantaneous transactions around the globe:

> Toward the end of the second millennium of the Christian Era several events of historical significance have transformed the social landscape of human life. A technological revolution, centred around information technologies, is reshaping, at accelerated pace, the material basis of society. Economies throughout the world have become globally interdependent, introducing a new form of relationship between economy, state, and society, in a system of variable geometry (Castells 1996, p. 1).

Such a prophetic vision was always an exaggeration. If previously there appeared to be no end to the triumphant march of information technology and global capitalism, the Asian economic crisis of mid-1997 put paid to such expectations. Taking stock of this series of unexpected crises in Asian countries, Castells tempered earlier views that 'this networked, global/ informational capitalism, powered by the most extraordinary technological revolution in history, seems to enable its expansion without limits, and without challenges' (Castells 2000, p. 53). According to more sober assessment:

> The naive illusion of a comprehensive, integrated global economy, enacted by capital flows and computer networks, and reaching out to most people in the planet, was shattered on 2 July 1997 as economic crisis struck Asia. At the turn of the millennium, we find instead that most people, and most areas of the world, are suffering from, but not sharing in, the growth of global info-capitalism (Castells 2000, p. 71).

China and India where most people live remain largely autonomous from world capital flows; whereas Indonesia and Russia are only two of the larger nations suffering from its market shocks and economic turmoil. There is also a gathering popular backlash against world economic organisations and the American neo-liberalist agenda that drives them. As a consequence, the fragility of the world system is now manifest, and a 'Great Disconnection' of countries seeking to control their own destinies more probable (Castells 2000, p. 72).

Even for countries with developed economies that are the main beneficiaries, globalisation has become increasingly contentious because of the enormity and differential impact of change that it entails. High technology industries, metropolitan communities and people with knowledge-based skills benefit but traditional industries, unskilled labour and rural and regional communities are marginalised. While cosmopolitan elites and neo-liberal economists extol the virtues of globalisation, noisy opponents are increasingly contesting its homogenising cultural influences, inequitable structural outcomes and adverse environmental effects. Globophiles embrace the extension of neo-liberal principles to global markets, whereas globo-phobes decry the loss of governmental control and inequitable distribution of benefits and costs. World trade and economic forums that celebrate and promote further globalisation of markets, such as those held at Seattle, Melbourne and Davos, have become rallying points for anti-globalisation groups based in affluent countries and organised on a global basis. Global-isation is creating its own dialectic of fragmentation.

Not surprisingly, globalisation has become a dominant theme in Australian public and scholarly discourse.[2] It has also become highly contentious. There is heated argument over the benefits and costs. Some resist the proliferation of global governance institutions, especially the monitoring of treaty obli-gations by United Nations committees. Critics claim that representative parliamentary democracy is being compromised or eroded through excessive treaty making that imposes international obligations and entails surveillance by foreigners. A backlash is evident in the Howard Liberal-National party government's decision to review Australia's involvement in treaty-making processes and UN monitoring committees. The politics of contemporary globalisation in Australia will be examined further in Chapter 7; here we are concerned primarily with its meaning.

Whatever the competing visions, arguments and accounts, the core of globalisation is the spread and intensification of free-market capitalism as a world system based upon advances in information and communication technologies, plus the changing social relations that are a consequence. Whether globalisation is considered novel or not depends upon whether we consider its particular form or generic structure. Certainly the modern form of globalisation based upon information technologies that enable instan-taneous, worldwide transmission of information is novel. So are the changes to world trade that the information revolution is producing and the particular impact upon the political economies of different countries that are a con-sequence. The transformative power of invention and markets, however, is as old as capitalism itself. Technological innovation and expanding markets have always been dynamic determinants of capitalism and identified as such by Adam Smith in *An Inquiry into the Nature and Causes of the Wealth of Nations* (1776). Inventions of cotton spinning and weaving equipment and the steam engine plus the expanding popular market for cheap cotton goods powered the Industrial Revolution. As Smith pointed out, capitalism was not restricted within national boundaries or to economic affairs, either in theory or practice. The wealth of nations owed just as much to specialisation in national production and trade with other countries based upon comparative advantage as it did to technological innovation in the domestic economy. The one reinforced and stimulated the other.

The globalisation of culture and capitalism is not new. From the late eighteenth century the Enlightenment cultivated belief in a New World Order based on reason and scientific inquiry. Numerous scientific expeditions and learned societies branched across the globe in the disciplined search for knowledge of the natural world. The Enlightenment also fostered humaneness in the treatment of other peoples based on belief in the universality of human dignity and the perfectibility of humankind. In the ethnocentric hope that all might become 'civilised' through instruction and demonstration, religious missions took Western Christianity to all corners of the globe to educate the denizens of settler societies and convert indigenous peoples. The globalisation of science and religion accompanied the spread of European imperialism and capitalism. These in turn depended upon new technologies in navigation, transport and communication. European settlement of Australia followed Captain Cook's voyage of discovery that was itself the extension of a scientific expedition. The telegraph and then the telephone shrank the world, helping to surmount the tyranny of distance in places as remote as the Antipodes.

The transformative power and global reach of capitalism have been both celebrated and criticised as attributes of capitalism since the eighteenth century. In his classic text *The Wealth of Nations* (1776), Adam Smith explained how trade among nations enhanced their wealth and powered the economic development of new lands such as the Americas. In the nineteenth century, Karl Marx railed against the powerful forces of capitalist production that were destroying traditional social and political relations and subjecting the great mass of humankind to exploitative and inhuman living conditions regardless of national boundaries. At the turn of the twentieth century, Lenin and other socialists claimed that colonialism was a late stage in the development of capitalism that had exhausted domestic opportunities for extraction of surplus value. In Karl Polanyi's terms, *The Great Transformation* (1944) achieved by capitalism had occurred on a world scale.

If globalisation is the face of world capitalism that transforms the political economy and society of nations and peoples, what is the role of the nation-state? More particularly, is the sovereign independence of nation-states being eroded and compromised by modern globalisation in its current phase of transformation through information and communication technology? As with globalisation itself, the answer is to be found partly from critical reflection on the concept of national state sovereignty and partly from the history of nation-states like Australia.

National Sovereignty

Many proponents and critics alike claim that globalisation is undermining the sovereignty of the nation-state. According to Castells, 'Nation-states will survive, but not their sovereignty' (Castells 1998, p. 355). Many lament the fact that, as Stephen Bell points out, 'the Australian state has lost considerable sovereignty' (Bell 1997, p. 97). The paradigm of national sovereignty is deeply embedded in public discourse as well as being a core component of international law and international relations. The rhetoric of national sovereignty has strong popular appeal and is easily exploited by politicians and popularisers who invoke national sovereignty and independence as fundamental values that are jeopardised by the transfer of powers to international bodies. Besides being the bogey of modern nationalism, globalisation is detrimental to citizenship understood predominantly in terms of membership in the nation-state. To the extent that the nation-state is undermined, national citizenship is diminished. In the next section we argue that citizenship is best understood as membership in multiple political associations, only one of which is the nation-state with others being subnational and transnational. If citizenship entails membership of multiple political associations, the demise of one, albeit the most significant modern one, is less crucial and might well be balanced by growth in the others – both global and local. In this section we show that national sovereignty, especially for countries like Australia, is largely a formal myth even if nation-states remain the most significant actors in domestic and world affairs.

Affirmation of the continuing primacy of the nation-state in modern domestic and world affairs is a corrective to more extreme claims about modern globalisation. Nation-states remain the primary promoters and regulators of global capitalism even if their control is neither sovereign nor complete. State sponsorship and partial control of capitalism on a global as well as a domestic scale are not new. From the late eighteenth to the early twentieth centuries the spread of capitalism worldwide and its domestic consolidation within nations was not inevitable but implemented and fostered through political intervention by the empires and nation-states of the day. Contrary to the claims of liberal economists, *homo economicus* was not natural but the product of market forces that in turn were put in place and sustained by government action and regulation. As Stephen Holmes points out, a major difficulty for establishing a market economy in post-communist Russia is the absence of a strong political regime to establish law and order and legitimise and police the rules of the game (Holmes 1998). Similarly, Linda Weiss argues that the economic regime required for membership in the competitive global economy can only be driven by strong politically motivated nation-states (Weiss 1998).

For better or worse, the nation-state is not as precarious or obsolete as the more fervent champions of globalisation claim. Apart from cyberspace, we are far from a borderless world. The nation-state remains the primary unit of political economy because most economic activity still takes place within the domestic economy (Hirst & Thompson 1996). In addition, the world economy remains 'more international than global' (Wade 1996, p. 61). National governments have been major contributors to the expansion of world financial markets through the myriad of trading, financing and settlement arrangements they have put in place or sanctioned. The global is mainly constructed by nation-states. As Ann Capling shows in her recent book, small countries like Australia can play an important role in working with larger countries to establish a global trading system (Capling 2001). If indeed there is a global system, argues Robert Holton, it is 'not constructed above and outside the reach of nation-states but largely through the needs of nation-states to cooperate with each other to resolve common problems' (Holton 1998, pp. 11–12). Even globophiles like Giddens affirm that globalisation is expanding the role of the nation-state: 'the nation-state is not disappearing, and the scope of government, taken overall, expands rather than diminishes as globalisation proceeds. Some nations, in some situations, have more power than they used to have, rather than less' (Giddens 1998, p. 32). As Frank Castles insists, 'globalisation does not prevent variation in domestic policy-making' (Castles 1996, p. 68).

We should be careful, however, not to overstate the power of the nation-state or its supremacy over either domestic or global capitalism. Nation-states have limited degrees of freedom in regulating capitalism at the domestic level in a neo-liberal environment. They are constrained to provide competitive conditions for investment, production and employment including moderate taxing regimes, competitive labour markets, prudent budgeting and restrained government expenditure. At the global level, control by nation-states is much weaker because there is no overarching governmental structure and agreement among states on regulatory arrangements and enforcement is difficult.

If nation-states are not sovereign today, nor were they in the past. Until relatively recently, nation-states were not the primary actors in world affairs, and nations like Australia made no claim to be sovereign and independent. In the nineteenth century, empires were more important than nation-states. For Australians well into the twentieth century, membership of the British Empire and of regional state polities remained more important than membership of the nation. When founded in 1901, the Australian nation-state was neither sovereign nor independent, remaining a loyal dominion of the British Empire and adopting a federal structure that preserved established self-governing colonies as states. Post-modern globalisation is reminiscent of Australia's past history. Australia's continuing federal structure as a nation is quite compatible with participation in international associations. According to Camilleri and Falk, nation-states will survive in the future but national sovereignty will not. In their words: 'Though the state will continue to perform important administrative and other functions, the theory of sovereignty will seem strangely out of place in a world characterised by shifting allegiances, new forms of identity and overlapping tiers of jurisdiction' (Camilleri & Falk 1992, p. 256). According to our argument, such a future will resemble Australia's past.

While the concept of national sovereignty has played a crucial part in the modern globalisation debate, its meaning is often confused or distorting. Even in Britain where sovereignty talk traditionally dominated parliamentary discourse, sovereignty was always an overstatement and is increasingly becoming a misleading concept. When Britannia ruled much of the world and the Westminster parliament was the supreme locus of British political power, constitutionalists like Dicey embellished this real supremacy with extreme formulations of an absolutist doctrine that neatly fused British politics and law (Dicey 1982, 1885). The sovereignty of the Westminster parliament is still proclaimed as formal doctrine, but in recent decades power has moved downwards to the sub-national region (Scotland, Wales and Northern Ireland) as well as upwards to the European Union. Britain has moved 'Beyond the Sovereign State', as Neal MacCormick has put it (MacCormick 1993).

While national sovereignty has been the key concept in international affairs and international law, its meaning has been ambiguous and confused. In a recent study *Sovereignty: Organized hypocrisy* (1999), Stephen Krasner argues that sovereignty is organised hypocrisy because the sovereignty of nation-states recognised by international law and diplomacy is often ignored and subverted in practice (Krasner 1999). While 'international legal sovereignty' is the recognition of the status and integrity of independent territorial entities, 'Westphalian sovereignty' that entails the exclusion of outside forces from the nation-state depends upon real political strength. While the two might ideally coincide, often they do not. The basic rule of Westphalian sovereignty is non-interference by foreign powers in the domestic affairs of a state, but this is often violated or compromised by intervention or invitation. Consequently, in Krasner's terms, a recognised international legal sovereign will not necessarily be a Westphalian sovereign (Krasner 1999, p. 23). It might be better to restrict the use of sovereignty as a formal term in international law while recognising that nation-states are more or less powerful and independent depending on their relative strength. In other words, sovereignty is a legal fiction.

Post-sovereignty theorists, intent upon showing how the forces of globalisation have eroded the political independence of nation-states, focus critically upon Westphalian sovereignty. They are at pains to point out that such sovereignty does not exist in practice, being infringed and eroded in all sorts of ways. They have joined with others in challenging the 'realist' school of international relations that dominated political science for much of the postwar period. The realists proffered a version of the sovereignty paradigm that assumed nation-states were sovereign and primary actors in international affairs (Goldman 1996, p. 429). A concept that better captures the greater complexity of relations involving democratic nations in an internationalised world economy is 'complex interdependency' (Keohane & Nye 1977). Multiple actors in addition to nation-states are engaged, and multiple goals other than national security, for example economic prosperity, enhanced human well being and mutual benefit, are pursued (Keohane 1996, p. 473).

Complex interdependency is a more appropriate paradigm than sovereign independence for understanding Australia, both as a dominion of the British Empire until the Second World War and subsequently as a more independent nation. Nationhood without sovereignty did not imply weakness and subservience, as F. W. Eggleston affirmed after a professional lifetime of involvement in Australian public and international affairs:

> The view that Australia showed a weak sense of nationhood because she did not adopt a completely independent position is, of course, nonsense. It ignores the factors in her strategic situation ... her isolation and the contraction of the world owing to new invention (Eggleston 1957, p. 4).

Using the paradigms of complex dependency and interdependency allows us to avoid the overblown notions of absolutist power that bedevil much thinking about national states in foreign affairs. Sovereignty statehood is especially misleading in studying Australia's national and international affairs and demeans its early experience as a nation. Those who assume such a paradigm inevitably bias Australia's political history and demean the status of its government. For example, Alan Renouf defines the first objective of Australia's foreign policy as being the preservation of the country from attack and from threat of attack, which is fine, but then identifies that with safeguarding 'Australia's independence as a sovereign state' (Renouf 1979, p. 1). While Renouf admits that Australia might freely decide to surrender part or all of its sovereignty as the European Union member countries have done, he does not recognise that this was in fact the strategy Australia has pursued during much of this century. 'Like a child', according to Renouf, 'Australia has shown a marked inclination to "stay with mother", first Britain and later the US' (Renouf 1979, pp. 14–15). Not surprisingly, using the bogus standard of independent sovereign state, Renouf finds Australia is a 'frightened country' that typically depends on, and shelters behind stronger countries.

Using different conceptual tools like complex dependency we can more accurately depict the Australian experience, especially in the first decades after federation.

Sovereignty affects citizenship as well as nationhood, where citizenship entails primarily membership in the national political community. As we shall see in Chapter 2, citizenship is possible without nationhood. That was the case for Australian colonials before federation when they were members of self-governing colonies and subjects of the British Empire. In modern times when citizenship is defined primarily in terms of membership of the nation-state, it is important not to overstate the significance of that association through claims of sovereignty or exclusivity. If the nation-state is by definition sovereign and citizenship is assumed to be tied exclusively to nationality, the demise of national sovereignty will inevitably jeopardise citizenship. In Australia's case, membership of a nation without sovereignty would mean an inferior type of citizenship. If nation-states do not have to be sovereign, citizenship is not compromised. Moreover, citizenship in non-sovereign polities is compatible with multiple membership in a variety of associations with complex interdependency. Such citizenship practice allows more flexible adjustment to a changing political economy.

Citizenship

Our study is concerned with the way that globalisation, mediated by the nation-state and other spheres of domestic governance, has shaped Australian citizenship. This is complex because citizenship is not uni-dimensional and exclusive to a single national political community, the nation-state, but multi-dimensional. A person can have membership in a number of political communities, one or other of which might be primary but not necessarily sovereign or exclusive. Because citizenship, like globalisation and sovereignty, is a popular but contested concept in political science literature and public discourse, we need to specify its meaning. This is also important for explaining the character of Australian citizenship and how it has developed over two centuries.

According to the Australian Citizenship Council's (ACC) recent Report, *Australian Citizenship for a New Century* (2000), Australian citizenship is poorly understood and largely taken for granted (Australian Citizenship Council 2000). These conclusions are sobering ones for a country that celebrated fifty years of Australian citizenship in 1999 (Rubenstein 2000) and its centenary of nationhood in 2001. They are also deeply puzzling. How can such a stable and robust constitutional democracy get by without the core political institution of citizenship being well understood and highly prized by Australians? How did we manage in the past? And how well equipped are we for a new century and millennium when the traditional institutions of nation-state and national citizenship are challenged by forces of globalisation? These large questions are addressed throughout the book, but first it should be helpful to clarify the concerns raised by the Australian Citizenship Council whose approach and findings are representative of widely held Australian views. Our book shows that Australia does have a robust and complex citizenship heritage that has developed over two centuries, but this has been poorly articulated both in critical scholarship and official discourse.

The Australian Citizenship Council claims that uncertainty and apathy are rife in current citizenship practice, that there is no unifying national symbol of citizenship, and that Australians are uncertain about what they hold in common. Unlike Americans who are said to celebrate their national virtues and venerate their political institutions, Australians are said to have 'an almost complete lack of interest in looking for the distinctiveness and the comparative success of the civic institutions that frame their citizenship'. This results in 'a strange situation in which one of the greatest elements in the Australian potential – its "polity" – is one of those that is least spoken about' (ACC 2000, p. 9). Nor are Australians clear about their national identity. To the questions 'What is distinctive about Australian political life?' and 'What is it that we can feel is our own way of doing politics?' the Council finds 'There is no particular answer' (ACC 2000, p. 19). To the fundamental question of what unites Australians, the Council can only give the answer that it is diversity: 'The Council believes public acceptance of diversity can be one of the bases of social harmony. A peaceful and fruitful social cohesion does not come from imposing uniformity. It comes from accepting difference and negotiating it' (ACC 2000, p. 12). Diversity and multiculturalism, however, are not the core attributes of Australian citizenship but consequences of a more pluralist and tolerant political society. While these are pleasing developments in Australian political life and civic culture in recent decades, they are premised on more fundamental shared liberal democratic values and citizenship arrangements.

Sensing that the truth about citizenship lies elsewhere, the Council advocates adoption of seven core civic values to improve citizenship awareness. These are commitments to the land, to the rule of law, to representative liberal democracy, to tolerance and fairness, to acceptance of cultural diversity, to the well being of all Australians, and to recognition of the unique status of Aboriginal peoples (ACC 2000, p. 11). While these commitments are laudable, they are couched as collective aspirations that do not add up to a foundational basis for Australian citizenship. The Council admits as much, remarking on the 'curious situation' that its favoured core values would be accepted by most Australians yet scarcely ever put to the fore when people 'sum up' Australia (ACC 2000, p. 15). The Council has little to suggest: that politicians provide leadership in championing these core values, and sponsor an international conference in the hope that international experts might help us to identify our own national distinctiveness.

If the Australian Citizenship Council is right in its general prognosis, Australia does have a major problem with national identity and citizenship as it goes into the new century. The Citizenship Council, however, was wrong in its findings; it was not looking in the right place to find Australian national identity and the foundations of Australian citizenship because of its fixation on diversity. Nor did it have adequate conceptual tools for the task of articulating and evaluating those aspects of national identity and political life that are relevant for citizenship. Its recipe of unity in diversity and championing abstract core values that, on its own account, are not to the fore in public or popular consciousness evidence its conceptual bankruptcy. As the latter part of the Citizenship Council's Report indicates, Australia does have a reasonably sophisticated and workable citizenship regime that is constantly developing and regularly fine-tuned. Citizenship does not operate in a political and cultural vacuum that the Citizenship Council supposes. What has been lacking is an adequate framework for understanding citizenship.

If the Citizenship Council's exploration of Australian citizenship was side-tracked by its concern for diversity and multiculturalism, others have been constrained by tying citizenship too closely to the paradigm of the sovereign nation-state. The paradigm of democratic citizenship based upon nation-state sovereignty has been the dominant conceptual model in postwar decades. According to Stephen Castles it is the foundation upon which democratic citizenship is constructed in Australia:

> Democratic citizenship, as we know it in Australia, is premised on a nation-state which has *sovereignty* over a specific territory demarcated by internationally agreed boundaries. In this model, the world consists of a multitude of such nation-states, each of which enjoys considerable *autonomy* in controlling its own economy, culture, and environment and society. The citizens are supposed to control the state through democratic processes, and the state is supposed to control what happens on its territory and to decide who or what may cross its boundaries (S. Castles 2000, p. 119. Emphasis in original).

This notion of citizenship based on the territorial nation-state has its origins in the treaties of Westphalia of 1648 that, among other things, empowered the prince to determine the religion of subjects throughout the prince's realm. In the transition to territorial states, old networks of feudal loyalties and superior religious claims of Catholic popes to secular authority were swept aside. European kingdoms such as England, France, Portugal and Spain were gradually transformed into nation-states and these progressively imposed religious and cultural homogeneity. Political power was consolidated and secularised by the French Revolution that centralised national power and legitimated popular sovereignty. As Habermas points out, nationalism added the 'specifically modern phenomenon of cultural integration' that shapes national consciousness and is used to mobilise otherwise isolated individuals. According to Habermas: 'Nationalism is a form of collective consciousness which both presupposes a reflexive appropriation of cultural traditions that have been filtered through historiography and which spreads only via the channels of modern mass communication.' It is a construct susceptible to manipulation by political elites (Habermas 1995, p. 257).

As Habermas also points out, this classic form of the nation-state is at present disintegrating (Habermas 1995, pp. 256–57). The fact that the Europe of today no longer fits the paradigm is the starting point for advocates of the 'post-Westphalian state' like Andrew Linklater:

> As the present century draws to a close, the subnational revolt, the internationalisation of decision-making and emergent trans-national loyalties in Western Europe reveal that the processes which created and sustained sovereign states in this region are being reversed ... What is required are appropriate visions of the post-Westphalian state (Linklater 1998, p. 113).

The post-Westphalian vision of Linklater and others draws heavily upon the earlier work of theorist Hedley Bull who suggested that international society was moving towards a form of 'neo-medievalism' (Bull 1977). Notions of individual rights and duties and a growing sense of 'a world common good' that extended beyond the nation-state were undermining the idea of national sovereignty. Bull saw in the complex layering of international, national and sub-national organisations and loyalties a healthy corrective to the system of self-contained nation-states. For him, neo-medievalism might help 'avoid the classic dangers of the system of sovereign states by a structure of overlapping structures and cross-cutting loyalties that hold all peoples together in a universal society while at the same time avoiding the concentration inherent in a world government' (Bull 1997, pp. 254–55).

A world of multiple loyalties and memberships on the part of citizens that are not restricted to the nation-state has profound implications for traditional understandings of citizenship and sovereignty, as Linklater acknowledges (Linklater 1998, p. 124). It is not simply the emerging world of the future, however, but also that of Australia's past when nationhood was forged within the British Empire. Australia was never a standard Westphalian sovereign nation-state to begin with, but one whose citizenship entailed multiple loyalties and membership of global, national and regional state political communities – the British Empire, the Australian Commonwealth and one or other of the regional states such as Victoria or Queensland. Until 1948, Australians called themselves 'British subjects' rather than Australian citizens, a formal title that indicated that their loyalties were not solely restricted to Australia but were to Britain as well. Even within their territorial nation-state, Australians had multiple memberships in national, state and local political communities.

The significance of earlier membership of the British Empire has been lost sight of in Australian thinking about citizenship, nationhood and globalisation, but is central to our account. Comparative scholars like Krasner also highlight the British Empire/Commonwealth, from about mid-nineteenth century to the Second World War, as one of the notable systems of nations that was not based on international legal sovereignty (Krasner 1999, pp. 228, 232–35). Others include the Holy Roman Empire that lasted from the ninth until the early nineteenth century, and the modern European Union. British imperial citizenship resembled that of other loosely organised empires, including most notably the Roman. The Romans extended the scope of citizenship from its classic origins in cities and small republics, freeing it from strict territorial boundaries by admitting whole communities. They admitted Latins from adjacent polities and subsequently other peoples from diverse regions as Rome's empire expanded. Roman citizenship became based more on political and legal entitlements and obligations and less on bounded locality. Reflecting upon imperial citizenship in its various forms helps us appreciate aspects of early Australian citizenship experience that are otherwise distorted by the sovereign state model.

Imperial extension, however, is only part of the more complex Australian tradition; federalism is the other part that transcends the neat sovereign state model. Federalism entails dual spheres of government, national and state, with government powers divided between them by an overarching constitution so that each government is one of limited powers and none are sovereign. As a result, federalism effectively entails dual citizenship or membership in two spheres of governance, each of which deals with significant citizenship rights and entitlements but neither of which is comprehensive or absolute. The Australian nation that was established at federation built upon and preserved established colonies with, in most cases, half a century of self-government. Included in colonial government was a system of local government that developed to provide an additional sphere of governance and citizenship participation. The colonies, along with their established systems of local government, were preserved in somewhat changed form as states and a new tier of national government was added in the process that created the Australian nation. Australian federation was not simply a compact between the colonies fixed by political brokers. It grew from grass roots nationalism. The framers of the constitution drafted a document that the people of the colonies would accept, and that was subsequently endorsed by their voting in referendum. This popular basis is reflected in the preamble to the Westminster Act that formally passed the constitution: 'the people of New South Wales, Victoria, South Australia, Queensland, and Tasmania, humbly relying on the blessings of Almighty god, have agreed to unite in one indissoluble Federal Commonwealth under the Crown of the United Kingdom and Great Britain and Ireland, and under the Constitution hereby established'.[3] Western Australians made up their mind to join federation at a late stage in the process and so were not included.

Because federal citizenship entails multiple memberships and loyalties in a complex matrix of domestic governance arrangements, adding an international dimension is not incompatible. Just as membership of the British Empire expanded early Australian citizenship by adding a transnational dimension, participation in modern international regimes where certain norms and standards are set universally can provide a positive extension of citizenship. The global dimension might properly be seen as enriching modern citizenship rather than undermining it, as the exclusive sovereign state model supposes. Citizenship is not completely 'bounded' to the nation-state, as David Miller claims. In Miller's view: 'All our experience of citizenship, then, has so far been of bounded citizenship within the walls of the city-state, later citizenship within the cultural limits of the nation-state' (Miller 1999, p. 69). But confining citizenship so narrowly ignores the more complex historical experience of nations like Australia that are formed within empires such as the British. In particular it fails to recognise Australian experience where political membership and loyalty of citizenship were not exclusive to the nation-state. The Australian experience shows that citizenship need not be bounded by the nation-state, just as nationhood need not be premised solely on sovereign independence. Furthermore, Australian experience with multiple spheres of domestic governance shows how citizenship can be grounded in ways that extend individual and group inclusion, participation and belonging. More complex and layered citizenship is possible where multiple spheres of domestic governance allow membership in, and loyalty to local, regional and national political associations.

Australian citizenship has its foundations in colonial history. A common mistake among commentators is to date its origins from the foundation of the nation-state at the turn of the twentieth century, or more superficially from 1949 when Australians were formally called Australian citizens for the first time.

The more significant formative era, when the character of Australian political institutions was initially defined, was the colonial. Accounts of Australian citizenship that present a progressive development 'from Subject to Citizen' since federation give a partial and distorted view (Davidson 1997). In considering citizenship, we need to take account of its different dimensions: the normative, or what people say they should do; the formal, what official documents say is the case; and the substantive, or what people actually think and do. Making these distinctions helps us take proper account of political culture and citizenship ideals that are often discounted or discredited. Proper distinction should be drawn between the formal policies of the state that articulate the rights and duties of citizens and the broader social contours of civil society that are shaped by popular culture and practice.

Citizenship and Civic Culture

While citizenship need not be entirely bounded by the limits of the nation-state, it does need to be extensively grounded in its land and culture represented by autonomous and distinctive political institutions. Otherwise residents remain colonial settlers from the mother country. Indeed this was the case for the first British penal settlements and for free settler societies in Australia well into the nineteenth century. Only gradually did these 'transplanted Britons' become Australianised, through growing attachment to the native land and developing a distinctive variant of British culture as well as self-governing institutions. Subsequently, as Australia's immigration policy was diversified, what was considered to be Australian became more multicultural with diffuse international associations and loyalties.

Political institutions and formal arrangements are necessary for establishing both a political community and its citizenship, but they are not sufficient. Human passions and aspirations have to be engaged, and habits of thought and action cultivated that support participation and reinforce compliance. Citizenship means membership in a particular political community that requires loyalty, patriotism and even heroism in times of war. Traditionally, national poetry, painting, literature, political rhetoric and historiography have extolled citizenship qualities and actions that are seen as desirable and worthy of emulation. Political communities are often endowed with mythical and imaginary qualities, as Benedict Anderson pointed out (Anderson 1983). Founding events and great leaders may be lionised, and shameful events such as the conquest and displacement of other peoples rendered as triumphant deeds. At a more mundane level, aspects of participation and association such as acquiring citizenship or casting one's vote are surrounded with reinforcing ceremony and ritual.

Citizenship and political participation are only a part of what is significant in human experience. Citizens live most of their lives in the private domain of family and friends, earning a living and providing for themselves and their dependants, perhaps joining voluntary associations and community groups ranging from churches to sporting clubs. This is the realm of private life and civil society where citizenship qualities can be enhanced by congenial practices and habits. For example, moral virtues of caring for others, co-operation and tolerance that enhance public life depend more for their nurturing on homes, schools and churches than on political fiat. A liberal democratic regime has as one of its main purposes the protection of large spheres of human activity for individual choice including the choice to form and join civic associations. People can go about their own private business without undue influence by the state. They can also form voluntary political associations to shape public opinion and organise political activities to change laws and policies including those that govern citizenship. Liberal democratic politics has the overarching role of preserving and facilitating civil society but is in turn strengthened by its independent vigour.

If the tendency in the past was to overemphasise the primacy of the political and the significance of formal institutions, in recent decades the pendulum has swung the other way. Communitarian theorists emphasise the significance of associations in civil society irrespective of whether or not they are politically oriented. Michael Walzer does allow a certain primacy to the formal institutions of the state, recognising that civil society requires these for its survival. Nevertheless, he insists with other communitarians that the social precedes the political as well as the economic (Walzer 1995). Robert Putnam argues that the political health of a society can be measured by the number and vitality of its civil society groups, such as choral societies and soccer clubs (Putnam 2000). Other more extreme communitarians like Selznick proclaim 'the primacy of the community over the state' (Selznick 1992). Important as the associations of civil society are, however, giving them precedence over the formal political institutions of the state is going too far. Just as political institutions of the state should not subsume and replace civil society, private and economic spheres of life cannot substitute for the political. Once political activity and the state replace all other forms of human association they become oppressive and degenerate into tyranny. On the other hand, if private or economic interests or religious groups rule in their own interests there is a comparable perversion of politics and citizenship practice.

In a recent study, John Ehrenberg sums up civil society as 'a sphere that is formally distinct from the body politic and state authority on the one hand, and from the immediate pursuit of self-interest and the imperatives of the market on the other' (Ehrenberg 1999, p. 235). While acknowledging the richness of civil society and the multiple memberships of people in various civic groups and associations, we should not confuse membership in any voluntary association with citizenship. It is important to restrict it to mem-bership of political parties, advocacy groups or social movements that seek to support or change the formal policies of the state. Wayne Hudson is correct in his recent observation that 'citizenship is not one thing' and monistic. As we have argued above, people can enjoy multiple membership in a number of political communities. However, Hudson's notion of 'differential citizenship' stretches the term to a plurality of 'cases and terrains of *sexual, educational, media, military, environmental, ecological,* and *religious citizenship'* (Hudson 2000, p. 16. Emphasis in original). This blurs the notion of citizenship with membership of non-political associations and groups. Schools are indeed common sites for training in good citizenship, as Hudson observes (Hudson 2000, p. 18), but to describe this as 'school citizenship' is confusing. Citizenship consists fundamentally of membership in a political association: this need not be exclusive or monistic, but it is political. Theoretical rigour as well as common usage support a more restrictive use of citizenship.

The problem with equating citizenship with membership in diverse civic, religious and vocational associations is the fragmentation and watering down that such usage entails. Some communitarians go further in actually privileging membership in voluntary political associations over the state as a reaction to liberal individualists who have sought to diminish the entire public sphere. The danger in both these cases is a weakening of focus on formal political institutions that is essential for good government. If individuals and diverse groups are too powerful and independent, common cause and political consensus are made problematical. Just as tyranny results if the state becomes too pervasive, anarchy or ineffective government are likely outcomes if diversity is too pronounced and civil groups have too much autonomy. Political unity can be undermined by a proliferation of intensely politicised groups in civil society. One reason why citizenship is especially salient today is fragility of political unity in many countries. In some countries, the re-emergence of ethnic nationalism has been sparked by changes in the international order with the collapse of the Soviet Union and the end of the Cold War. In others there have been major dislocations due to mass migration or economic restructuring. According to Ronald Beiner, such modern 'political dilemmas have raised anew deep questions about what binds citizens together into a shared political community' (Beiner 1995, p. 3). In various parts of Europe there has been a tendency for ethnic nationalisms to replace civic nationalism, with disastrous consequences in ethnically diverse countries (Beiner 1995, p. 8). According to Kymlicka and Norman, the challenge for many countries is to construct a common political citizenship out of people who participate in the political in diverse ways. They ask : 'How can we construct a common identity in a country where people not only belong to separate political communities but also belong in different ways – that is, some are incorporated as individuals and others through membership in a group?' (Kymlicka & Norman 1995, p. 309). Acknowledging 'deep diversity' such as one finds in Quebec is one thing, but finding a sufficient basis for Canadian unity that respects such deep diversity is quite another, and so far an intractable, challenge.

Citizenship and political unity have traditionally been linked themes in political science that become prominent at times of rapid change and national transformations. In the early 1930s prominent American political scientist Charles Merriam coordinated an eight-volume comparative study of citizenship and nationhood in a selection of countries with vastly different political cultures and circumstances. These included fascist Italy, Germany and communist Russia that were mobilising around totalitarian ideologies of the right and left; Switzerland and Austria-Hungary where central political allegiance had to be reconciled with conflicting religious and ethnic populations; as well as France, Britain and the United States. The country studies ranged from *Making Fascists* to *Civic Education in America*. In a book that remains one of the best accounts of what makes up citizenship and is relevant for our purposes, Merriam drew together the lessons learnt from the eight studies, focusing on the role of civics in forging and sustaining national cohesion and loyalty from the large and complex collection of groups that make up modern nations. At a time when national cohesion and loyalty were being radically reshaped in some countries, Merriam retained a pluralist perspective of concern for the 'broad range of pluralist patterns of group behaviour developed in a wide range of social settings' (Merriam 1931, p. 319). As well as political interest and loyalty, there were interests and loyalties to religious, racial, regional, economic, and cultural groups, all at times and in part in cooperation, competition or conflict with one another. Forging national unity from such disparate groups and interests was problematical given 'the intricate whirl of competing loyalties, alternatively attracted and repelled by one and another, in an endless series of forming and dissolving interests' (Merriam 1931, p. 2).

National unity was for Merriam a primary purpose of politics and was to be facilitated by citizenship formation through civics education. Its techniques were the familiar ones that are nevertheless worth listing: 'the formal school system; the governmental services – naval, military, bureaucratic; the political parties; the specific patriotic organisations' (Merriam 1931, p. 16). Symbolism and ceremony also played a key role:

> In all systems there is found a cult of group coherence, expressed in various forms of ceremonialism and symbolism. Of these the flag expresses the most vivid symbol of political unity. Holidays, music, art, memorials, ceremonial rites, and observances of various kinds are included ... In each state there is found an impressive array of vivid and colourful pictures, rhythms, events, in which the prestige and power of the political authority is presented, and the individual is identified with their beauty and strength (Merriam 1931, p. 22).

Our own study is much concerned with the civic aspects of Australian citizenship formation; hence there is a good deal of focus on civic institutions, ceremonies and symbols and the ways in which these were gradually transformed from transplanted British to native Australian.

Merriam's comparative conclusions about citizenship and civic cohesion in the early 1930s remain valid today. What it is that makes people of diverse loyalties and interests cohere sufficiently so that they share common citizenship in a stable polity is both deeply problematical and difficult to analyse systematically. Moreover, the process is continually evolving either because of developments within or influences and shocks from outside, or combinations of both. As Merriam summed it up:

> the process of developing civic cohesion goes ceaselessly on, in great part the unconscious and uncontrolled impact and equilibrium of social and economic forces blindly struggling for expression, recognition, dominance. A whirling mass of social groups with their loyalties, codes, and personalities finds in some way a territorial locus, a population, a political order, a ruling personnel – a balance which may last for a hundred years or a hundred days, until its habits of domination and subordination, its crowns, its flags, its pains and penalties, and its prestige melt into some other imposing hierarchy of power. Fear, force, routine, magic, and mumbo jumbo play their part in producing the cohesion and the morale necessary for the performance of the functions of the political order. ... But in time there emerge consciously organized and directed ways of generating loyalty and giving the desired direction to the attitudes of the mass of the political group (Merriam 1931, pp. 359–360).

Our account of Australian citizenship examines how citizenship ideals and practices have been shaped and reshaped over two centuries, since the colonial era. The focus is political – upon disputed ideals within political culture, differing views over the rights and responsibilities of Australian citizens, and political contests over policy and legislation. Grounding such contestation, evident in its political rather than violent resolution, is a deeper consensus on legitimate process and core values. This consensus is also political but in a more fundamental way than the ongoing contestations of day-to-day politics. The political is linked to and, to an extent, depends upon civic society and associations. Hence we emphasise the small 'c' citizenship of civic society and culture as well as the large 'C' citizenship of political institutions.

Our study corrects the Citizenship Council's depressing and superficial conclusions that citizenship is not a unifying national symbol; that there is no consensus on what is held in common and a lack of interest in civic institutions; and that there is no distinctiveness about Australian political life except, perhaps, its diversity. We document a robust and complex civic culture and evolving set of citizenship arrangements that have developed as Australians changed from being transplanted Britons and formally British subjects to distinctively Australian citizens. That change is reflected in the switch from the oath of allegiance to the citizenship pledge. Those becoming naturalised a century ago were required to swear faithfulness and 'true allegiance to Her Majesty Queen Victoria, Her heirs and successors according to law'. Today there is a simple pledge to Australia, its people and institutions:

> From this day forward, under God, I pledge my loyalty to Australia and its people, whose democratic beliefs I share, whose rights and liberties I respect, and whose laws I shall uphold and obey.[4]

Modern Australia is proudly multicultural, and some like Mary Kalantzis interpret this as 'moving to a new civic pluralism' that 'has the potential to lead the world with its practical example' (Kalantzis 2000, p. 99). Kalantzis' optimism is based on Australia's weak sense of nationalism and its more recent history of government commitment to policies of cultural and linguistic diversity. In light of these, Kalantzis believes, 'Australia has a chance of producing the nation of the future: a nation with a post-nationalist sense of common purpose, a nation without nationalism' (Kalantzis 2000, pp. 107–108). This vision attributes too much significance to ethnic diversity and understates the continuing strength of Australian cultural identity and English language paramountcy. Despite the garnish of multiculturalism, in contemporary Australia there is a melding of cultural diversity around an English-speaking Australian polity and its civic practices, even though these may be transformed, to some extent, in the process.

Civic pluralism enhances citizenship providing it is not taken too far. A nation-state without nationalism is fine, but there does need to be shared membership in, and commitment to, political community. Australian citizenship entails just that: sharing in the Australian polity and civic life, enjoying equal rights and entitlements in its democratic system of governance, and having responsibility for maintaining and obeying its laws. Historical origins are also important because what Australia is today and might reasonably become in the future depend on its past foundations and development. The richness and detail of what this entails, and how it has been influenced by global forces and mediated by domestic governance, is the subject of the following chapters.

Chapter 2

Citizenship without Nationhood

While citizenship today is commonly regarded as membership of a nation-state, Australian citizenship has its origins in British imperial and colonial self-governing polities. Federation created the Australian nation at the beginning of the twentieth century, adding a national sphere of government and a national sphere of citizenship. There was no revolutionary break with the past, however, since national government and citizenship did not replace either the British imperial link or established colonial polities. Forging nationhood through adding a national overlay to existing global and local political associations produced a complex system of layered governance and citizenship. The British imperial link was inevitably weakened by Australia's becoming a nation, but it was not severed. Australia remained a loyal dominion within the British Empire for several generations; it retains the British monarch as its formal head of state a century later; and Australians continued as British subjects for another half-century after federation. Independent nationhood for Australia was evolutionary rather than revolutionary, and Australian citizenship developmental with residual British elements continuing for generations. Subsequent chapters examine in detail the non-exclusive character of Australian nationhood and citizenship at federation and beyond. This chapter is concerned with the pre-federation elements of Australian governance and citizenship that provided the foundation for subsequent federal government and the additional citizenship that attached to a nation-state. The chapter makes two key arguments, both of which are alluded to above. The first is that citizenship is not necessarily linked with a nation-state; indeed, it can flourish as it did in the nineteenth-century Australian colonies without a nation-state. The second is that globalisation is not new or unique to the late twentieth century, but has shaped Australia since first European exploration and settlement.

We have already argued in Chapter 1 that nation-states are typically not sovereign and independent, and that national citizenship or membership in the nation-state is not exclusive. In this chapter we go further and show that there can be a reasonably full and complex citizenship without a nation-state at all. This was the case in the Australian colonies before federation. The privileging of the nation-state as a political community is of relatively recent origin, becoming dominant only after the First World War that precipitated the demise of dominant empires. The primacy of the nation-state was boosted by the League of Nations and the formation of the United Nations after the Second World War and has been reinforced by the paradigms of international law and international relations. The history of nations reveals a more complex reality. Australia was not founded as a sovereign nation-state in 1901, and Australian citizenship cannot be understood in those terms. Those who characterise Australian citizenship in the twentieth century as a bipolar linear progression from subject to citizen give a partial and distorted account. Australians did not become formally Australian citizens until 1949, yet experienced a rich and complex citizenship that provided them with membership in multiple political communities, both supra-national and sub-national as well as national. To understand this layered complexity, it is necessary to take account of the earlier formative experience of citizenship in the Australian colonies.

This chapter traces the origins of Australian citizenship to British colonisation and colonial self-government. The colonial experience of British subjects was one of civic entitlement and engagement rather than subservience and passivism. There was pride, for the most part, in the British imperial legacy, and colonials volunteered to serve Queen and Country in the Maori wars, the Sudan and the Boer War. Imperial loyalty did not preclude domestic autonomy and self-government. Even during the period of direct rule, distance conferred opportunities for autonomy in political decision making. Economic opportunity and the absence of traditional social structures inspired endorsement of broader participation in colonial politics and Australians devised constitutions that were amongst the most democratic in the world. The darker side of Australian settler societies was a political culture with strong elements of hierarchical ethnocentrism that was manifested in an oppressive panoply of prejudices and manners. Practices of British overlordship and cultural prejudice were emulated by colonials in ways that shocked and concerned even the British Colonial Office. It was evident in discrimination against the Catholic Irish, vilification of the Chinese and the dispossession of indigenous peoples. Colonial capitalism was distorted by patronage and perpetuated structural inequalities that undermined citizenship rights and entitlements. Moreover, colonial capitalism was dominated by British investment and trade and subject to the ravages of global capitalism.

Colonisation as Globalisation

The second main theme of the chapter is that globalisation is hardly novel, but has shaped Australia since British colonisation in 1788. British colonisation followed earlier exploration by British and European powers that had been global colonisers since the late fifteenth century. Mercantilist expansion and strategic advantage fanned colonisation in the sixteenth and seventeenth centuries with trading companies increasing the reach of European states, and then becoming de facto governments in colonial territories. European monarchs granted charters to favoured companies to establish overseas plantations and estates that conferred the commercial advantage of monopoly as well as the authority of governance. Commercial expansion was followed by migration, contractual or enforced, as those with capital gained access to lands and required labour to work them. Impoverished agricultural workers from the Old World became the indentured labourers in the New, while convicted felons were transported to forced servitude in exile. The slave trade was revived in the fifteenth century on a scale unprecedented since the days of antiquity, reaching its height in the eighteenth century. Millions of Africans were shipped across the Atlantic by Portuguese, Dutch, English and French slave traders who obtained their human cargo through commodity exchange with native chiefs and slave raiders. Free settlers were often political or religious refugees from the clashes of Reformation and Counter-Reformation Europe. New colonies offered better prospects for more radical and non-conformist politics than did post-Westphalian Europe in the process of building nation-states and imposing established state religions. The Enlightenment stimulated European churches to bring 'civilisation and salvation' to foreign populations. The Enlightenment also prompted patronage of scientific expeditions of naturalists, botanists, geologists and astronomers to probe new worlds of knowledge. Piracy flourished alongside trade in the restless traffic of colonial globalisation where private plunder differed little from public exploitation except for its scale and formal legitimacy.

The imperial European powers introduced their own political institutions and culture of governance, ruling by various combinations of fiat, negotiation and devolution. The British used monarchical edict, parliamentary oversight and civil administration. As early as 1625, King Charles I had established the Commission of Trade that would become the British Colonial Office as the flag supplanted the contractual government of mercantilism. This Office was somewhat chaotic in its dealings, which was hardly surprising in view of the rapidly growing and diverse nature of the colonies it was to administer (Morris 1968). Nonetheless it was not without a mission. While agents handled trading matters, the Colonial Office focused on governance issues. The civil servants who ran the Colonial Office (if not from the upper echelons of society whence came parliamentarians, cabinet ministers and the prime minister) were drawn from the ranks of the genteel and schooled in civil society and governance. In dealing with colonial governments and British subjects in the colonies, they and their emigrant emissaries – gubernatorial officers, civil administrators and military officers – exercised an authoritarian overlordship that linked dignity, refinement and compassion with unquestioning authority.

The British were by no means the first to be interested in the great southern continent. The Portuguese may have visited Australia's shores as early as the sixteenth century. In the seventeenth century the Dutch Governor-General of the East Indies, Anthony van Diemen, authorised numerous expeditions that pieced together a map outline of the continent: New Holland. The Dutch did not become colonisers because the continent's apparent barrenness could not be reconciled with the fabulous prizes associated with the Great South Land. The British buccaneer, William Dampier, had explored some of the north-west coast in 1688 and concurred with the earlier Dutch assessment, a decision he endorsed following a subsequent expedition. By the mid-eighteenth century both French and English writers were taking stock of the region's territory and the colonial purposes to which it might be put. Charles de Brosse's *History of Navigation to Southern Lands* (1756) suggested that it could be used for placement of foundlings, vagabonds, paupers and criminals. A decade later, John Challender's *Terra Australia Cognita* echoed similar themes. The Frenchman Louis de Bougainville and James Cook made expeditions to the Pacific. Cook, following scientific observation of the Transit of Venus for the Royal Society made from Tahiti, was directed by the British Government to sail in search of the Great South Land. On 22 August 1770 he took possession of the eastern coast in the name of George III.

This political claim by the British might never have led to colonisation because establishing and maintaining territorial possessions was expensive. By the eighteenth century the British Government had taken over rule of Canada and India from mercantile trading companies. Added to these administrative costs were the expenses of the Seven Years War with France and the War of Independence with the former American colonies. Loss of the latter left Britain without a dumping ground for convicted felons so New Holland, with its additional prospects of flax and timber for naval supplies, was proposed instead. In 1786 Captain Arthur Phillip received a commission from the British Government to found and govern the colony of New South Wales as a penal settlement. After an eight-month voyage by the First Fleet, Foundation Day was proclaimed on 26 January 1788 in the centenary year of the first British sighting of the continent. New South Wales was proclaimed a Crown Colony of the British monarch, King George III. The onset of King

George's attacks of mental debility began in the same year, but that was of little consequence since 1788 was also the centenary of the Glorious Revolution. One hundred years before, the British parliament had asserted its sovereignty in putting a tame monarch, King William of Holland, on the British throne in place of the Stuarts who had pretensions to absolutist rule. Within its constitutional monarchy, British institutions of parliamentary government, civil administration and the common law were the envy of progressive Europeans.

The British Empire of the nineteenth century competed with other European powers, most notably the French, for military supremacy and colonial expansion. Great Britain pursued supremacy as a world power for economic purposes of expanding trade and opportunities for private enterprise and wealth. The political economy of British imperialism was a unique blend of power politics and liberal economics, with the one reinforcing the other. Imperial expansion increased British trade and markets for buying its raw materials and selling its finished goods, while imperial power ensured British advantage in such markets. Classical liberal political economy, that was a strong component of British political orthodoxy, defined the task of government as a constrained one of providing the framework and conditions suitable for private enterprise. This led to scepticism about establishing elaborate machinery of colonial governance that would be a drain on finances. The challenge was to provide only such administration as would ensure law and order and facilitate commercial enterprise. But that was clearly not sufficient either in theory or practice, as Adam Smith, the great architect of a liberal economic order as the foundation of the wealth of nations, had also pointed out. Labour and capital were far from producing a self-regulating equilibrium that was either socially acceptable or adequate in providing the necessary infrastructure for the economy and civil society. Government would need to ensure that public goods such as ports and schools were provided and perhaps provide them itself; and labour markets would need to be regulated to ensure that workers received a decent minimum wage. The political economy of distant settler colonies would obviously require greater government intervention and provision.

Colonial government was a curious hybrid of global and local rule – Colonial Office instructions, the Governor's discretionary rulings, and increasing input from influential locals. Because of the physical and cultural distance from the metropolitan centre, colonial settler societies became increasingly self-reliant and established linkages and regional affiliations among themselves. The power distribution under colonial globalisation is a matter of contention. Some scholars have characterised imperial governance as supremacist rule over subordinate colonial settlements. According to this interpretation, imperialism was 'power viewed from above' while colonialism, in contrast, was 'power from below' (Thornton 1963). This neat paradigm has a certain attraction, and has been used to explain emergent nationalism in colonial societies and the progressive evolution of national citizen from imperial subject. It is too linear and mechanistic, however, and distorts the historical complexity of real power relations. Human agency allows reflexivity and differential power relations, while ongoing relations between colonial peripheries and the imperial government allowed scope for accommodation and adaptation of imperial edicts to local conditions. Within settler societies there was no simple movement from subject to citizen but rather more complex negotiations between cosmopolitan subjects and parochial citizens, or people with differential shares in both.

The permutations of citizenship within any given settler society depended on the local political community that was partly derivative of British political institutions and culture but also reflected colonial particularities. Because Australian colonisation was established for penal purposes, early government was firmly authoritarian. A gulf separated the ruling elite of governor and administrative military officials from the population of exiled prisoners and indigenous inhabitants (Atkinson 1977). One was a world of literate and comfortable cosmopolitan rulers – albeit in an antipodean backwater – while the other was vernacular and tied to local community. The challenge of governance was balancing authoritarian and sometimes repressive control with policies for including emancipated convicts and protecting displaced indigenous inhabitants.

This chapter is concerned with two distinct eras of colonisation: the first, the period of direct British rule; and the second, the subsequent era of colonial self-government. It shows a layering of citizenship, or multiple memberships of overlapping political communities that reflects the historical origins and development of colonial settler societies in Australia.

With varying degrees of loyal sentiment, absent altogether among Irish patriots, colonists were British subjects of a global empire. As well they belonged to particular colonies and identified with local governments. The multiple spheres of governance contributed in various ways to a colonial system of 'glocalisation' that combined global and local parts. Although authoritarian, British government was constrained by distance and the relative insignificance of antipodean settlements. British administrators displayed the kind of enlightened standard setting that distance itself can afford. There was no political vacuum, however, as aspirant colonial elites, well schooled in the principles of hierarchy that supported the 'Great Arch' of British governance (Corrigan & Sayer 1985) were eager to reconstruct domestic institutions that would perpetuate their privileged position.

Direct Rule

The presence of the global and its influence in shaping local political institutions were inherent in colonisation. British imperial rule and colonial governance were facilitated by cultivation of personal loyalty and allegiance to the reigning monarch who provided a benevolent human face to a harsh convict settlement. The founding of the new colony of New South Wales in 1788 was celebrated with the raising of the British flag and a free issue of liquor so that all might toast His Majesty, the personification of the British state (Bagehot 1963). Royalty had less power but was enjoying renewed popularity as the rallying point of nationalism and imperialism. When news of the Battle of Trafalgar reached Sydney on 20 April 1806, military volleys were sounded and thanksgiving services were held. The monarch was portrayed as the moral guardian of civil liberties, before whom as before God, all might appear equal. Gubernatorial tradition enshrined aspects of this tradition to soften its image. Governor Arthur Phillip, faced with the prospect of rapidly diminishing supplies for the first settlement, took the same portions as others, and on the monarch's birthday ensured that all could rest from their labours. The Royal Pardon was available to all British subjects, and petitioning the monarch enabled emancipists to publicise their claims for rights and colonists the cessation of transportation. In return, under threat of French invasion or Irish convict uprising, colonial subjects would volunteer to supplement the military regiments through the formation of Loyal Associations, parallel to those formed in Britain (Dozier 1983).

If the monarch remained the symbol of British governance across the globe, more prosaic matters of law and order rested with the political insti- tutions of British colonialism. Typically trade preceded the flag, but that was not the case in the Antipodes where colonisation provided a destination for convicted felons. With Britain engaged in intermittent warfare with France and burdened with other domestic, colonial and imperial concerns, however, direct rule was relatively diluted. It consisted of generalised instructions to the governors, occasional British parliamentary inquiries and a light military presence. This was only possible because of the efficacy of transplanted British culture and practice and the vigour of local adaptations of British institutions of governance.

Australian colonisation occurred during a time of great political and social upheaval in Europe. In Britain, the established oligarchy was being chal- lenged by an increasingly prosperous middle class, while industrial artisans and dissatisfied labourers clamoured for greater equality and political repre- sentation. The entire period of direct British rule coincided with Europe's 'age of revolution', 1789 to 1848 (Hobsbawm 1962), when the British Government perceived itself to be under threat of imminent rebellion. It passed repressive legislation that limited voluntary association within Britain and, following the Irish uprising of 1798, dismissed the Irish parliament and orchestrated the 1801 union. British rule in Ireland was especially brutal as the Catholic Irish were dispossessed and their religion suppressed. But even in England civil liber-ties were curtailed in the interests of maintaining law and order, and tough measures imposed following demilitarisation at the end of the Napoleonic wars. While uprisings were suppressed and revolution averted, British politics and society were gradually transformed by the transfer of power to middle-class industrialists and property owners. Radical evangelists set about enculturating and empowering those without property so that they could make their presence felt in public life.

British social and reform movements spread quickly to the colonies and were often more transformative here than in Britain because of less entrenched opposition, but that was during the latter period of self-governing colonies. During the first forty years, colonial governance was more authoritarian. The governors issued proclamations that were read from the church pulpit and, from 1804, printed in *The Gazette*. Rather than being advised by ministers who were accountable to parliament, governors relied upon a cadre of administrative officers: a secretary, the surveyor-general, the principal surgeon, the provost-marshall and a judge advocate. Their authority was buttressed by a resident contingent of roughly a thousand soldiers, as well as the global reach of the British navy. From 1790 to 1808 the Governor was supported, and sometimes thwarted, by the infamous New South Wales Corps whose officers and soldiers were recruited specifically for the task. Subsequently, detachments of regular regiments were sent from other parts of the Empire for tours of military duty in the colony. Their function was one of keeping guard over the civil community, protecting it from attack from other imperial powers and reprisals from indigenous warriors. They were also at hand to check prisoner rebellions.

Authoritarian colonial government was leavened by the rule of law. A rudimentary judiciary was set up by a Charter of Justice with courts of civil and criminal jurisdiction being established. As might be expected for a penal colony, the scales of justice were often weighted in favour of the authorities at the expense of civil liberties. The first Judge Advocate, David Collins, who was also Secretary to Governor Phillip, had no legal training and his only experience in formal legal proceedings was in courts martial. In this incomplete civil society there was no trial by jury. Civil cases were presided over by government appointees and criminal ones by military officers. Acts of insubordination or deeds of transgression on the part of convicts were severely punished. The first sitting of the New South Wales Court of Criminal Jurisdiction occurred just weeks after the founding of the colony and adopted the same tradition of harsh punishment observed in Britain, augmented by notions of secondary punishment for already convicted felons. Hangings and floggings were regular events designed to strike fear into the hearts of all felons as a deterrent to possible future acts of defiance. Such repression proved effective as there was only one small uprising at Castle Hill in 1803 that was inspired by Irish political prisoners. Nor was escape an easy alternative, although some took their chances in unfriendly bushland or attempted to stow away in trading vessels.

Ironically, the threat to established authority came less from convicts than from the ranks of the military guardians. Some military officers prospered through trading enterprise and grants of land, and sought to secure further advantage through challenging lawful authority. In the initial four-year interregnum following Phillip's resignation and the appointment of John Hunter, the powers of the civil magistrates were suspended and those powers vested in the officers of the New South Wales Corps. When Hunter's successor, Bligh, attempted to rein in such excesses, key officers staged a mutiny. As influential officers and gentlemen, however, the treasonable act of the two leaders was dealt with by recall to England to face trial rather than flogging or hanging. While the officer was stripped of his command and both were exiled for a period, they returned to resume their business interests and land holdings in the colony.

The establishment of multiple colonies across the continent was due to strategic foreign policy considerations of consolidating the British presence. Fears of French occupation led to an offshoot settlement in Van Diemen's Land in 1804 and, twenty years later, to settlement on the north of the continent at Melville Island and on the south-west coast at King George's Sound. In this way Britain secured a continent that could, by right of earliest navigation and exploration, have partially belonged to the Dutch, or through contemporary exploration to the French. Thus Australian colonialism was made uniquely British and protected from competing colonial powers and cultures.

If British foreign policy was expansionary, colonial policy was focused on cost containment and the promotion of self-reliance – concerns of public administration that have strong resonance in our own time. Such policies two hundred years ago exacerbated the gulf between the governing class and the governed; they fuelled a tradition of counter-authoritarian politics on the part of the Irish (O'Farrell 1986) and increasingly alienated and marginalised indigenous populations. The British Government's focus on cost containment increased colonial harshness and the brutality of penal repression. The provisioning of the first fleets was so minimal that meagre rations had to be further rationed to levels that jeopardised survival. The transportation of convicts was contracted to merchant shipowners who profited by limiting rations and selling the remainder at journey's end. Despite complaints from the colony's Surgeon-General, effective regulation was slow in coming: until 1801, the voyage out killed 1 in 10, and even by 1812 the number was 1 in 46. In February 1791, Prime Minister Pitt had to defend the establishment of the antipodean colony as the cheapest means of disposal for convicts. Cost economies led in 1793 to assignment of convicts as servants to civil and military officers, and in 1794 as servants of landowners. In 1798, a parliamentary Select Committee on Finance questioned the economics of penal colonisation in the Antipodes that had cost over one million pounds for the transportation of 6,000 convicts.

Cost pressures sometimes had favourable outcomes. In 1801 Governor King extended the pass system so that convicts with good behaviour records could be granted 'tickets of leave' to free them from government keep and allow them to pursue their own material independence. Free settlers and private enterprise were encouraged as a means of fostering colonial self-sufficiency and lessening the burden of public expenditure. In July 1792, Governor Phillip was authorised to make land grants to civil and military officers, and from 1793 a small number of free settlers started to arrive in the colony of New South Wales with ambitions for farming. In steering the embryonic command economy from subsistence towards profitable export industries, the governors fostered agriculture and promoted expeditions to discover seas and lands favourable for new investment opportunities. Livestock were gradually acquired so that by 1800 there were 6,000 sheep in the colony. Earlier government plans for establishing a flax industry failed when the flax proved to be of poor quality, and wine was tried as an alternative. In April 1800 the Home Secretary, the Duke of Portland, sent two French prisoners to New South Wales for three years to establish viticulture and paid them an annuity of 60 pounds. Unfortunately the venture proved unsuccessful and the vintages produced only poor quality wine. Sealing and whaling proved more lucrative. By the turn of the century, merchants such as William Campbell were exporting oils and fur to China, whaling vessels were built locally and whaling stations established. Commercial conditions were quite primitive with rum serving as an early medium of exchange. Under Macquarie's rule, 10,000 pounds worth of Spanish dollars were put into circulation with discs cut from the centre and a bank was established. Civil and military officers as well as emancipated convicts engaged in commercial ventures, with some like John Piper, Simeon Lord (Hainsworth 1971) and Samuel Terry (Dow 1974) making fortunes (Hainsworth 1968, Steven 1965).

Establishing Civil Society

The policy of encouraging wealthy settlers was pursued for the dual purposes of fostering capital investment and raising the moral tone of colonial society. Governor Macquarie initiated grazing rights and auctions of colonial wool in London to attract British private investment and 'settlers of responsibility and capital'. In 1821 John Macarthur proposed the establishment of an 'aristocracy' of landowners by supporting immigration of men of substantial capital. Soon he and others were securing the huge land grants that might make that possible. In 1824, Edmund Curr of Hobart formed the Van Diemen's Land Company and applied for half a million acres as a land grant. The same year Macarthur obtained agreement for the formation of a joint stock company, the Australian Agricultural Company, and secured the allocation of a million acres of grazing land. Five years later Captain James Stirling established the Swan River colony on the western coast based on the private capital of large colonial developers such as Thomas Peel. Private capital and initiative were behind settlement in Victoria. In 1834 Edward Henty, from the prosperous Henty family that had settled in Van Diemen's Land and Western Australia, landed in Portland Bay with stock and indentured servants. The following year, John Batman arrived in the Port Phillip District to negotiate a treaty with the indigenous inhabitants for 6,000 acres on behalf of a Van Diemen's Land syndicate known as the Port Phillip Association. The agreement was not accepted by colonial authorities, but unauthorised settlement was eventually recognised and legitimated with the appointment of Captain Lonsdale as resident magistrate from the colony of New South Wales.

Hierarchical social relations were reproduced as settler capital acquired its necessary labour. In New South Wales, assignment of convicts expanded with an upsurge in transportation following the end of the Napoleonic Wars. Although conditions varied according to the circumstances and predispositions of the property owner, the assignment system was one of virtual slavery that cruelled development of a free labour market. An immigrant labourer complained in 1846 that 'the upper classes of New South Wales settlers have so long been used to deal with the poor wretched convicts ... that the habit and the feeling at the bottom of it have become rooted in their very nature; and they would wish to treat free people in the same way' (Martin 1986). The Master–Servant Acts of 1828 and 1840 were modelled on British legislation, making infringement of contractual arrangements a civil misdemeanour for masters but a crime for servants.

Social hierarchy was built into Edward Gibbon Wakefield's *Sketch for a proposal for Colonising Australasia* (1829) that was self-funding and free from 'convict taint'. He argued that a respectable social order could be achieved by selling land at prices sufficient to attract bidders of considerable capital and using the revenue to provide assisted passages for labourers and servants. The idea gained popularity. In 1831 the British Government began auctioning land in the older colonies of the eastern coast, and in the following year the Land and Emigration Commission was established in Britain to implement a scheme of assisted passages. Wakefield's proposal was behind the South Australian settlement that was founded through the joint auspices of the British Government and a Commission representing investors who had adopted Wakefield principles in forming the South Australian Land Company. In 1840 the same ideology informed a Western Australia Company that settled the Australind district, in the south-western region of the continent, and two years later led to the colonisation of New Zealand. Thus Australia was colonised in a series of bold schemes and by a combination of public and private initiative and capital.

Social hierarchy was fostered and reproduced in colonial settlement in ways that furthered capital development in a market economy while per-petuating structural social inequalities. Nevertheless in the early years of colonisation opportunities were sufficient in expansionary local economies to engender sentiments of hope that even the lowliest might be propelled up the ranks of material achievement and privilege. The acquisition of property, especially land, was an all-consuming passion, and colonials were charac-terised as ruthless money-grubbers. Personal betterment was achieved by assimilation into the cultural habits of respectability as well as by material success. It was assumed in British colonial rule that good governance was as much the product of moral behaviour as of appropriate political institutions. Educational and religious instruction were seen as promoting the growth of domestic and social harmony built on shared ideals of good character and independence (Nadel 1957; Roe 1965). The humanitarianism of the Enlightenment influenced responses to groups as marginalised as the indig-enous inhabitants and transported felons. Governor Macquarie established 'a Native Institution' for the education of children and set aside a reserve where adults could be taught land cultivation. An annual gathering of 'friendly natives' was convened on 28 December where, amidst feasting on roast beef and plum pudding, the Governor conferred badges of chieftainship, or King Plates, and celebrated the achievements of the children at the Institution. Industrial schools, probation and other penitentiary reform measures were trialled for the reform of convicts and their assimilation to ways of virtue, industry and thrift. In the end, however, both policies were abandoned.

Colonial conditions challenged humanist sentiments and government measures often curtailed civil liberties. Aborigines, gender imbalance and the Irish posed special difficulties. In August 1837 a Select Committee on Aborigines in the British Settlement tabled its report in the British House of Commons and recommended that funds from the sale of Crown lands be deployed for the purposes of protecting the indigenous inhabitants. A Chief Protector of Aborigines was appointed for the new Port Phillip District with four assistants. This protectionist policy remained virtually intact until a new wave of assimilation a century later. Gender imbalance caused concern because of the disruption to the niceties of domestic society. Exile and transportation tended to be the lot of men rather than women, and this was exacerbated by the predominance of males freely seeking their fortune in the new world. Governor Macquarie issued ordinances designed to foster marriage and family life, banning work on Sunday and restricting Sunday trade. Later, assisted immigration schemes were established to foster families and women of 'good character'. British colonial authorities responded to the 'the troubles' at Home by cracking down on the Irish. The Irish rebellion and subsequent Act of Union in Britain triggered surveillance of religious wor-ship and house-to-house searches for weapons. Freedoms of worship, speech and association were precarious. Both Governor Darling and Lieutenant-

Governor Arthur in Van Diemen's Land were nervous that criticisms might fan unrest among dissident groups.

The colonial settlements were fraught with tensions and quarrels over the distribution of power and property. Exclusives argued with emancipists over the extent to which former convicts were to be integrated into civilian life once their sentences were served. As the colony became more sophisticated in its commercial dealings, law suits escalated: in the first quarter of 1810 alone almost 400 writs were issued by the Court of Civil Jurisdiction. New charters of justice were issued but achieving greater liberality in the courts was as difficult and contested as it was in the political arena. Nevertheless from the 1830s there was more fostering and growth of civil society. Governor Brisbane took great pains to encourage the development of mediating institutions that he saw as necessary for cultivation of the citizenry and civilised community. He granted 10,000 acres to the London Missionary Society for proposed work with indigenous Australians. He encouraged the Wesleyans to form a Bible Tract Society. He also requested Lord Bathurst to send out more Catholic priests. Governor Bourke built upon this openness by revoking the monopoly of the Anglican Church and extending government grants to all denominations in 1836. From the 1830s trade societies, friendly societies and mechanics' institutes all started to make an appearance in the colonies.

The 1830s was a decade of political reform globally in Britain and Canada as well as locally in the Australian colonies. In Britain the ascendant Whigs passed the 1832 Reform Bill and the 1835 Municipal Corporation Act. The 1837 rebellion in Canada led to the Durham Report that was to transform colonial governance. 'Radical Jack' Durham's proposals for responsible government in local matters, while retaining imperial direction in foreign affairs, won endorsement as a model for the governance of British dominions. In the Australian colonies, the Australian Patriotic Association was formed in 1835 to press for self-government and an end to transportation that stood in the way. Sir Robert Molesworth's Committee of Enquiry to the British parliament recommended the discontinuance of transportation. Despite lobbying from the landed colonials, transportation to the mainland ceased in 1840.

In 1842 a form of representative democracy was introduced comprising a unicameral legislature with both nominated and elected representatives and the possibility of municipal government. Concerns that local democracy would degenerate into mob rule gained some credence from the conduct of the first elections in 1843 (Thompson 1996). There were 41 candidates from a broad range of occupations who contested 24 seats (Thompson 1996, p. 89). Sydney polling took place on 15 June, which local observers noted was the anniversary of King John's signing of the Magna Carta (Thompson 1996, p. 106). The day began peacefully enough with rival candidates parading their colours through the streets, but degenerated as faction fights broke out and a mob of four to five hundred went on a rampage. Polling in the other boroughs took place at later dates and was mostly without the violence of the Sydney poll. However, there was loss of life in the rural county of Durham, at Paterson (Thompson 1996, p. 115), and in Melbourne, riotous disorder (Thompson 1996, p. 118). Such aberrations confirmed the worst fears of conservatives about popular democracy.

While British colonisation of the Antipodes took place at the height of revolutionary upheaval in Europe, the establishment of local political communities coincided with the second wave of European revolutionary upheaval. From the mid-1840s there were stirrings of popular democratic agitation and mounting objection to the continuance of transportation to Van Diemen's Land on the part of smaller entrepreneurs and free settlers wanting to get rid of the 'convict taint'. An Australasian League was formed with membership in all the colonies as well as New Zealand that mounted a petition and organised advocates in London for discontinuance. Residents in the Port Phillip District had a particular grievance with their electoral representation on the New South Wales Legislative Council, staging their own protest in 1848 by nominating Lord Grey, the Home Secretary, as their local member. Sweeping change was not long in coming with the Port Phillip District being made the separate colony of Victoria by the 1850 Australian Government Colonies Act. The Act also gave each colony powers to alter their constitution so as to attain self-government. Thus by mid-century, the Australian colonies were also beneficiaries of the British Government view, confirmed by Canadian experience, that the government of dependencies was best left to loyal colonial nationalists. This view was reinforced by John Stuart Mill in his treatise on *Representative Government* published a decade later in 1861:

> It is always under great difficulties, and very imperfectly, that a country can be governed by foreigners; even when there is no extreme disparity, in habits and ideas, between rulers and the ruled. Foreigners do not feel with the people. They cannot judge, by the light in which a thing appears to their own minds, or the manner in which it affects their feelings, how it will affect the feelings or appear to the minds of the subject population (Mill 1972, 1861, p. 383).

Beginning as distant extensions of an expanding empire, the Australian colonies were essentially unbounded except by distance and geography. As time went by, the interplay of global and local reinforced social hierarchies and the divergence of aspirations and life chances. Senior officials and those with wealth and connections enjoyed a certain cosmopolitanism. The governors were at the pinnacle of the system with careers in imperial service that took them to many countries where they played host to visiting dignitaries. Members of British, Spanish, French, Russian and American scientific expeditions called at colonial ports at various intervals and sometimes ventured into the hinterlands. Italian, German and Spanish missionaries also arrived to work with indigenous communities. Governors and rising members of colonial society retained a primary focus on the mother country. Many of the colonial elites visited Britain and sent their children to British boarding schools; others, such as Wentworth, retired there. All the early narratives on the colonial experience were published in Britain from the memoirs of early administrators through to the accounts of explorers, scientists and naturalists.

Global colonisation produced a different life expectancy for the less well to do. Emancipated convicts, indentured labourers and assisted immigrants put down local roots that would form the nucleus of new attached communities. These more parochial settlers were also transplanted British, but were necessarily focused on and limited to the colonies. For some, shared Britishness and loyalty to the British Empire (embodied in the institution of the monarch) helped bridge the divide. For others from Irish Catholic background or with republican disposition, Britishness and British rule were sufficiently permeable and decent to be tolerated or supported. Self-government tipped the balance of political power in favour of the parochial and the native born who could now forge new alliances around local issues. While the British connection would continue to provide a significant globalising link and a protective strategic umbrella, colonial self-government and citizenship became increasingly dominant from the mid-nineteenth century.

Colonial and Local Governments

By the end of 1851 the colonies of South Australia, Van Diemen's Land and Victoria had all elected representatives to their respective legislative councils, along the lines already in operation in New South Wales. As the colonies moved towards self-government, the issue of whether political privilege should be offered to those of wealth and social standing became a contentious one. The British policy of encouraging men of property and substance to form large companies and emigrate suggested some potential for a local aristocracy. As de Serville noted of the Port Phillip District, however, genuine aristocrats were too few in number to form a governing class (de Serville 1980). Moreover, of those who did migrate, many lost fortunes in the crash of the 1840s and others retired back home.

The claims of the large landholders to a monopoly on political power were challenged by the merchant entrepreneurs and free labourers, but more significantly by fortune seekers to the gold-rushes, many of whom were middle class professionals and artisans. Indeed the goldfields were to be the site of a popular political skirmish. The biggest rushes initially were in Victoria from 1851 and the colonial government imposed a monthly licence fee on miners to help defray expenses of policing the areas. These were imposed on all and were resented as another expense in already ruinously expensive conditions. Protests were launched as early as December 1851 at Mount Alexander and, as licence fees were raised, further protests ensued. Many of the gold diggers were literate and were prepared to make the issue a political one: no taxation without representation. The culmination was the Eureka Stockade rebellion at Ballarat on 3 December 1854 that resulted in a pitched battle between miners and government troops. It was over in a mere twenty minutes or so, but there was loss of life on both sides. Nothing further came of this republican outburst because political reforms soon gave all the democratic rights of representative government that the miners demanded. Colonists, new and old, resumed 'the rush to be rich' as self-governing institutions were put in place and democratised (Serle 1977).

Legislative councils drafted constitutions for their colonies modelled on the British constitution and included the monarch, an upper house based on a nominated and restrictive franchise, and a lower house with a more liberal franchise. The colonial constitutions reflected progressive British opinion while going some way to protecting the interests of conservative property owners. The most flamboyant debate was in New South Wales where conservatives argued with liberals and radicals. William Charles Wentworth advocated a Westminster system closely modelled on the British Government, with an Upper House stocked by a local nobility. Daniel Deniehy derided this 'bunyip aristocracy' in a famous speech, and in his paper, *The Southern Cross*, attacked colonial patrician snobbery and championed the natural rights of man. John Dunmore Lang pushed for Chartist principles and founded an Australian League to work for a federated Australian republic independent of Britain that he had advocated in *Freedom and Independence for the Golden Lands of Australia* (1852). Neither conservatives nor radicals won the day. The 1855 constitution for colonial self-government included a restrictive franchise that went some way towards satisfying conservatives. Within three years and despite vociferous opposition from the Council, the Electoral Reform Act brought in more radical measures. It adopted the secret ballot already in operation in Victoria, abolished property qualifications for candidates, established population as an important criterion in drawing electoral boundaries and introduced manhood suffrage after six months residence.

The colonies of Victoria and Tasmania also gained British assent for their Constitution Acts in 1855, with South Australia following suit the next year. Victoria's restrictive franchise was liberalised in 1857 for the Assembly and 1869 for the Council. In 1870 it became the first of the Australian colonies to introduce payment of members of parliament. South Australia's constitution gave adult male suffrage from the beginning, although the restrictions of the Upper House remained to the end of the century. Tasmania remained the most conservative of the self-governing colonies, liberalising qualifications to its franchise for both houses in 1871 but not revoking them until 1900. Queensland and Western Australia were slower in moving to self-government in 1867 and 1890 respectively and when they did their constitutions replicated the franchise restrictions evident in the mid-century constitutions.

Alastair Davidson laments that Australian political institutions were developed through legal process rather than popular struggle and that they still reflect legalism rather than populism (Davidson 1997). While this might be true in the sense that constitutions were drafted predominantly by middle class lawyers, nonetheless there were fierce political struggles between the Upper and Lower Houses over issues such as land ownership. *The Australasian Sketcher* (7 June 1879), commenting on land settlement in the colonies, noted 'each colony finds itself in possession of an enormous territory ... (that) is often found to be a constant cause of heartburning and class animosity'. Between the claims of the squatters and selectors, free traders and protectionists, pragmatism and compromise prevailed.

John Hirst attributes the popular disregard for political affairs in Australia to the excessive liberalism from the inception of parliamentary democracy in the nineteenth century (Hirst 1988). The easy triumph of liberal democracy in mid-nineteenth-century Australian colonies did obviate the need for sustained political struggle and patriotic leaders. As a result, politics was pragmatic and politicians rather colourless, as contemporary observers noted:

> The best class of politicians we have is composed of men of commonsense ability and plodding disposition who are content to deal with our politics as matters of business rather than imagination and to bring plain business like views to bear upon them. We cannot be enthusiastic about men who at the best manage the affairs of the country pretty much as they would manage those of a grocer's shop (*The Australasian Sketcher*, 10 July 1875).

Without the formation of party machinery until the end of the century (Loveday, Martin & Parker 1977), politics in most of the colonies was also very fluid as politicians attempted to establish alliances on common ground while doing battle to gain pecuniary advantage for their local constituency. In Victoria during the first twenty years of self-government there were eighteen changes of government. The franchise disparity between the houses of parliament reproduced social and economic inequalities and resulted in bitter constitutional battles. These were lamented by *The Australasian Sketcher* that adopted a typically conservative stance:

> [F]rom time to time the various colonies of Australia wax exceeding wrath with the Upper Houses. These bodies were called into existence in order that they might check hasty legislation, but whenever they attempt to discharge this, their primary function, there is what is commonly called 'a row' (8 October 1874).

The same paper expressed alarm at 'the peril of class legislation arising from our democratic form of government' with the danger, ironically, of 'the wisdom of the few being overborne by the folly of the many' (Ibid., 4 September 1875). An attempt by Liberal Premier Berry to have the Imperial Government amend the constitution so as to break the power of the Legislative Council – he led a personal delegation to the Colonial Office in 1879 – was unsuccessful. Berry forced the issue to an election in 1880 that coincided with a recession and lost. His critics had a field day:

> [T]he Premier had fallen into hopeless discord with the spirit of the community over which he ruled. His objects were not, as the result shows, the objects of the people; and his methods were not their methods. His system was one of revolution, and nothing can be more remote from the desires of the English community and from those of the people of Victoria ... (Ibid., 27 March 1880).

Each self-governing colony cultivated its own political heritage and responded to the economic vicissitudes and fortunes of the times as best it could. Rivalry between colonies and their political elites hampered the cause of greater cooperation and unity. Nonetheless there was remarkable family resemblance in governance, born of common colonial ancestry. The remainder of the chapter examines the similarities in political institutions and political cultures among the colonies. They all had a multi-layered citizenship in which their people were subjects of the British Monarch, represented in each colony by the Governor, and citizens of both colonial and local political communities. The running of day-to-day affairs and the mediation of global forces was carried out by colonial parliaments and municipalities. These functioned in comparable and routine ways throughout the nineteenth century until they came under new challenges from progressives and the labour movement towards the end of the century.

Colonial Governments

While the origins of each of the Australian colonies were distinctive in a way that gave a unique profile and character to the societies established in each of the colonies, nonetheless, through British rule, there was a strong family resemblance in the political institutions and practices of each of the colonies. In the same way that the monarch commanded unity and allegiance throughout the empire, the local representative, the colonial governor, was the pinnacle of the colonial government who symbolically ruled over all. In addition to being the local head of state, surrogate for the distant monarch and representative of the imperial government, the governor also presided over colonial society. This provided an opportunity for local aspirants, of whom there was no shortage, to stay in touch with a more global and cosmopolitan world. Commenting on the Victorian gubernatorial celebratory ball of 1874 at which some 2,000 invitations had been issued, *The Australasian Sketcher* observed:

> Owing to the limited extent of colonial society there is not the strict division of classes on such occasions that exists in England and everyone who has gone through the formality of calling at Government House expects an invitation (8 August 1874).

The task of drawing the line somewhere was the unenviable task of the Governor's wife who exercised final judgment as to who was accepted into government circles. This circumscribed those who held exclusive entitlement to the prestige of leadership in public life from those who were exiled to second-class circles. *The Australasian Sketcher* observed:

> The wife of a colonial Governor has a very difficult part to play. She is necessarily the head of colonial 'society' and as such compelled to discharge certain public functions under the eyes of critics who are not always prepared to place the best construction on action or motives. To avoid making some enemies, especially in an ultra-democratic country, is almost an impossibility. If she is exclusive, then, in the eyes of one section of the people, she is proud and 'stuck up'; if she extends the boundaries of her hospitalities widely, then she falls a prey to the wrath of the 'upper 10' and is accused of courting vulgar popularity ... (8 October 1874).

Defence was one area where the colonies participated globally in supporting Britain's imperial interests. Although the British maintained a military presence in the colonies until 1870, every colony formed voluntary defence regiments as they became self-governing from the 1850s. They also set about purchasing their own warships: Victoria's first warship *The Victoria* arrived in local waters in 1856 and South Australia's *The Protector* in 1884. There was a strong sense of affiliation with the British and a willingness to join British imperial forces around the globe. Volunteer colonial troops went to fight in the Maori wars in New Zealand in the 1860s, to the Sudan in 1885 and to the Boer War at the end of the century. Colonial governments were also concerned about matters of local defence and were sensitive to threats of invasion from foreign powers hostile to Britain, such as Russia during the Crimean War. The eastern colonies were deeply concerned about the occupation of the Pacific islands by foreign imperial powers, and resented French annexation of New Caledonia in 1853. In 1872 the Governor of New South Wales, Sir Hercules Robinson, accepted sovereignty over the Fiji Islands on behalf of the British. Queensland was especially assertive, annexing the Thursday Islands in 1872 and the Torres Strait Islands in 1879. In 1883 this northern state took a bolder step in attempting to annex Papua-New Guinea, a move that was initially repudiated by the British. Following German annexation of the northern section of New Guinea, Britain belatedly undertook possession of the southern section of Papua in September 1888.

With their economies dependant upon international trade in primary products, the colonial states were keen to expand and develop overseas markets. They were early participants in international exhibitions inaugurated by Britain's Great Exhibition of the Works of Industry of All Nations in London in 1851 and the Paris Exposition Universelle in 1855. The colonies shipped cargoes of exhibits and pamphlets to subsequent exhibitions held regularly in London and Paris, as well as to those held from time to time in America – at Philadelphia in 1876, New Orleans in 1884 and Chicago in 1893 – and elsewhere, such as Calcutta in 1883. Overseas investment and technology were also important for local services and industry. The colony of Victoria benefited from American, Canadian and British commercial enterprise. From 1854 Freeman Cobb and Partners operated a coach service to the goldfields using American stock built in Connecticut. From the 1870s, the American Clapp Company gained a near monopoly on omnibus services throughout greater Melbourne. In the late 1880s, Canadian brothers George and William Chaffey initiated a large irrigation project in Mildura based on their experience in California. British investment capital not only provided for much of the public debt, but also fuelled speculative land development in greater Melbourne that culminated in 'the land boom' of the 1880s.

The colonies and colonial residents were linked to foreign affairs in other less self-interested ways. They were assiduous in establishing networks for the receipt of charitable donations to help relieve distress caused by natural disasters, war and industrial disputation within Britain (Walker 1982). Subscriptions were raised for the Irish in 1846–47, 1879–80 and 1889. A decade later Patriotic Funds were established to aid war widows and families of veterans killed in the Crimea, the Indian Mutiny, the Sudan and South Africa. Struggling workers in the industrial Midlands and the north of Britain were assisted in the early 1860s after the American Civil War cut off cotton supplies to factories, and in 1889 funds were sent to help striking dockworkers. Money was sent to help famine relief in China despite the pointed resentment against the Chinese living in Australia.

Colonial governments were noted for their large investments in publicly owned infrastructure that has been called 'colonial socialism' by some commentators (Butlin 1959). They developed infrastructure that would overcome the tyranny of continental distance and link the colonies to London and other metropolitan centres. Communication and transport were colonial priorities with huge investment in telegraph lines and cables, railway lines and shipping facilities. In providing such infrastructure within the public domain, colonial states were meeting economic and social needs in vital areas for which there was inadequate private capital. As the French visitor Albert Metin pointed out after a study tour at the turn of the century, this was not really socialism at all but rather colonial pragmatism: 'from a distance it is socialism; from close at hand it is simply a colonial experiment' (Metin 1977, p. 165). In supporting the development of infrastructure, the colonies were quick to take advantage of the new technologies of the nineteenth century that transformed economic activity and social relations. These technologies enabled the colonial states to quickly expand continental development and link that to global markets. Although communication and transportation technologies have changed, the social and economic geography of Australia still reflect its nineteenth-century origins with large coastal cities being the population centres and connecting hubs between regional and country hinterland and the outside world.

As well as providing extensive infrastructure for development, colonial governments were also active in shaping the population through assisted immigration policy. Immigration was unrestricted and resulted in disproportionate numbers of men, many of whom regarded themselves as sojourners. The early colonial governments sought to promote the stability of settled family life by sponsoring the assisted passage of single women and families. The assisted immigration program was opposed by some as sweeping up the dregs of British paupers, and there was notable hostility towards the Catholic Irish from sectarian bigots. John Dunmore Lang's early campaign against Irish immigration was taken up by Henry Parkes who, in November 1880, stated that Irish immigration to New South Wales would be restricted to ensure people of English descent would remain the dominant group. Irish nationalism and grievances inevitably spilled over to the Australian colonies where so many Irish had settled. There were periodic tensions: in 1867 over 'the Fenian scare' at the time of the assassination attempt on Prince Alfred, during the commemoration of the anniversary of Dan O'Connell's birth, during the tour of the Redmond brothers in 1883, and on the centenary of the 1798 rebellion. There was also regular brawling between Orangemen and Irish. Secularists as well as sectarians resented the Catholic bishops' decision to remain independent of the government education system and develop their own Catholic schools.

The White Australia policy has its origins in this period when colonial governments restricted Chinese during the gold-rushes. From the 1850s, the influx of Chinese to the goldfields heightened xenophobia and led to hostility and violence on the diggings. Victoria's Goldfields Commission inquiry into the Eureka uprising revealed considerable opposition to these 'Mongol strangers'. When the numbers of Chinese rose sharply from 2,000 in April 1854 to 17,000 in June 1855, the Victorian government passed an Act to Make Provisions for Certain Immigrants. This Act imposed a poll tax of 10 pounds on all arrivals of Chinese descent and restricted the carriage of Chinese to one per 10 tons of shipping. Ships with Chinese passengers then diverted to Robe in South Australia and Chinese fortune seekers travelled overland to the diggings. After an attack on Chinese miners at the Buckland River goldfield, the Victorian government prevailed upon the South Australian government to pass similar legislation to its own in November 1857. After mob violence against the Chinese at Lambing Flat in June 1861, the New South Wales government passed the Chinese Immigration Act that was similarly restrictive. The Queensland government passed its own legislation in August 1877. Despite the tight restriction on Chinese immigration, opposition increased. When the trade union movement began organising on an inter-colonial basis in the 1880s, one rallying cause was opposition to Chinese labour, although at the time there were only 50,000 Chinese in a total population of some two million. Inter-colonial conferences of the premiers endorsed this position, despite the representations of two commissioners sent by the Emperor of China in 1887.

Colonial opposition to non-white immigrants and workers was not uniform. Queensland allowed Kanakas from the Pacific islands to work as labourers on sugar cane plantations. The 'blackbirding' practices followed by unscrupulous traders continued despite legislation that ostensibly outlawed them. Their consequences would divide Queensland politics and complicate its participation in the federation process at the end of the century. On the other hand, the need to address this breach of an ostensibly White Australia and prevent further inroads provided a catalyst for federalists in Queensland and the other colonies. A significant plank of the federalist cause was creating the machinery of national government that would ensure a uniformly white immigration policy and obviate the need for cheap coloured labour through industry protection and generous bounties.

Across a range of policy areas, the colonies acted as semi-independent nation-states as well as being virtually autonomous in domestic affairs. They mediated issues of defence, commerce, diplomacy and immigration in ways that preserved allegiance to their common British heritage and advanced opportunities for people. Each colony was dominated by a large metropolitan city that was both the seat of government and the centre of population, commerce, communications and transport that fanned out from there into the hinterlands (Hirst 1973). Although secondary in political significance, local communities were an important part of colonial experience. In colonies without a history of transportation, municipal government was regarded as an essential element of governance.

Municipal Government

Despite extensive global penetration and the movement of immigrants and settlers, property owners constituted a solid nucleus of those attached to local communities that began to develop their own distinct identities. Municipalities added an additional layer to the multiple political communities in which colonial Australians lived that also included the larger polities of colony and empire.

These overlapping communities shared a political culture that was reinforced by the institution of monarchy and personalised in the resident governor. While governors set the tone of cultivated society for an aspirant elite, they also personified the monarchy for ordinary people in local communities. The Marquis of Normanby, who arrived in Victoria in 1879, was exemplary in this respect, as reported at the time: 'The new Governor has already paid many visits to different districts in the colony and is evidently endeavouring to make himself acquainted with the country over which he has come to rule' (*The Australasian Sketcher*, 12 April 1879). Governors regularly travelled to local communities for social and civil events such as inspecting voluntary fire brigade services, laying foundation stones for churches and opening charitable bazaars. Royal visits helped keep the monarchy alive. Prince Alfred made the first of the Royal tours in 1867–68 and travelled extensively in the colonies he visited. This was the occasion for enthusiastic monarchists to demonstrate their loyalty and the opportunity for others to register expressions of gratitude, as did the Chinese at the Ballarat goldfields:

We, strangers of the Tai-tsing dynasty of China, respectfully present this address to your Royal Highness. We sincerely congratulate your Royal Highness on your arrival at Ballarat, and view with pleasure the loyal demonstrations which greet your Royal Highness on every side. The influence of your visit is felt to be salutary to all classes of people, but strangers who have come from a distance to get gold in this far-famed country are grateful for the protection we here enjoy in equal measure with people from other countries. In our dwellings we have had no annoyance, and in our streets we have felt no fear. This state of things has diffused satisfaction everywhere, and renders this country a most desirable place to reside in. We fervently hope that friendly relations may always subsist between our countries, and that Her Majesty the Queen may long be spared to reign in peace. We also

sincerely wish and pray that your Royal Highness may have
favourable breezes, wherever you may go, in the noble ship your
Royal Highness commands and that her presence, whatever seas
she sails, may inspire confidence to all kinds of shipping carrying
on honest and beneficial trade, and diffuse terror and dismay
among corsairs and pirates. Presuming to take a glance at you
Royal Highness, and respectfully making our nine prostrations,
we look to your Royal Highness's acceptance of this address
(McKinlay 1970, p. 103).

At Castlemaine, Chinese leaders in ceremonial procession made a deputation
to the Prince that included a similar address: 'We assume a low posture,
before England's lesser Lord, and the son of the Great Empress. We acknow-
ledge her greatness, which allows us to follow our calling (*The Australasian
Sketcher*, 12 April 1879).'

While patriotic fervour was no doubt spontaneous among many, it was
cultivated by colonial governments and civil groups as a means of coalesc-
ing colonial sentiment and interests with those of the Empire. The British
Government was manipulating the monarchy for the same purpose, embel-
lishing the image of the homely Queen Victoria as an august Empress. The
Queen's Jubilee in 1887 was the occasion for spectacular displays of loyalty
from Australian colonials. Church-minded, civic-oriented citizens used their
own money to present young scholars with a Jubilee edition of the New
Testament. Local businessmen illuminated their shops and decorated them
with Royal memorabilia and insignia to provide a display of loyalty.

Local communities were important for forging colonial as well as imperial
allegiances, and as well provided the location for voluntary associations
and civil society groups considered vital for a healthy citizenry and polity.[1]
Volunteer defence corps marshalled and drilled in local halls. Members of
parliament were active providing patronage for mutual improvement
societies and sporting teams. They also provided leadership in public debate
on civic issues raised by branches of colonial political leagues. The colonial
public service relied on local personnel to implement their services and carry
out regulatory functions. The colonial governments, mindful of cost containment, also relied extensively on the voluntary efforts of educated middle
class burghers. Defence corps were drilled by honorary officers, local schools
were supervised and endowed by locally elected Boards of Advice, and courts
functioned through the services of honorary magistrates. Colonial regulation
was delegated to local councils where it often foundered on vested interests.[2]
Charity relied on support for local fundraising and supervision of the local
benevolent asylums, hospitals and visiting societies. In turn, councillors
regarded local parliamentarians as lobbyists and advocates for obtaining
colonial funds to improve civic infrastructure and amenities. In these ways

colonial and local interests were inextricably linked and colonial matters etched in local concerns.

A large part of citizenship was expressed in municipal affairs. The most successful, self-made men of the town purported to rule for the good of all but were often more oppressive than busy colonial administrations or distant British officials. Leading citizens of the town identified their own prosperity with that of the municipality over which they governed, developing something of an overlord's attitude to his fiefdom and imitating the customs of landowning gentry in Britain. Even into the 1880s municipalities carried out annual Beating of the Bounds to inspect the state of repair of their lands. Honorary magistrates sitting in judgment on vagrancy cases in local courts recalled the old Laws of Settlement, 'looking after your own' while bidding strangers on their way. Councillors promoted local boosterism and built bigger and better town halls to reflect their public importance.

Other aspects of political life were less parochial. Global movements fostered the growth of local branches of leagues and reform causes that set sparks of controversy amid local colonial communities. Sabbatarians lobbied for the closing of sporting fixtures, publican trading and places of public education such as museums and libraries on Sunday. Temperance movement members pressed for an abstemious populace and the closure of public houses. Officers of the Salvation Army campaigned for saving the souls of the poor by working with them. Women's suffragists championed the place of women in public affairs.

Municipalities were significant in promoting a culture of sturdy independence as the basis of citizenship. Sunday Schools, Mechanics' Institutes and Schools of Design trained young people in public virtue. Charity was rationed to the deserving poor. Those who lacked the credentials of citizenship, through ownership of property and cultivation of civility, were excluded from public affairs. Attitudes towards the marginalised were patronising and prejudice was rife. The poor and those lacking respectability lived on the margins of local communities in the worst areas – along watercourses, beside flooding and polluted river embankments. This was the downside of nineteenth-century colonial culture and the local legacy of the political economy of largely unregulated capitalism. Despite the positive statism of colonial governments, colonial economies were driven by private interest and global markets and subject to the cycles of boom and bust. A casualised labour force and freedom of contract defined the precarious existence of the working poor.

By the end of the nineteenth century the Australian colonies had reached a plateau of self-governance with complex citizenship associations that were part global, part colonial and part local. While formally British subjects, Australian colonials had become primarily citizens of their own colonies that nevertheless embodied local variants of a predominantly British political culture. The very strength and vitality of colonial self-government and civil society meant a weakening of direct British links and influence. At the same time, the combination of strong self-governing colonies and weakened British imperial rule was structurally inadequate for dealing with the large problems and challenges facing Australia. Managing the domestic economy, securing international capital investment, mediating the impact of global markets and promoting continental markets and infrastructure were all hindered by colonial boundaries and jealousies. Maintaining strategic defence and regional security as well as controlling immigration could not be readily achieved by separate colonies. Supra-colonial structures of governance were required to address these continental challenges.

The following chapter focuses on the political construction of a national sphere of governance and citizenship that built upon, and incorporated, the legacy of the colonial era. In constructing a new national sphere of governance there were those who wished to emphasise their imperial citizenship and enter into an imperial federation. There were others who wanted to sever imperial ties and form a strongly colonial and nativist citizenship. The majority of citizens, however, regarded both of these more extreme alternatives as unacceptable. They opted for a new Commonwealth of Australia with a federal form of government that preserved existing colonies as regional states and British imperial links. A new sphere of national citizenship was added that extended and complemented existing supra-national and subnational polities.

Chapter 3
Nation-state and Citizenship

Like the United States a century before, the Australian nation-state was created through a political process of federating established colonies that were already proudly self-governing. The formation of a nation-state gave political structure to an emerging cultural nationhood of people from predominantly British origins and similar colonial experiences. Federalism entailed establishing a new sphere of government and endowing it with sufficient powers for national purposes while retaining the colonies as states with jurisdiction over their own regional and local affairs. The new nation-state was established within the protective shelter of the British Empire in ways that partly facilitated and partly restricted the process of nation building. Nationhood was achieved without revolution and bloodshed while strategic matters of defence and foreign affairs remained with the British Imperial Government as had been the case for the Australian colonies. This left Australia as a dependent British dominion until the Second World War, as we shall see in Chapter 4.

Australia adopted the form of federalism devised by the American founders that differed fundamentally from the earlier confederal form of alliance among governments of independent states that was previously known as federalism. In this older form, the people remained solely citizens of their respective states with political participation restricted to membership of those states. There was no common citizenship and government of the federal alliance was carried on by delegates of the member state governments. This was clearly a weak form of rule because collective decision making depended on each member government instructing its delegates on a particular line of action. The new federalism invented by the American founders changed that by creating a national polity of which the people were members and a national sphere of government in which they were directly represented. In effect this meant establishing a system of dual citizenship. Given the existing imperial links as well as municipal affiliations, Australian citizenship had even greater complexity and entailed multiple membership in international, national, regional and local political associations.

The Australian nation-state was constructed through a deliberative political process of consensus building, negotiation and institutional design that required both sustained political leadership and popular support. Federation presupposed the development of a popular culture of Australian nationalism and a thickening of civil society on a national scale. It was an endorsement of a nationalist principle that envisioned a larger sphere of governance in which the Australian colonies could, collectively, take their place in the world while retaining imperial alliances and local loyalties. Such a process was facilitated because people came to identify with a distinctive and vernacular culture as well as intensifying their inter-colonial networks and associations in the latter part of the nineteenth century. Federation was built upon a popular nationalist sentiment evident in local communities from the 1870s that reached its height in 1888, the anniversary of the centenary of British colonisation. Politically, federation was achieved through the practices of democratic citizenship that had already been established in the separate colonies. Leading colonial politicians drafted the constitution and, for most of the colonies, were elected as delegates to the drafting convention of 1897–98 by the voting population. The draft constitution was approved in popular referendums before being sent to London for formal ratification by the Westminster parliament. The new national constitution was Australian made through a political process that was radically democratic for its time.

This chapter begins with an extended examination of the development and quickening of Australian nationalism and civil society in the nineteenth century. These provided the sustaining political culture and associational networks that made federation possible. The constitutional foundation of nationhood that is analysed in the second part of the chapter both pre-supposed and enhanced this earlier civil foundation. The chapter highlights the complementarity between national citizenship and the pre-existent supra-national and sub-national citizenships of British colonial subjects in Australia. We show that while retaining the formal language of 'British subject' and some of its attributes, the Australian citizenship adopted at federation was both substantial and robust from the beginning.

Nationalism and National Civil Society

To understand the push for the establishment of a national political community with a national sphere of citizenship, it is important to emphasise the significance of nationalism and how this complemented both imperialism and political parochialism. As we have already seen, British subjects living in the Australian colonies were already citizens of the British Empire. Membership of this empire was attractive because it was global in extent and offered protection and status to those who were members. Imperial membership, however, was shared by multiple and diverse peoples and cultures. In contrast to this, nationalism emphasised a particular cultural homogeneity and a distinctive way of life in a unique land. This very distinctiveness had developed because British subjects living in Australia, through self-government, possessed a citizenship that had allowed them to shape their own immediate circumstances. At the same time, colonists were deeply aware of the parochialism and difficulties inherent in governing their separate colonies and municipalities. Creating a nation-state would enable them to establish a self-governing political community on a continental scale. This would facilitate further development of a distinctively Australian way of life and enable better mediation of global challenges and opportunities. The national project was shaped by the desire to retain both imperial linkages and parochial self-governance that allowed a diversity of political agendas and interests reflecting regional and local variation and choice.

Australian nationalism was a hybrid of mainly British influences and a common colonial experience. Despite being separate units of governance, the Australian colonies shared ideas, knowledge and cultural developments of English-speaking peoples around the globe. British cultural influence was pervasive. Francis Adam, the British writer who visited the Australian colonies and published *Australian Essays* in 1886, recorded with sardonic humour the metropolitan influence:

> The first thing that struck me on walking about Sydney, looking at the place and the people, was the appalling strength of British civilisation. These people have clung, not only to the faith, but the very raiment of the giant … (Adam 1886).

Nonetheless by the final decades of the nineteenth century the proportion of those born in the colonies exceeded those born overseas. This permitted an upsurge of pride in and respect for colonial achievements and cultural expression. As settlers put down permanent roots and the native born became dominant, colonial society became self-assured and colonials more confident of their identity. Whereas in the earlier days of exile, there was subservience to the standards and ideals set in London, majoritarian embrace of vernacular practices gave greater confidence in their validity. Indeed colonial boosterism even claimed superiority. The novelist Anthony Trollope, visiting the colonies in this era, remarked on the propensity of colonials to blow their own trumpets (Trollope 1967, 1873). The burgeoning colonial self-awareness had all the narcissistic self-importance of the adolescent. The contemporary metaphor used in the popular press was that of the strapping colonial youth. The British colonies on the Australian continent were viewed as Young Australia, and favourably contrasted with Old Britain (Inglis 1981, pp. 1–23). Moreover, Australians were seen as a New Race, triumphing over the indigenous inhabitants who were seen as a Dying Race (*The Australasian Sketcher*, 25 December 1875). Curiously, in developing a distinctive local culture, Australia used predominantly derivative British cultural forms, but also retained something of indigenous Aboriginal cultures. In the homogenising process, British regional variation was lost and blurred as was the cultural integrity of traditional Aboriginal clan and moiety linguistic groupings.

This is not to say that the majoritarian culture was universal. Indeed there were significant minority groups, perhaps the most important of which continued to be Irish nationalists and Irish Catholicism. Not all aspects of colonial civil society presaged an emerging consensus of shared national values. Anti-Irish sentiment and religious sectarianism were rife within colonial Australia. Veteran New South Wales Premier, Sir Henry Parkes, an immigrant British tradesman who had prospered, exploited the tradition of anti-Irish sentiment that had begun with religious bigots such as Samuel Marsden and John Dunmore Lang. In November 1880, Parkes voiced his opposition to Irish immigration, arguing for the preservation of 'the British character of the population as it now exists'. Sectarian differences were also pronounced in the colony of Victoria, where there were regular outbreaks of violence between the followers of the Orange and the Green. In Sydney, when the Redmond brothers were scheduled to undertake a fundraising tour of the Australian colonies to raise money for the Irish National League, a large protest meeting attracted some 8,000 opponents. Invoking 'the purity of public life', Parkes preached communal harmony over tolerance for sectional debate:

> Let Irishmen cherish the memory of the bright and heroic passages in her history; let them, if they wish, cherish with a burning indignation the ways they have evolved. But they have come here for a very different purpose, and I at once take my stand on this very simple rule that when Irishmen, or Englishmen or Scotchmen or Germans come to this land, they have no right to revive the animosities of the land from which they have come. Our public life ought not to be disturbed, ought not to have its very heart torn, by the revival of injuries of other countries.[1]

That Parkes couched his sectarian posturing in the rhetoric of public consensus evidences the strength of the broadly civic culture that was emerging.

The construction of nationhood and its political expression, through federation, also depended on the maintenance and enhancement of social ties between those living in the separate colonies. *The Australasian Sketcher* that began publication in 1873 with coverage of news of all the colonies as well as islands of the Pacific both represented the growth of social affiliations as well as being an advocate for them as a necessary precursor to political unity.

> [I]t would be wrong ... to conclude that federation is a mere dream, and that no conditions are being prepared for its becoming a fact. It has grown to be recognised that when federation takes place it will be less due to the conferences and compacts of our statesmen than to the blending of interests that must arise and is arising between the different populations. Everything that facilitates intercourse and mutual exchange, the construction of railways that weave the colonies together, and so to speak destroys the space by which their communities are kept apart by artificial and sometimes almost hostile, divisions, will blend into the unity of a great Dominion of Australia (26 December 1874).

This blending of colonial into national interests was a precondition of federation: civic culture would precede constitutional form.

Similar views were expressed in 1875 by Sir William Stawell, the Victorian Governor, at a dinner in Melbourne:

> Rest assured that the legal fruition of that long wished for object will be more the giving of a formal effect to a result produced by other causes than the social production itself of that result. Federation will really be established before it is actually proclaimed. We must appreciate our fellow colonists, must give up the ideas that our colony is the only colony to be considered. We must give up the feeling that we are merely living for ourselves in our own colonies. We must become citizens of the world, of our own world at all events ... (*The Australasian Sketcher*, 30 October 1875).

Governor Stawell's comment that 'Federation will really be established before it is actually proclaimed' evidenced his appreciation of the importance of the growth of shared national aspirations over colonial parochialism. Being an imperial officer speaking to imperial subjects, Stawell could appeal to the international as a means of leveraging the national: 'We must become citizens of the world, of our own world at all events'. In his view at least, the global was congenial with the national.

Among ordinary people, a view of a commonwealth was being formed from shared memories, perceptions and links forged and inspired through common experience and endeavour. Aspirations of immigrants, together with the freedom of contract for labour that prevailed in a deregulated market, meant that workers regularly moved between the colonies. Former convicts frequently went to South Australia and Victoria to escape the convict taint of their past. Within colonies, there was a similar restlessness, as goldfields were discovered and new settlements established. Labourers in this highly mobile workforce had a collective experience of the Australian colonies that would increasingly translate into national aspirations. From 1879 trade unions, although established in the separate colonies, began holding inter-colonial conferences once they became committed to advancement through political rather than industrial means. In going national, unions were following the patterns of industry and private capital that, unlike colonial statist capitalism, paid scant attention to colonial boundaries. Business interests had always gone beyond colonial boundaries and exploited commercial opportunities and speculative investment in other colonies. Rural entrepreneurs such as the Henty family from Tasmania brought the pastoral industry to Victoria. When land in Collingwood was first sold in Melbourne, much of it was bought by wealthy property holders in New South Wales (Barrett 1971). In Melbourne, astute businessmen, such as the agricultural implement maker and entrepreneur, John Buncle, sent their commercial travellers to agricultural shows throughout their own colony and into those of neighbouring colonies. The successful fish merchant, Robert Langford, extended his business dealings beyond Melbourne to Sydney and Brisbane.

Inter-colonial interests and associations were more extensive than the protagonists of capitalist production. Churches and friendly societies were experienced in establishing hierarchical organisational structures that encompassed the associations of smaller territories with affiliations to larger territories. Mostly the affiliations were from the local, to the colonial and to the imperial. However, there were some moves to form national affiliations. One friendly society was dedicated to this cause. Formed in Melbourne in 1871, the Australian Natives' Association carried forward the tradition of mutualism, but it did so through exploiting indigenous cultural forms rather than British ones. It also aimed to be as inclusive as possible, with aspirations to more universal membership of young native Australians in all the colonies. The symbols chosen as mastheads of a new cultural identity were appropriated from indigenous ones: meetings were called corroborees and boomerangs were used as insignia for membership of the brotherhood. There were also other groups wanting to construct national associations. By the late 1880s professionals were meeting regularly on a national basis: in April 1887 the first inter-colonial medical conference was held in Adelaide, and in June the Australian Economic Association held its inaugural meeting.

Sporting events were a further means of fostering inter-colonial interests and signalling cultural unity, while at the same time cementing colonial loyalties. Inter-colonial test cricket dates from the 1869 match between Victoria and New South Wales. The first inter-colonial rowing competition was held in 1878 and the following year the first inter-colonial Australian Rules football match was played between the colonies of Victoria and South Australia, in Melbourne. In 1882, the first inter-colonial match of Rugby Union was held between New South Wales and Queensland.

In the 1880s national aspirations and imaginings were given a fillip by intellectual endeavours and publications in anticipation of the 1888 Centennial Celebrations. *The Bulletin*, first published in Sydney in 1880, became the knock-about champion of a national cultural identity. *The Bulletin* was home to 'the bush poets' whose voices mythologised the land and the loyalties of battlers whose lives were tied to its harsh seasons. Political union presupposed claiming the land as territory for the imagined nation-state even though the settler population was sparsely scattered over its surface and concentrated in metropolitan centres rather than the bush. In 1881, almost a decade after the separate colonies agreed to a common census, the first census for all six colonies was held and revealed an Australia-wide population of some two million inhabitants. In the boom era of the 1880s there were Utopian visions of a magnificent destiny for the Australian colonies as a nation.

Australia was receiving more attention on the world stage, and had always been seen as a collective entity rather than as separate colonies. In London, a series of reflections on life in the Australian colonies was being published that followed on from Trollope's 1873 journalistic impression. This included Richard Twopeny's *Town Life in Australia* (1883) and Francis Adam's *Australian Essays* (1886). An enterprising American book firm, S. C. Moffat and J. W. Lyon, who had previously published a visual representation of Canada called *Picturesque Canada*, set about achieving a similar publication on the Australian continent. This *Picturesque Atlas of Australasia* included an extensive text interspersed with copious illustrations of all the colonies as well as related countries in the Pacific. Initially published in separate volumes, a combined publication was produced in 1886. One of the commissioned compilers, Professor E. E. Morris, an Indian-born Englishman who had settled in Melbourne for an appointment to the university, undertook a further laborious project in philology and lexicography. This was published in 1898 as *Austral English: A dictionary of Australian words, phrases and usages*. Images of Australian life received wider popular attention when Ethel Turner's *Seven Little Australians*, published in November 1894, became an international bestseller.

The 1888 Centenary of Foundation was a milestone for colonial Australia and a grand occasion for national imaginings. Since the Jubilee celebration in 1838, the arrival of the British at Botany Bay on the 26 January 1788 had been celebrated with an annual holiday called Foundation Day. The Centenary celebrated British colonisation but in a way that emphasised common origins of British heritage and shared aspirations for the future.

Shared economic challenges and technological benefits reinforced this commonality. Colonial governments had invested heavily in infrastructure development through borrowing in the British capital market and, following the 1890s recession, would benefit from adopting a collective approach to such capital markets. In part, they invested in telegraph lines and the interconnection of the separate railway lines of the colonies to facilitate inter-colonial trade and commerce that would be a major purpose of federation. Linking the separate railway gauges adopted by the separate colonies was more problematic and took a further twenty years. In 1883 the key link was made between New South Wales and Victoria and hailed as a 'federal event' by *The Argus*:

> It was a federal event, celebrated in a possible federal capital, and under these circumstances in turn it was as natural that the celebration should be of a federal character as that squatters should converse about sheep or ladies about their dressmakers and children (Barrett 1971, p. 394).

By 1887, the rail network was extended further with Adelaide being linked to Melbourne and Sydney.

Federation and Popular Support

The construction of a nation-state built upon a popular sentiment for, and articulation of, a homogeneous and distinctive vernacular culture. Apart from national imaginings, Victorians were eminently aware that nation-states needed to be socially constructed and economically viable. Infrastructure and demographics were the nuts and bolts of establishing an enlarged political community. But the whole point of creating a nation-state was taking a place in the larger world politically: being able to represent distinctive interests, maintain them and, above all, defend them. Such concerns were always the stimulus for more concerted political action on the part of the separate colonies in the Australasian region.

The political development of Australian nationhood was a gradual process, unhurried by necessity or political imperative. Paradoxically, British imperial administration provided a benevolent shield that undercut any urgency for federation but was quicker to perceive its attractions than the colonial governments themselves. Governor Macquarie in an 1817 dispatch to the Colonial Office first suggested that the continent be named 'Australia' in preference to 'New Holland'. Thirty years later, when the colonies were de-manding responsible government from the British Government, the Colonial Secretary, Earl Grey, recommended that a federation should be considered.

Grey was following up Governor Fitzroy's earlier concern with administrative delays, and saw a centralised authority as the answer. While Grey's suggestion was rejected by the colonies, in a prescient symbolic gesture in 1855 the British Government appointed a governor-general of all the colonies, resident in the colony of New South Wales.

Although the colonies shared a common cultural identity and were becoming more interdependent, their distinctiveness was sustained by separate self-governing political systems. Forging national unity would require transformative political action in establishing institutions of national governance. Overtures for political unity commenced in the more populous colonies from the 1870s onwards. Success would depend on both astute political leadership and popular will to forge a national polity that would consolidate and expand the shared experience, memories and aspirations of colonial Australia.

In March 1867 a conference was convened on the part of the five self-governing colonies (New South Wales, Victoria, Queensland, South Australia and Tasmania) and New Zealand and there was agreement to lobby for improved imperial postal services. They also discussed the advantages of federation, although its immediate prospects were not promising. Only the south-eastern cluster of colonies attended a subsequent inter-colonial conference in July 1870: Victoria, New South Wales, South Australia and Tasmania. Cooperation was achieved on matters such as inter-colonial postage and telegraph charges and on keeping uniform statistical records. Defence was to become a more urgent consideration only a month later. In August 1870, British troops were withdrawn on the grounds that the British Government could no longer afford to maintain the garrison. As a colonial newspaper writer observed:

> The circumstance is important as marking an event in the history not only of this colony, but of Australia; it is the first step towards nationality, not the result of direful conflicts and years of suffering, but the well considered conclusion of men who rule the destiny of a great nation.[2]

There was more hope than reality in this sentiment. The eminent Irish radical politician, Charles Gavan Duffy, who had immigrated to the colony of Victoria and become its premier, established a Royal Commission to inquire into the matter of federation. But this came to nothing. A major stumbling block was the leadership rivalry between Victoria and New South Wales and the additional fact that each had chosen different economic policies. Victoria was committed to protection of local industry and manufacture, whereas New South Wales followed a free trade policy. When the Franco-Prussian war threatened, New South Wales unilaterally passed legislation to raise its own military force.

Political federation was revived in the early 1880s, the catalyst being concerns about immigration and the ambitions of rival imperial powers in the Pacific. In January 1881 an Australasian inter-colonial conference met to consider the contentious issue of Chinese immigration. There was a groundswell of hostility towards the Chinese in the eastern colonies sparked by the growth of the trade union movement and alarm that the colony of Western Australia had been considering a proposal for assisted immigration of Chinese. The conference agreed that Chinese immigration should be restricted. Mindful that the British Government would likely be disapproving, the conference prepared a communiqué claiming that the decision was not based on racial prejudice but on the 'rational' dangers of 'aliens'. A Chinese delegation toured the Australian colonies in 1887 to raise concerns about such discriminatory attitudes, but to no avail: 'White Australia' became increasingly a central plank of the federation movement.

As discussed in Chapter 2, concern for keeping other European powers out of the region was also behind the new wave of enthusiasm for federation in the 1880s. An 1883 inter-colonial conference supported a motion put by Queensland's premier, Samuel Griffith, that a bill be submitted to the British parliament for the formation of a Federal Council of Australasia that would include New Zealand and Fiji. The conference was concerned with the possible incursion of France or Germany into the region and urged that the British Government annex as much of New Guinea as possible. When the British Colonial Office was unmoved, Queensland took the unprecedented action of issuing an annexation of eastern New Guinea that was subsequently repudiated by the British Government. Following intense lobbying by the premiers of the Australian colonials and New Zealand, Britain finally proclaimed south-eastern New Guinea as a British protectorate following Germany's move on north-eastern New Guinea. The first meeting of the new Federal Council of Australasia took place in Hobart in January amid concerns that France had its imperial eyes on the New Hebrides.

Despite Britain's apparent insensitivity to the threat of foreign powers in the Pacific, the Australian colonies were enthusiastic supporters of British imperial concerns elsewhere in the globe. In February 1885 the colonies provided troops to fight in the Sudan. Months later, when tensions appeared in relations between England and Russia, all the colonies set up successful recruitment drives for volunteer defence forces. European power rivalries did eventually cause concern among military strategists regarding the adequacy of colonial defence forces. British defence expert, Major-General Sir Bevan Edwards, inspected colonial military arrangements and advised that the separate colonial forces were inadequate and required 'federation of the forces of the different colonies'. This was an additional reason for political federation.

The celebration of Queen Victoria's fifty years as sovereign set the occasion for the Australian colonies to consider their place in the world. This occurred at a time when British historians and publicists were proposing ambitious

schemes for further consolidating the majesty of the Empire. As if to compensate for Britain's losing her lead as the great industrial power of the
nineteenth century, enthusiasm for British cultural imperialism waxed
stronger than ever. The flag was to lead trade, not trade the flag. One of the
precursors to the movement for a more integrated global empire was Charles
Dilke. His *Greater Britain* (1868) highlighted the importance of the colonies
he had recently visited on a grand tour that included Australia. The historian
John Seeley in *The Expansion of England* (1883) advocated a federal system
of government for the colonies of the Empire. J. Froude, who had visited
Australasia in 1885, published *Oceana* (1886) which supported a federal
British parliament. Charles Dilke's *Problems of Greater Britain* (1890) advocated the unification of the Empire. The grandiose vision of such theorists
was taken up by the Imperial Federation League established in 1884 to
proselytise on the issue. At the first Colonial Conference that met in the
Jubilee year in London, however, the premiers from the Australian colonies
were not enthusiastic about British imperial federation. Their concerns were
more mundane and they were successful in getting a ten-year agreement for
stationing a British naval squadron in Australasian waters.

A different kind of national federation was in the air, as the colonies celebrated the centenary of British colonisation in 1888. In October 1889 Sir Henry
Parkes called for abolition of the Federal Council (which New South Wales
had never joined) and establishment of a federal system of unification among
the Australian colonies with a federal parliament and federal government. In
February 1890 the colonial premiers and New Zealand representatives met to
discuss Parkes' proposal and agreed to a Federal Convention in 1891 at which
delegates from all the parliaments would meet to draft a constitution. At the
convention banquet, Sir Henry Parkes, after toasting the Queen, saluted a future
Australia of 'one people, one destiny'. In grandiose rhetoric, Parkes proclaimed:
'The time has come when this Australian people should be one – henceforward
and forever – should make common cause and inherit one common destiny'.

There has been much debate as to whether federation was a hollow
agreement or built on broader political foundations. Scholars of constitutional jurisprudence are divided on the issue of the extent to which the
constitution was founded on and legitimated by popular participation. Those
who celebrate federation have argued that Australia, for its day, provided the
most democratic model of constitution making ever to be attempted (Quick
& Garran 1976, La Nauze 1972, Galligan 1995, Irving 1997). Critics, like
George Williams, have a contrary view:

> The making of the Australian constitution was neither repre-
> sentative nor inclusive of the Australian people generally. It was
> drafted by a small privileged section of society. Whole sections of
> the community were excluded from the Conventions or from
> voting for the draft constitution ... (Williams 1999, p. 30).

Historians have also presented differing accounts. Stuart Macintyre's recent review of Australian historiography shows how the earlier celebratory accounts of federation gave way to more sceptical and critical ones (Macintyre 2000, pp. 3–20). Revisionist historians have characterised federation as something of a political hoax, involving an elite and curtailing rather than enhancing democratisation.[3]

The centenary of federation in 2001 has stimulated the entry of new proponents reworking and extending older positions. Bob Birrell adopts a celebratory approach by drawing attention to the mobilisation of popular opinion through the Australian Natives' Association (Birrell 1995). Many others, however, denigrate its achievement. Professor McMinn claims that, although there was popular sentiment, this was not translated into political involvement. (McMinn 1994). Peter Botsman goes so far as to claim that the whole process of appearing to frame 'the people's constitution' was in fact a 'swindle' (Botsman 2000). Curiously, he uses total population figures including children, instead of total eligible voting population, to argue that only the smallest minority actually supported federation. Phillip Knightley alleges that Australians showed little interest in federation because they were captured by the more immediate concerns of plagues and drought and because of utter weariness that 'politicians had been talking about it but doing nothing for too long' (Knightley 2000). So dominant have the revisionist and critical accounts become that many have lost sight of the original story of federation and its positive achievements. According to Birrell, such accounts have so obscured the original story of federation that it has become 'The Secret Story', as he subtitles his recent book (Birrell 2001).

In fact Australian federation was probably the least secretive and elitist of any comparable process of nation-state building. While political elites dominated the process of constitution making throughout the 1890s, they were either appointed by colonial parliaments or directly elected by the people. Although voting was not compulsory in the referendums and women, children and most indigenous and other non-white people were excluded, the process of constitution making was truly democratic by the standards of the time. Moreover, the constitution making of the 1890s was premised on the existence of a popular national consciousness and a politically active citizenry (Roberts 2001). Federation was built on firm foundations of popular support and discursive democratic practices inherent in existing colonial citizenship and imperial association. The extent of active involvement in politics by ordinary people is evidenced in the range and extent of political agitation and mobilisation on a broad range of issues, including the women's campaign on temperance.

The performance of civic roles in local communities helped school citizens in politics and public life. Leading citizens worked on establishing civic cohesion and promoting general interests rather than particular ones. They saw themselves as setting an example of public duty by assuming municipal office, sitting on the local courts, convening meetings on public issues of the day and acting as patrons for various leagues and clubs. Professionals and qualified artisans established and ran courses at the local Mechanics' Institutes and Schools of Design. Leading townsmen sat on the Board of Advice that supervised and supported the provision of public school education. Men and young boys were encouraged to become school cadets or senior cadets and join volunteer brigades in order to build their character. They were also urged to train and become members of local fire brigades. Their uniformed ranks were accorded a place of honour in colonial pageants and municipal ceremonies. Boys marched in playgrounds, young men drilled in halls and reel-houses and young women, two by two, went about visiting the heathen and destitute. The unions, the friendly societies and cooperatives offered the means for small property owners to sustain their independence and improve their circumstances. The churches established societies for self-improvement in refinements such as music and debating as well as for civic education.

Voluntary associations provided training in political skills, probity and organisation. If the heart of politics lay in argument and debate, then voluntary associations provided training in cooperative resolution of issues in an orderly and public manner through patronage, meeting procedures and the art of debate. Serving in voluntary associations had a civic as well as vocational role, with elected office-bearers being responsible for ensuring that the aims of the organisation were met and that subscribers' funds were appropriately administered. Associations of civil society preceded those of national government in setting up elaborate structures of devolution and federation. Amid the chaos of laissez-faire capitalism, the Victorians were great organisers and particularly adept at devising political structures to organise political advantage or economic efficiency. Municipal councillors and council officers regularly contended with wardship contestations over annexation or secession. Voluntary associations were veterans at federating to achieve greater political influence. By the mid-1880s, local mutual improvement societies, professional organisations, the trade union movement and employer organisations were all federating to form national associations.

Public issues were regularly debated in a society that retained strong oral traditions and a propensity for public debate. Federation was a topical issue throughout the 1880s, even in working class suburbs like North Melbourne. For example, in September 1883, the North Melbourne Literary and Debating Society sponsored a talk by Mr Taverner on Federation. In July 1884 there was a joint debate between the local Mechanics' Institute and the Footscray Debating Society on the question of the 'Federation of the Australian Colonies'. In 1885 the Australian Natives' Association sponsored a debate as to whether Australian Federation was to be preferred to Imperial Federation.

De Tocqueville considered freedom of association and the organisations of civil society to be the life-blood of democracy. The voluntary associations of civil society played a significant role in nineteenth-century public life in Australia. In particular, the Australian Natives' Association played a key role in promoting nationalism and the federation movement through its network of local branches. Equally important was the civic involvement evident in local communities and polities. The homogeneity of colonial political regimes allowed political agitation, mobilisation and socialisation to be directed towards continental uniformity and a new sphere of federal governance.

In sum, the establishment of national government in 1901 extended the project of self-governance that had developed during the nineteenth century and had been manifest in most colonies since mid-century. Queensland was a laggard in the federation process of the 1890s and failed to send delegates to the 1897–98 convention. Western Australia was the latecomer, achieving self-government only in 1897 and belatedly ratifying the draft constitution in 1899. Federation entailed the blending of established traditions of British parliamentary responsible government (that colonials were familiar with) and a federal constitution modelled on the American prototype. The Australian founding was an evolutionary rather than a revolutionary mutation, building upon a national civic culture and extending tried political practices of the colonies to a new sphere of national government. The constitution was Australian made: designed by political leaders elected for that purpose and endorsed by the Australian people voting in referendums in their respective colonies. At the same time, this antipodean experiment in democratic constitution making and nation building relied heavily upon the protective umbrella of the British Empire. The British Government supported federation but, for the most part, left constitution making to Australians. Importantly, the British Government took care of national security and foreign policy, as Chapter 4 will document. Secure in international affairs, the Australian founders could get on with the business of nation building.

Constitution Making

The making of the Australian nation was completed through the process of framing and adopting the federal constitution. This occurred in the elaborate series of constitutional conventions during the 1890s, formal passage of the draft bill by the Westminster parliament, and proclamation of the new nation in January 1901. The groundwork for nationhood had been laid by colonial nationalism and the development of a politically active citizenry. Nevertheless the design and implementation of a federal constitution that satisfied the majority of political leaders and people in the various colonies was a political feat of great significance. Without it there would have been no Australian nation and no national citizenship. Given the continuities of colonial life and British imperial association, however, creating a federal nation that retained the colonies as states and remained a British dominion was not as dramatic or as radical as some national foundings have been. That does not mean, however, that the establishment of a nation-state was not a momentous political event. The eventual outcome was always precarious given that it relied on the partial coalition of polities that had been separately established and were already experienced in exercising their own independent power. Nevertheless, contestation, argument and compromise – processes crucial to democratic politics – were successfully employed to make the Australian constitution.

Alastair Davidson claims there was a democratic deficit in both the constitutional process and its product. He laments the overall legalism of Australian citizenship and claims that the constitution was foisted upon a passive population (Davidson 1991). He complains that the citizenry did not agree 'as an active majority to its terms'; it 'did not make that citizenry formally sovereign'; it 'did not enshrine the basic rule of a democracy'; it contained no 'definition of what it is to be a citizen'; and it 'contains no bill of rights, despite the fact that such rights are the cornerstone of "modern liberties"' (Davidson 1997, p. 51). Davidson's point of positive reference is the French people and the 1791 constitution of the French Republic, which is curious because ordinary French people were still struggling to establish democratic participation in the final decades of the nineteenth century (Hazareesingh 1998; Nord 1995). What Davidson prefers is a different approach to constitutional design and democratic citizenship from the one followed in Australia. In the Australian model, citizenship and rights were not spelt out in the constitution partly because, unlike the French revolutionary situation in 1791, they did not have to be and partly because they were quite deliberately left for parliament to determine.

Although unlike the French in manner and form, Australia's constitution making was remarkably democratic. A Federal Convention was held in Sydney in 1891 and produced a draft constitution. Although not adopted, it did provide a blueprint for the second round of successful constitution making in 1897–98. The 1891 draft constitution was strongly federal in character and copied substantially the American model. James Bryce's *American Commonwealth* (1888) was conveniently available and would be saluted by Alfred Deakin as the bible of the Australian constitution makers. Individuals like Inglis Clark from Tasmania championed American design principles. So strong was the support for federalism at this convention that responsible government was left somewhat open as the executive form of government: depending on how it fitted with federalism and a powerful Senate in practice, it might need to be changed. Hence responsible government was not constitutionalised by this first convention.

The 1891 draft was never implemented for a number of reasons. One was a lack of popular support. The 1891 convention had consisted of delegates appointed by colonial governments, and the draft had to be approved by colonial governments. A second reason for the 1891 draft bill's not being adopted was the greater urgency of other issues of the day. The 1890s depression and drought raised more immediate concerns for colonial parliaments, and the rise of the Labor party re-focused attention on immediate political adjustments in various colonies, especially New South Wales. It was left to businessmen and affected interest groups to press for the dismantling of inter-colonial barriers to trade and commerce, and the Australian Natives Association to kindle a grass roots movement of federation leagues. Popular conventions were held to mobilise support, and imperialism and republicanism were argued as causes alongside federation. The groundswell of support for federation through the mid-1890s was sufficient to trigger a second round of constitution making towards the end of the decade.

In 1897, Queen Victoria's Diamond Jubilee year, a new Federal Convention met in Adelaide for a second attempt at drafting a constitution for the new nation. This time delegates were directly elected by the people of the colonies and provision was made to submit the completed draft to the people of the colonies voting at referendum. The 1891 draft constitution provided a blueprint and once again the American federal model dominated the thinking of the convention. This time, however, there was more protracted discussion and debate with delegates meeting for three successive sessions of the convention, at Adelaide and Sydney in 1897 and in Melbourne in the summer of 1898. Under Edmund Barton's leadership, this convention was more confident in adopting a uniquely Australian blend of federalism and responsible government. The draft constitution was reviewed by the colonial parliaments and their suggestions considered at the Melbourne session. It was then put to referendum for endorsement as required by the Enabling Acts of the colonies. Although supported by majorities of those voting in the four colonies in which referendums were held, the draft constitution failed to win the special majority of 10,000 that had been prescribed in New South Wales. Neither Queensland nor Western Australia was quite ready at this point, so no referendums were held in those colonies: Queensland had refused to send delegates to the 1897–98 convention, and Western Australia played a wait-and-see game.

Further concessions were necessary to swing additional support in New South Wales and these were considered at a Special Premiers' Conference attended by all the colonial premiers. They agreed that the new national capital should be in New South Wales, although not within a certain radius of Sydney. Until it was built, the seat of national government would be located in Melbourne. The other changes made were termination of the Braddon financial clause and substitution of a simple for a three-fifths majority at joint sittings of parliament when the two Houses were in disagreement. Both were seen as measures favouring the larger states like New South Wales. Although the changes were not major ones, the amended draft constitution was re-submitted to the people of colonies, including Queensland, for endorsement. This time it passed with strong majorities in all the participating colonies. Western Australia again dragged its feet until goldfield settlers, many of whom had come from the depressed eastern colonies, pressed for a successful referendum in that colony as well. The final step in the process of ratification was formal passage of the constitution by the British parliament, after slight modification to broaden appeals to the Privy Council.

The outstanding feature of the Australian constitution-making process, from the point of view of citizenship, was its thoroughly democratic character. While the British imperial parliament provided a certain formal legitimacy at the final stage, popular sovereignty was its foundation and spirit. This was evident in the process of constitution making: direct election of delegates to the 1897–98 convention and approval of the draft constitution by popular referendums. It was also reflected in the constitution itself. The preamble stated the agreement of the people of the various colonies to form 'one indissoluble Federal Commonwealth'; both Houses of parliament were to be 'directly chosen by the people'; and the constitution could be amended only by popular referendum.

The democratic character of the constitutional process and the constitution itself were eloquently acknowledged at the time. The 1900 Premiers' Conference affirmed that the draft constitution belonged 'in a very special sense to the people of Australia, whose only mandate to governments and parliaments is to seek enactment by the Imperial Parliament in the form in which it was adopted by the people' (Quick & Garran 1976, 1901, p. 237). In insisting upon the broadening of Privy Council appeals that he claimed were necessary for Imperial interests, Joseph Chamberlain nevertheless acknowledged that 'the Bill had been prepared by the Australian people' (Quick & Garran 1976, 1901, p. 242). And from a comparative perspective, the Australian constitution, both in its making and its provisions, was more radically democratic than any of its close counterparts. The Canadian constitution of 1867 was the product of an elite process that eschewed popular input; so much so that even today it is problematical whether Canadians can constitute themselves into a sovereign people (Russell 1993). The Americans had been more democratic in using specifically elected constitutional conventions (Beer 1993), but had not gone so far as popular endorsement of the draft constitution.

The Australian nation-state was built upon a sturdy colonial tradition of democratic civic culture. It was founded not on the boldness of poetic imagining or ideological fervour, though this formed a leavening influence, but on solid, pragmatic bargaining and compromise. Australian rule was the achievement of immigrants and settlers who were dedicated to the pursuit of material prosperity and democratic politics. Nationhood for them was essentially a political union for consolidating and furthering political, economic and social goals. International influences of the labour movement and the women's temperance and suffrage movements subsequently shaped and influenced national policies but they did so in ways that reflected indigenous aspirations. Australian rule was to establish fifty years of White Australia, which restricted global immigration in the interests of Advancing Native Australians and preserving their British stock.

National Citizenship

Not only did federation create the Australian nation-state as 'one indissoluble Federal Commonwealth' that preserved the colonies as states and established appropriate institutions of national government, its more significant, but less well recognised, purpose was to enhance Australian citizenship. It did this by adding a national sphere of enlarged governance while continuing, albeit in modified form, sub-national and supra-national polities and affiliations.

This key federation purpose of enhancing and extending democratic citizenship has been neglected for various reasons. The complexity of dual citizenship that federalism entails – being a citizen of one's state for local purposes as well as a citizen of the nation for national purposes – was alien to unitary assumptions inherent in dominant British discourse. This assumed that citizens were members or subjects of a sovereign state; and that sovereignty was single and undivided. The leading British exponent of this view, Oxford don A. V. Dicey, dominated British constitutional thinking in the latter part of the nineteenth century (Dicey 1982, 1885) and had a profound effect on Australian constitutional jurisprudence. His teaching on parliamentary sovereignty bedevilled the thinking of generations of Australian lawyers and commentators who struggled to apply the Dicean doctrine of parliamentary sovereignty to Australia's Commonwealth and State parliaments that had only limited constitutional powers. The Dicean mindset cannot appreciate or tolerate federalism. That is because sovereignty is essentially a unitary as well as an absolutist concept whereas federalism entails duality and limitation of powers.

The other side of the Dicean sovereignty paradigm is the unitary citizen. An absolute and undivided sovereign or sovereign state can only allow a unitary citizen or subject who is undivided in their allegiance and loyalty. This clearly does not fit with federalism where citizenship is dual, and a citizen's allegiance divided between national and state governments. Put another way, citizens in a federal country are members of two distinct and non-sovereign political entities, each of which has limited powers and both of which are controlled by an over-arching constitution. Broadly speaking, the national community exists for purposes of national governance and the provincial state community for regional or more local governance. The unitary concept of sovereignty does not fit a federal constitutional system like the Australian where a constitution defines and limits the powers of national and state parliaments and governments. Sovereignty in such a system lies beyond any one sphere of government or parliament, either with the over-arching constitution, which allocates and limits jurisdictional powers, or with the people whose instrument of government the constitution is. Obviously, unitary notions of citizen or subject do not fit federal citizenship where people are members of two political entities each of which has separate governmental jurisdiction.

A more mundane reason for the neglect of citizenship in the Australian founding and during the first half-century of nationhood is the simple assumption that it did not exist. The formal title of 'British subject' used in the constitution and official government documents for the first half-century of federation has often been taken at face value. It is naively assumed there were no Australian citizens until Australian people were officially designated as such in the Commonwealth's Nationality and Citizenship Act 1948, that came into force on Australia Day 1949. Many critics and commentators have ignored Australian citizenship during the first half-century of nationhood because they wrongly assume it was either non-existent or insufficient. Yet as we have seen, British subjecthood in the Australian colonies comprised citizenships in both an imperial sphere and in more parochial self-governing spheres.

As Chapter 2 has shown, Australian colonists and their colonial governments were extensively interconnected with Britain and the British Empire. This continued at federation and well into the twentieth century. British subjecthood was more than a formal correlate of constitutional monarchism. It included a certain status and various entitlements that flowed from membership in a global empire, especially for those who could afford to travel and engage in more cosmopolitan activities. For many Australians but not all, it also entailed a strong sense of personal and group attachment to a cherished motherland and its language and culture. Whatever the value of this British connection and the formal title of subservience to British monarch and empire, Australian citizenship entailed much more. Just as the Australian nation was formally a constitutional monarchy but in effect a federal republic based on popular consent, (Galligan 1995) Australian citizenship was similarly complex and entailed democratic self-governance. This was manifest in the most fundamental way: in making their own constitution that enshrined a federal system of government that was fundamentally democratic. Australians thereby became members of a new national, as well as continuing state, political communities where governments could provide social and economic benefits and entitlements as well as the standard legal and political ones (Chesterman & Galligan 1999).

Federation added an additional sphere of national citizenship to colonial citizenship while retaining the blend of colonial and imperial elements that were already in place. Australians retained British subjecthood that formally recognised their membership of a global empire as well as their established colonial citizenship that made them members of local self-governing communities. At federation they extended this to national membership of the new Commonwealth of Australia. If we include local government that had been established in the colonies in the nineteenth century, Australians shared in four different political communities – empire, nation, state and local. Add to this the mix of rights and duties attaching to each polity, and one has the structural elements of Australian citizenship. To say the least, it was both rich and complex.

Capturing that richness and complexity, either at federation or even today, is not straightforward because Australian citizenship has no core definition or constitutional statement of rights and duties. The Australian Citizenship Act of 1948 defined Australians as citizens for the first time but it did not spell out what that citizenship entailed. Nor did the founders in the Australian constitution a half-century earlier. After considerable debate, the founders decided not to constitutionalise citizenship, preferring instead to leave its definition and development to the new Commonwealth parliament and continuing state regimes. Neither the Commonwealth nor the States have come up with a core instrument of citizenship, but have provided particular rights, duties, entitlements and benefits in a piecemeal way. With two spheres of federal government involved, the process of defining Australian citizenship and specifying the rights, entitlements and benefits that it confers has been a contested and developmental one. Whether we like it or not, the founders did not specify citizenship in any detail, as we shall see in the next section. They preferred to leave its definition and development to legislative and administrative processes under the constitution, that will be examined in some detail in subsequent chapters.

Original Intent

Citizenship was at the heart of the new Australian political community established at federation. Two of the most prominent founding fathers signalled this in their inaugural messages to the Australian people on 1 January 1901. Alfred Deakin said that Australians would be 'for the first time in our history the possessors of a common political citizenship', while Samuel Griffith confirmed that 'henceforth, every Australian is a citizen of the new-born Commonwealth' (Quoted in Irving 1997, p. 169). What federation did, however, was not to provide constitutional definition of national citizenship but to set up the institutions of national government that would do so.

Those who drafted the constitution had a robust notion of the new Australian citizenship they were instituting. Citizenship was considered at length during the Melbourne session of the Federal Constitutional Convention in March 1898. The founders debated two different proposals concerning aspects of citizenship: one was to include a guarantee of a citizen's privileges and immunities modelled on the Fourteenth Amendment of the American constitution; the other was whether to include an enumerated power to enable the new national government to make laws with respect to 'Commonwealth citizenship'. In the event, neither was adopted but in the discussion the citizenship purpose of federation was articulated and reasons for not including citizenship in the constitution exhaustively debated.

A brief sampling of the convention debates shows that its leaders had both explicit concerns for, and complex notions of, citizenship. Richard O'Connor, a key person on the three-man drafting committee, confirmed: 'we are creating now a new and a larger citizenship. We are giving new rights of citizenship to the whole of the citizens of the Commonwealth' (Federation Debates 1898, p. 689). More precisely, Josiah Symon, a leading South Australian, reminded delegates who were advocating 'equal citizenship' and 'one citizenship' under the new Commonwealth that 'the whole purpose of this Constitution is to secure a dual citizenship'. According to Symon, that was 'the very essence of a federal system. ... dual citizenship must be recognised as lying at the very basis of this Constitution' (Ibid., p. 675). The radical Victorian liberal, Henry Higgins preferred to articulate this as 'double citizenship' or 'two citizenships' – with citizens having certain privileges and immunities 'as a citizen of the Commonwealth' and others 'as a citizen of the state' (Ibid., p. 684). Others like Charles Kingston from South Australia preferred such terms as 'federal citizenship' and 'Australian citizenship' (Ibid., p. 677). Isaac Isaacs laid out the rich citizenship menu that would be available to Australians: 'We have the citizenship of the British Empire on the one hand, and the citizenship of the state on the other', he said. What was further required was provision for a new national citizenship that should not be defined in the constitution but left to the new Commonwealth parliament (Ibid., p. 1759).

The convention majority in voting down mention of citizenship in the constitution was swayed by several key concerns. Many who freely used the term 'citizen' in debate nevertheless thought that its technical meaning was unclear, and therefore its inclusion in the constitution would raise more problems than it would solve. In any case, as Isaacs insisted, the Australian situation did not require an American-style Fourteenth Amendment guarantee of a citizen's privileges and immunities that had been passed to force recalcitrant Southern states to extend citizenship rights to Black Americans after a bloody civil war (Ibid., p. 670). Besides, the American practice of spelling out rights guaranteed in the constitution was not one that the Australian founders were used to or favoured.

The other main consideration was a federal or states' rights one: not interfering with the right of states to make laws. Indeed, fear that the Commonwealth might use a power to make laws regarding 'Commonwealth citizenship' for just such a purpose was the reason why many opposed John Quick's proposal to put citizenship in the constitution. Quick wanted 'a citizenship of the Commonwealth higher, more comprehensive, and nobler than that of the states' (Ibid., p. 1766). However, other key figures like Edmund Barton and Richard O'Connor thought constitutional entrenchment of citizenship was unnecessary because they had already provided for the new Commonwealth to legislate with respect to the franchise. Barton claimed: 'We have provided in this Constitution for the exercise of the rights of citizenship, as far as the choice of representatives is concerned, and we have given various safeguards to individual liberty in the Constitution.' In other words, basic democratic citizenship was sufficiently ensured by providing representative institutions of government.

Barton clinched the argument for excluding any mention of citizenship in the constitution on the grounds of conventional constitutional usage. Despite using the terms subject and citizen interchangeably himself, Barton pointed out that 'citizen' was not a technical term used in British and colonial constitutional lexicons. He cited *Stroud's Judicial Dictionary*, a standard authority of the day that contained no definition of citizenship as applied to a British subject. Moreover, Barton observed: 'No such term as citizen or citizenship is to be found in the long roll of enactments, as far as I can recollect, that deal with the position of subjects of the United Kingdom, and I do not think we have been in the habit of using that term under our own enactments in any of the colonies' (Ibid., p. 1764). Subject was 'the ordinary term to express a citizen of the empire', Barton insisted when the matter came back to the convention for yet another attempt at formulating section 116: 'We are subjects in our constitutional relation to the empire, not citizens. "Citizens" is an undefined term, and is not known to the Constitution. The word "subjects" expresses the relation between citizens of the empire and the Crown (Ibid., p. 1786).'

In this extensive discussion of citizenship, the founders finally moved from using the more substantive term 'citizen' to the technical term 'subject', not because they did not have strong ideas about the new Australian citizenship that they were creating but because subject was considered appropriate constitutional terminology. Nor is the constitution's relative silence on citizenship issues evidence of neglect; it simply reflects the majority preference against putting such matters in the constitution. The issue then was not whether a new Australian citizenship was being created but rather how that was to be done. The options were spelling out citizenship in the constitution or leaving its definition and development mainly to continuing state and future Commonwealth parliaments and governments to determine. They chose the latter course that was entirely consistent with their constitutional traditions and practice.

Even when the Commonwealth's Nationality and Citizenship Act 1948 came into force on Australia Day 1949, the rights of the Australian citizen were not spelt out. One became an Australian citizen by being born in Australia or naturalised, but substantive citizenship rights did not necessarily attach to such status. Australian citizenship was a formal category like British subjecthood which, as Geoffrey Sawer pointed out, was 'by itself worth little; it is the foundation on which further conditions of disqualification or qualification are built' (Sawer 1961, p. 37). The conditions of disqualification or qualification that were built onto formal Australian citizenship came by way of separate Commonwealth and State statutes and administrative practices, as had been the case when Australians were formally subjects during the previous half-century. The new federal constitution adopted the established colonial and British way of handling citizenship.

Substantive Citizenship

To understand the substance of Australian citizenship, one needs to look beyond formal Australian citizenship terminology and legislation to Commonwealth and State laws and practices that determine basic citizenship rights, entitlements and responsibilities. There is much more to citizenship than legal status. Citizenship, as T. H. Marshall's influential characterisation makes clear, also entails consideration of civil, political and social rights (Marshall 1992, p. 8). While Marshall assumed there was a progressive implementation of a rights regime, it is worth stressing that citizenship rights are highly contested and, as the subsequent chapters will show, citizenship entitlements in Australia have been, and continue to be, subject to political contestation.

Divorcing citizenship status from rights and benefits facilitated exclusions on racial and other grounds, in a way that debased Australian citizenship status as a hollow, even hypocritical, formality for minority groups. At the same time Australians were also confident of using government and state policy for majoritarian social and economic well being, rather than seeking individual protection from the state through a bill of negative rights as the Americans had done. For Americans, founded in part by political refugees suffering religious persecutions, government and the state were potential predators that the individual needed to be protected from. Hence the Bill of Rights specifies areas where 'Congress shall make no law', such as establishing a religion or abridging the freedom of speech; or individual rights which are not to be violated, such as the right of peaceable assembly or the right to keep and bear arms. In contrast to this, many Australians viewed government and the state positively, as a powerful collective means that could improve economic and social well being for the majority, if not minorities. In documenting how Australia has managed citizenship and in assessing how well it has done so we need to include social and economic policy, in particular health, education, wages policy and social welfare.

Although 'citizen subjects' of the British Empire, Australians, at the time of federation, created their own national democracy based on, for the time, quite radical democratic principles. The Depression had exposed the shortcomings of an unregulated global market place that progressives sought to remedy through state regulation. According to W. K. Hancock, one of its greatest critical exponents, the prevailing ideology of Australian democracy was 'the sentiment of justice, the claim of right, the conception of equality, and the appeal to Government as the instrument of self-realisation' (Hancock 1961, 1930, pp. 51–58). Each individual, Hancock claimed, was 'a citizen, a fragment of the sovereign people; each of them is a subject who claims his rights – the right to work, the right to be happy – from the State and through the State'. Successive generations of British and Irish migrants had brought the latest waves of progressive ideas – Chartism, positive liberalism, radicalism and labourism – to the Australian colonies. Combining a statist political economy suited to settling and developing a harsh continent with policies that left immigration, capital flows and labour largely unregulated produced an experience of Australian citizenship that was quite different in kind from either the British parent or the American alternative. Australians were independent democratic citizens, not subservient subjects of a distant motherland.

Federation created a new sphere of Australian government and citizenship that gave its members an enhanced means of protecting, maintaining and enhancing their collective benefits and interests. The nation-state provided a powerful instrument for mediating the impact of globalisation on citizenship through external affairs and domestic policies. Hitherto Australian citizens had been members of political communities that were almost totally global in their concerns or at the other extreme essentially parochial. As members of the British Empire, they were citizens of a wider world and privy to the rights and duties that such imperial association entailed. As members of particular colonies and municipalities they were concerned with advancing community life within a defined locality. Once the Australian nation-state was constructed, the citizens of the new Commonwealth would be concerned with protecting, maintaining and enhancing their own distinctive way of life in a global context as well as domestically. Within the nation-state there would be two spheres of politics and policies that would mediate the impact of globalisation on citizenship through external affairs and domestic policies.

In examining the experience of Australian citizenship in the century since federation, we examine the politics of mediation in both these fields: external affairs in Chapters 4 and 6, and domestic politics in Chapters 5 and 7. Globalisation had been significant in shaping and defining what was distinctively Australian. The political expression of that distinctiveness was the formation of an Australian nation-state that was also the chief means to its achievement.

Chapter 4

Imperial Dominion to Pacific Nation

The people of the Australian colonies formed a nation-state to extend self-government and build a distinctively Australian political community on a continental scale. In the rhetoric of Sir Henry Parkes in celebrating the opening of the 1891 Sydney convention, there would be 'One People – One Destiny' for a nation uniquely occupying a continent (La Nauze 1972, p. 34). Shaping that nation and its people was a developmental process in which the nation-state, created at federation in 1901, would play a major role. As we saw in Chapter 3, the Australian founding was an evolutionary rather than a revolutionary mutation that built upon an established civic culture and traditions of colonial self-government that were strongly British in origin and character. The creation of the Australian nation-state did not entail an assertion of national sovereignty or becoming independent from Britain but took place within the protective umbrella of the British Empire. The Australian nation-state happily left the crucial matters of national security and foreign policy primarily to the British Government, remaining a loyal dominion throughout the first part of the century. The fact that the Australian nation was neither sovereign nor independent in its early decades does not mean it was aberrant or incomplete. As we saw in Chapter 1, sovereignty is an obsession of modern formalist thinking about nations that exaggerates the real status of most nations and distorts the founding of nations like Australia that were formed within the British Empire.

While lacking sovereign independence in external affairs, the Australian nation-state nevertheless played a significant role in mediating global forces in ways that shaped a distinctive nation and citizen body. In the process and as the global balance of power changed through two world wars, Australia developed from being a British dominion to a more independent Pacific nation. That potent and complex process of nation building and maturation as a nation-state is the subject of this chapter. The parallel evolution of Australians from being formally British subjects, but in effect distinctively Australian citizen subjects at federation, to Australian citizens by mid-century is examined in Chapter 5.

Distinctive Nation

In its beginning, Australian settler society had been predominantly British but in ways that made it distinctive from the rest of the colonised world. As a legacy of its colonial history, Australia's homogeneity was unrivalled outside European home nations. The overwhelming preponderance of British people resulted from British possession and settlement that narrowly pre-empted that of the French, as we saw in Chapter 2. It was also due to Australia's geographical isolation away from the bustling trade routes of world commerce, and the dispersion of Australia's indigenous peoples as hunter gatherers across an inhospitable land. Once the British had established a few strategic settlements, other European powers stayed away. The Australian pattern of colonisation was quite dissimilar from that of India or Africa where massed indigenous peoples required varieties of shared and indirect rule. It was also different from Canada and South Africa where prior French and Dutch settler societies had to be accommodated. Even New Zealand was different because of the concentration and organised strength of its Maori people.

Australia's founding as a nation-state was underpinned by its British heritage and that in turn reinforced a strident monoculturalism that only gradually matured into a more tolerant nationalism and accommodation of multiculturalism. Drawing upon a potent mix of notions of the superiority of British culture and the white race, the first Australian government implemented a White Australia policy that would shape the nation and its people for generations. The Immigration Restriction Act 1901 adopted the 'relatively gentlemanly' method of a dictation test that officials could apply in excluding non-whites (Sawer 1956, p. 23). The sting was in the administration of the policy rather than its legislative formulation, but its effectiveness was not diminished. It reflected the same racial prejudices as segregation in the United States and apartheid in South Africa; the difference was that it excluded non-whites at the national border. Canada and New Zealand, and even Britain itself, were not too dissimilar but restricted the migration of non-whites on somewhat more subtle grounds. Asian countries were probably more racist and exclusive, but they did not encourage immigration as Australia did.

The White Australia policy brought to a close the free movement of people that had been a feature of the nineteenth century and anticipated a world trend towards immigration restriction. Passport controls were introduced uniformly by nation-states in the course of the First World War and became an accepted fixture of the international order by the 1920s (Torpey 2000). Despite remaining part of the British Empire with its citizens called British subjects, Australia maintained its own more restrictive immigration policies. Leaders like Prime Minister Billy Hughes unashamedly championed such policies in international forums to ensure that racial equality was not enshrined as a founding principle of the League of Nations.

Immigration restriction was only one of a series of protective national policies that Australia put in place. Australia, as a nation-state, was in retreat from the globalised free market economy of the nineteenth century. The labour movement had become politicised and sought to influence industry policy, advocating protection of Australian industry as a means of providing jobs for Australians. The 1902 Customs Tariff Act signalled a national commitment to protection that would last for most of the twentieth century. Australia was not alone in this. There was a global swing towards protectionism. Germany and America both embraced tariff protection, while Britain too became protectionist and had its waning Empire adopt imperial preferences on tariffs at the 1932 Ottawa conference.

The Australian nation-state tried to mediate the impact of global forces and threats in other routine ways. The Commonwealth established a customs service to police imports and quarantine stations to combat the spread of diseases, although that did not stop the arrival of the global pandemic of deadly influenza that struck with the demobilisation of overseas troops in 1919. Wartime surveillance led to strict national security regimes. Press censorship, controls over broadcasting, the formation of Commonwealth police, the stripping of citizenship rights of naturalised aliens from enemy countries and changing German place names reflected a narrowness of culture and parochialism. The openness of nineteenth-century cosmopolitanism that went with a more liberal political economy was superseded by a more closed and insular society. By the 1930s, book censorship on moral and political grounds became government policy through the office of the Minister for Customs. Like quarantine requirements, cultural closure was by no means complete or unchallenged; the banning of books such as Huxley's *Brave New World* was ridiculed and contested.

While the Australian nation-state was building barriers at its borders to protect and enhance what it saw as a distinctive, desirable and indeed preferable way of life – nonetheless it was far from globally isolated. The first fifty years of Australia's nationhood coincided with sweeping technological advances in communications and transport that resulted in a rapidly shrinking globe. The 1920s saw the beginning of radio broadcasting, wireless linkage to Britain, commercialisation of powered flight, significant private and commercial investment in vehicular transport and the beginning of 'talking movies'. Australia and Australian people were part of an increasingly interconnected and interrelated world from which there could be no real political or civil isolation.

Nor was Australia sufficiently strong to stand alone as an independent nation without close affiliation with Britain. Although some had Utopian visions of a limitless future for the newly constituted nation, the reality was more sobering. Australia's population was limited, its defence capacity was marginal and its resources were undeveloped. During the first decades of Australia's nationhood, the Commonwealth and State governments relied heavily on Britain. Population increase under the White Australia policy relied upon immigration promotion and assisted passage agreements with the British Government. Australia's naval and military capability was reliant on the advice of British experts and the use of British industrial technology. The massive investment in state infrastructure largely depended on British capital, as did the financing of much of private industry. Australia's enormous effort in the First World War was tailored to British strategic interests in Europe, and its terrible losses the price of such an association.

Global influences affecting Australia and its people during the first half-century of nationhood were obviously more varied and extensive than British and strategic ones. An idealistic internationalism was evident in the revival of the modern Olympics. Annual Esperanto conferences, to forge a common world language, were held from 1905 onwards. The militant and anarchic wing of the labour movement, the syndicalists, founded the International Workers of the World. The Bolshevik revolution in 1917 gave earnestness to the establishment of the Internationales and inspired the formation of national communist parties. Such movements were the stuff of non-government organisations that took root or were stifled within the various nation-states depending on the governments of the day. National governments conceded the need to scrutinise domestic and international practices through the construction of supra-nationalist government organisations. The establishment of the International Labor Organisation (ILO) and the League of Nations were forerunners of the more complex supra-national organisations that evolved during the second half of the twentieth century and are discussed in Chapter 6.

Nonetheless, for its first decades of nationhood, Australia's membership of the British Empire was critical to the way it defined its place in the world and mediated global forces and influences. The imperial connection was evident in the way the constitution prescribed the handling of foreign affairs and the way it was practised for decades after federation. Australia was a dependent nation in foreign and defence matters that chose to participate in world affairs through the medium of empire. The remainder of the chapter explores the meaning and implications of Australia's dominion status in the first part of the twentieth century and how it became an independent Pacific nation and member of the community of nations by mid-century. It shows that this peculiar status enabled the development of independent nationhood while at the same time circumscribing Australia's international activities. Australia was a distinctive nation but with dependent dominion status.

Dominion Status

Using the term 'Dependent Dominion' to describe Australia's international status for several decades after federation needs some clarification. Although applied to countries like Australia and Canada in the British Empire, the term never had much currency or affection among Australians. Unlike Canada that had proudly called itself a 'dominion' when it federated in 1867, Australia chose the more independent term 'commonwealth'. The eminent University of Melbourne jurist, Professor W. Harrison Moore suggested in 1900 that:

> Rightly or wrongly the title 'Dominion' has come to suggest that prevalence of the central power which is the mark of Canadian union, and the domination of the Union government in State matters is the very thing which from 1890 has been seen to be impossible in Australia (Moore 1900, p. 35).

Moore was referring to the centralist constitutional arrangements for domestic governance that Canada had adopted in 1867. We are concerned with the imperial use of the term to denote the international status of countries like Canada and Australia that chose to remain dependent on Britain for their foreign affairs and defence policy.

'Dominion' was not used consistently or exclusively to refer to the member nations of the British Empire in legislation or other official proclamations and memoranda. According to the Oxford-based Australian scholar, K. C. Wheare, dominion was used in two senses. One was as the descriptive title of a particular member country, as in the Dominion of Canada; the other was to differentiate the group of self-governing member countries including Canada and Australia from non-self-governing member countries like India. The title 'Dominion of Canada' was used in the British North America Act of 1867, although in section 3 the British North America Act declared that the provinces 'shall form and be One Dominion under the Name of Canada'. Hence, Wheare argues that despite British insistence on the title 'Dominion of Canada', 'Canada' was the name given to the new political community on its birth certificate (Wheare 1953). To complicate matters further, most dominions eschewed the term in their own constitutional discourse. Australia chose to call itself a Commonwealth in 1901; South Africa preferred the term Union in 1901; whereas the republic of Ireland joined the Commonwealth as 'the Irish Free State' in 1922. Preferred domestic usage aside, the term 'Dominion' was used in a resolution of the first Imperial (previously called Colonial) Conference of 1907 (Latham 1929, p. 7). This was done at the request of the 'self-governing' dominions, a group of privileged members – Australia, New Zealand, Canada, South Africa and Ireland – to distinguish them from other members like India that were governed by Britain. Although retained by Canada in its constitutional discourse, the term 'dominion' became increasingly obsolete as the British Empire metamorphosed into the British Commonwealth.

Imperial, and previously Colonial, Conferences held from 1887 provided a consultative forum where the views of colonies, and later dominions, could be aired on a range of external affairs, even if Great Britain retained control. At an earlier conference, convened at the time of Queen Victoria's Diamond Jubilee celebrations in 1897, Colonial Secretary Joseph Chamberlain had tried to keep alive the hope of Imperial Federation, with its promise that the colonies would have a greater say in imperial foreign policy. Enthusiasm for such an arrangement was at best lukewarm. Nevertheless, Chamberlain did encourage all the members to follow the 'patriotic course' of Australia and South Africa and make a financial contribution towards the maintenance of the British Navy in the far-flung outposts of the Empire.[1] For the most part, however, colonial members wanted a free ride: enjoyment of the peace and security that the Empire provided without contributing much to its upkeep. According to one British commentator, Eric Walker, it was already clear at the 1887 conference that colonial self-interest stood in the way of Imperial Federation: the colonies 'cherished their present liberties, desired more, and so long as Britannia ruled the waves saw no reason why they should part with any they had' (Walker 1943, p. 219).

John Latham, writing in 1929 when he was Commonwealth Attorney-General, painted the 1907 first Imperial Conference in a much more positive light. It had been presided over by the British Prime Minister rather than the secretary of state for the colonies, and 'marked the real beginning of the era of consultation upon affairs of common interest' (Latham 1929, p. 7). Still, at the 1911 Imperial Conference, Australian Labor prime minister Andrew Fisher made no headway in proposing that he should be consulted about international agreements affecting Australia. He received no support from the Canadian or South African governments, and British Prime Minister Asquith asserted Britain's sole authority over foreign policy (Millar 1978, p. 72). That was soon to change because of the massive participation of Australia and other dominions in the Imperial Forces in the First World War. As had been foreshadowed during the war, the dominions' equal status with Great Britain in foreign as well as domestic affairs was affirmed in the postwar Imperial Conference and spelt out in the 1926 Balfour Declaration. As discussed earlier, Australia was caught in the backwash of imperial lethargy, and would not take advantage of this hard won equality in foreign affairs until threatened by Japanese invasion and virtually abandoned by Britain in the Second World War.

In the meantime, Australia had constituted itself as a federal nation in 1901 under its own Commonwealth Constitution. The design of foreign affairs machinery in the constitution and its early use in foreign affairs reflected Australia's continuing membership of the British Empire and its reliance on the protective umbrella of British foreign policy and defence. The irony was that Australia ended up with full and plenary executive and legislative powers with respect to foreign affairs and treaty making. It is to those issues that we now turn, beginning with the drafting of the relevant constitutional sections.

Constitutional Treatment

In constituting a new nation one might expect to find a dominant concern with matters of foreign affairs and defence because self-preservation is a necessary condition of nationhood. The country must be able to defend its citizens from hostile attack and deter potential aggressors. Moreover, national prosperity for a developed country in an interdependent world requires ongoing relations with other countries for purposes of trade, communications, travel and association. Because Australia's constitution was made under the protective umbrella of the British Empire, however, relatively little attention was given to foreign affairs. This section examines the origins and influences, particularly imperial ones, on the drafting of the Australian constitution's external affairs provisions.

The provisions which are relevant to the external affairs power of the Commonwealth, particularly treaty making, are sections 51, 61 and 75 of the Constitution. Section 51 (xxix) gives the Commonwealth the power to make laws with respect to external affairs. It provides the legislative power that enables the Commonwealth parliament to translate international obligations into domestic law. The executive power to enter into treaties is provided by the broad monarchical language of section 61: 'the executive power of the Commonwealth is vested in the Queen and is exercisable by the Governor-General as the Queen's representative'. In practice this means responsible government with the Queen and Governor-General acting on the advice of the prime minister and ministers who are in turn responsible to parliament. At federation, foreign affairs was left with the British Imperial Government so that the power to enter into treaties was exercised by the Queen on the advice of the British Government. As Australia acquired control over its foreign policy, this royal prerogative was subsumed under the executive power of the Australian government in section 61. It should be emphasised that the power to enter into and ratify treaties and conventions is an executive power that is separate from the legislative power of implementing those treaties as domestic law. Section 75 (i) of the Constitution gives the High Court original jurisdiction in all matters arising under any treaty, though, as Saunders notes, this jurisdiction has never been used by the court (Saunders 1995, p. 176).

This broad constitutional framework allows the Commonwealth Government and parliament full and plenary powers over external affairs and treaties today. Indeed some critics see the powers as too unspecified and open-ended. In the federation conventions, however, these matters received scant attention because it was assumed that they would remain primarily the responsibility of the British Imperial Government. Nevertheless, it is important to examine the founders' treatment because that reflected the assumptions of the time as well as putting in place the design for the future.

Preliminary discussion commenced at the Melbourne 1890 conference convened at short notice to determine whether the time was ripe for framing a national constitution. There Samuel Griffith, then Queensland opposition leader, signalled the need for the new Commonwealth to have power over 'external relations'. Fellow Queenslander John Macrossan extended this to include power over 'external territories'. The Queenslanders were concerned with foreign affairs and defence, especially with hostile powers acquiring colonies to the north. The state was also deeply divided over the continuing importation and use of Kanaka labourers in its northern sugar industry.

A power over external affairs was included in the first draft of an Australian constitution produced at the Sydney conference held in March 1891, but just how the external affairs power made its way into the first draft is not clear. In early 1891 both Andrew Inglis Clark, Attorney General of Tasmania, and Charles Kingston of South Australia had prepared drafts for a constitution. Neither of these drafts used the phrase 'external affairs' or 'external relations', although Clark's draft did provide for a range of such matters. He proposed that the new parliament's powers would include: 'criminal process beyond the limits of the Province in which it is issued, and the extradition of offenders'; regulation of fisheries outside Australasian waters beyond territorial limits; regulation of Australasian affairs with the islands of the Pacific and a general power to 'make laws for outside territory'.[2] It seems most likely that the term 'external affairs and treaties' was inserted by Griffith while working with the drafting committee aboard the Queensland government's yacht, *Lucinda*, during the Easter recess. 'External affairs and Treaties' first appeared on Griffith's list of Commonwealth powers and was most likely his own phrase (La Nauze 1972, pp. 50–51). When the convention reconvened it approved without debate a Commonwealth power to make laws with respect to 'external affairs and treaties'. The choice of the term 'external affairs' reflected the contemporary imperial usage and Australia's perception of itself in the British Empire and the rest of the world. It encompassed Australia's relationship with Britain, which, although physically 'external', was certainly not considered 'foreign', and the rest of the world, which Australia saw as both external and foreign.[3]

Treaties were also mentioned in Covering Clause 7 of this draft which provided that:

> The Constitution ... and all laws made by the Parliament of the Commonwealth in pursuance of the powers conferred by the Constitution, and all Treaties made by the Commonwealth shall ... be binding on the Courts, Judges and people, of every State, and of every part of the Commonwealth ... (Federation Debates 1891, p. 944).

There was some brief discussion of this with concern being raised over whether Australian laws would apply on British ships. Griffith acknowledged that the words might appear 'rather startling' to some delegates, but sought to allay fears by pointing out that these words had been used previously:

> They are taken from the Federal Council Act of Australasia, and were inserted by the imperial authorities after consideration and in substitution for more limited words that were proposed by the Convention that met here in 1883. Finding those words there ... it was felt perfectly safe to adopt them (Ibid., p. 559).

That seemed to be sufficient and the words remained in the draft bill.

The 1891 draft constitution was not implemented but provided a blueprint for the second series of conferences in 1897–98. The first meeting in Adelaide in 1897 did not alter the 1891 provisions relating to 'external affairs and treaties'. Doubts were again raised about including treaties in the covering clause and Griffith's earlier assurances were repeated. The Adelaide draft constitution included both mentions of treaties, but other bodies were soon to be drawn into considering the matter. The Adelaide convention broke up on 23 April 1897 in time for the premiers of the Australian colonies to sail to London for Queen Victoria's Jubilee celebrations and an associated Colonial Conference. While Australian colonial parliaments were considering the draft constitution, the Colonial Office did its own scrutinising. Its concerns were passed on by Joseph Chamberlain, Secretary of State for the Colonies, to Sir George Reid, Premier of New South Wales.

The Colonial Office was concerned about including any mention of external affairs and treaties in the draft constitution (de Garis 1969, pp. 98–102). It recommended deletion of Clause 7's stipulation that 'all treaties' made by the Commonwealth should be binding on the courts and people of all States. The Colonial Office surmised that this wording had been copied from the US Constitution but insisted that it 'was not applicable in British countries where treaties technically were made by the Crown rather than the State, and did not have the force of statute law unless specific legislation was passed'. The Colonial Office also raised the same concerns about imperial shipping laws that had troubled Convention delegates at Adelaide, claiming that uniformity of shipping laws throughout the Empire under the Merchant Shipping Act of 1894 was critical to imperial trade. That was despite almost identical wording to that of the draft constitution having been used in the Federal Council Act of 1885, as Griffith explained in Adelaide. The Colonial Office also objected to the Australian parliament's being given a power over 'external affairs and treaties' in the enumerated listing of Commonwealth powers. This was part of the Empire's foreign relations, it was claimed, and the responsibility of the Imperial Government.

In early September 1897 the convention delegates reconvened for the second session of the convention in Sydney. There the concerns of the Colonial Office, that had also been raised in the New South Wales parliament, were addressed. Convention leader Edmund Barton successfully moved that the mention of treaties be removed from covering clause 7 giving the reasons advanced by the New South Wales Legislative Council that were similar to those of the Colonial Office:

> inasmuch as the treaty-making power will be in the Imperial Government, we should omit any reference to the making of treaties by the commonwealth; in other words, while they concede that we should make certain trade arrangements, which would have force enough if ratified by the Imperial Government, the sole treaty-making power is in the Crown of the United Kingdom (Federation Debates, Sydney 1897, p. 239).

Not surprisingly, Reid endorsed Barton's view, relying on arguments from the Colonial Office for which he had been the chosen repository:

> This is an expression which would be more in place in the United States Constitution, where treaties are dealt with by the President and the senate, than in the constitution of a colony within the empire. The treaties made by her Majesty are not binding as laws on the people of the United Kingdom ... The expression, I think, ought to be omitted (Ibid., p. 240).

At the final Melbourne session of the Conference in 1898, Barton moved that the words 'and treaties' be omitted from sub-clause 52 (xxix) in conformity with the amendment previously made to covering clause 7. Because of minor objections by South Australian delegates, Patrick Glynn and Josiah Symon, Barton agreed that the matter be considered during an adjournment (Federation Debates 1898, p. 30). Deakin was concerned that such an omission might unduly limit the federal parliament's powers:

> I understand that the leader of the Convention will look at the words 'and treaties', with the view to see how far, by omitting them, we would limit the powers of the Federal Parliament within the range of the powers that the Canadian Parliament already enjoys (Ibid., p. 31).

The issue was laid to rest with no further discussion and the additional words 'and treaties' were omitted from the final version of section 51 (xxix), which referred only to 'external affairs'.

As one might have expected, such narrowing of the Commonwealth parliament's power by deleting mention of treaties raised some uncertainty that continues even today. Some commentators have argued that the deletion of the words 'and treaties' from section 51 (xxix) of the constitution implied that the Commonwealth does not have unlimited power to enter into treaties (McDermott 1990). The weight of authority and High Court decisions since federation, however, strongly support the opposite conclusion. Professor Harrison Moore suggested very early on that the power was a plenary one (Moore 1900, p. 39). This was in contrast to Quick and Garran's view that the power had 'obvious limitations' and that no executive power of the Commonwealth to enter into treaties had been contemplated:

> There is nothing in it indicative of an intention of the Imperial Parliament to divest itself absolutely of all authority over the external affairs of Australia and to commit them exclusively to the Parliament of the Commonwealth, any more than it divests itself absolutely of any other of its supreme sovereign powers (Quick & Garran 1976, p. 631).

Nevertheless Quick and Garran claimed that the legislative power to make laws giving effect to treaties 'must be deemed to be included in section 51 xxix – "External Affairs"' (Quick & Garran 1976, p. 770).

While treaty making and foreign affairs remained firmly in British imperial hands after federation, some of the earliest Commonwealth-state disputes were over which sphere of government had the right to speak for Australia, via the Imperial Government, in international affairs (Saunders 1995, p. 151). Before federation, colonial governments had exercised this function, but after federation the Commonwealth claimed sole prerogative. Whether there was any ongoing role for state governments in treaty making was contentious, as was the status of pre-federation agreements made by colonial governments. Perhaps not surprisingly, Commonwealth attorneys-general were quick to resolve the issue in favour of the Commonwealth. Consideration of such questions stimulated the first articulation of the scope of the Commonwealth's external affairs power. Alfred Deakin set the ball rolling as Attorney-General in 1902 by claiming that the deletion of the words 'and treaties' during the course of the convention debates in no way diminished the Commonwealth's legislative power over treaties:

> The omission, as it appears from the debates, was solely to prevent any assumption arising that the Commonwealth claimed an independent power of making treaties. Legislation with respect to the enforcement of treaty obligations is clearly within the scope of 'external affairs' (Brazil 1981, p. 134).

This view was echoed in 1906 by another leading nationalist, Isaac Isaacs, who stated that:

> the Commonwealth has, by Imperial Statute, been invested with the power and responsibility – and so far as Australia is concerned with paramount power and responsibility – with respect to 'External affairs' (Brazil 1981, p. 323).

This interpretive issue was clearly a crucial one for future national development when Australia would take over responsibility for its own foreign policy and treaty making. Although correctly predicting that the external affairs provision of the constitution would be 'a great constitutional battleground' (Quick & Garran 1976, p. 631), Quick and Garran would be proved wrong in claiming only a limited executive power for the Commonwealth. Rather it was the expansive views of committed nationals like Deakin and Isaacs that would carry the day. As Australia became more independent and responsible for its own foreign affairs and treaty making, Australian governments would claim an unlimited executive power and the High Court would oblige with legitimating interpretations of the sparse constitutional clauses. External affairs and treaty making have become major pillars of Commonwealth status and power in recent decades, not only with respect to international affairs but in the Commonwealth's inter-governmental relations with the states. This large expansion of the Commonwealth's domain is examined in Chapter 6.

Nation Building and the Great War

Nations are not made by constitutional design or judicial interpretation alone, or perhaps even primarily. An emerging national civic culture supported federation, as Chapter 3 has documented; and the accelerated growth

of national consciousness and national associations and groups helped consolidate nation building through the early decades of the twentieth century,
as subsequent chapters will show. Australia's constitution making had been
intensively discursive through the prolonged series of constitutional conventions in the 1890s and, given comparative standards of the day, widely
consultative and democratic. Nevertheless, something was missing. The
Australian nation had not been forged in a noble war of independence, nor
had it been sealed with the blood of patriots. This was to change with
Australia's participation in the Great War.

Hundreds of thousands of young Australians volunteered for service and
fought in the main battles of the war on the other side of the world: at
Gallipoli, in the Middle East and in the trenches in France. Huge casualties
were suffered in terrible battles. The ANZAC legend, that gave remembrance to the bravery of its soldiers in battle, helped forge a collective spirit
that signalled the coming of age of the Australian nation. But it was a
deeply ambivalent remembrance: of service and death for shared values,
but far from home in battles to uphold British imperial dominance and
the European balance of power. The young Australian nation might have
been blooded in this war, but British imperial ties were reaffirmed at the
same time.

It had all begun on a more optimistic wave of imperial bravado. Apart
from regional and domestic concerns that Australia regarded as vital, 'she
recognised the authority of the British Government in imperial Policy'
(Eggleston 1933, p. 534). When war broke out in Europe, Australia considered itself involved and immediately put all its armed forces at the disposal
of the British. The small Australian navy was put under the control of the
British Admiralty, and Australia's volunteer soldiers were placed under
British army command as they left Australia. While close consultations
between dominion and British governments reflected the emerging equal
status of the dominions that would be confirmed in Imperial Conferences
after the war, the broad hierarchy of empire persisted in strategic decision
making and military command structures.

Australia had 'changed little from her pre-war position', Sir Frederic
Eggleston concluded in a survey of Australia and the Empire up to 1921.
While retaining certain national objectives, such as the White Australia
policy, Australia, for the rest, was 'prepared to let Empire policy be conducted
by Great Britain and to accept the results. If they lead to war, Australia would
be bound and would cooperate in the same way as she has done in the past.'
Being so bound could entail enormous sacrifices, as had been the case in the
Great War, but it could also allow a certain amount of free-riding and
irresponsibility. Australia made no contribution to the general defence of
the Empire after the war, and wound down its defence forces. Ominously,
Eggleston noted in 1933 that 'Australia obviously does not think that the

Pacific is as dangerous as was thought some years ago, and the popular opinion seems to be that the only armaments really required in the Empire are those dictated by the position in Europe' (Eggleston 1933, pp. 544–45).

There had been a limit to Australia's cooperation during the war that divided the nation politically. The wave of imperialism that galvanised Australians behind the war effort broke over the contentious issue of conscription. Religious, ethnic and political differences were exposed and conflagrated. Australian imperialists, intoxicated with war and serving the British Empire, saw no bounds to the sacrifices Australia should make. In successive referendums they sought to impose compulsory military service to top up volunteer forces and meet the further demands of British imperial forces bogged down in trench warfare in France. Australians of a more nationalist and republican bent shared in the war effort but drew the line at conscription. This group included most of the Labor party, many Catholics, especially in Melbourne where Archbishop Daniel Mannix was influential, and many of Irish-Australian descent.

Championed by the firebrand Labor prime minister, Billy Hughes, conscription was twice forced to popular vote, and twice defeated. This was despite 'the expectation that the influence of all the leading newspapers and most of the prominent public men in Australia would be effective' (Scott 1933, p. 579). It was also despite framing the questions in ways that softened the issue. The first referendum on 28 October 1916 asked:

> Are you in favour of the Government having, in this grave emergency, the same compulsory powers over citizens in regard to their military service for the time of this war, outside the Commonwealth, as it now has in regard to military service within the Commonwealth?

The negative vote won by a narrow margin with three states – New South Wales, Queensland and South Australia – voting no (Scott 1933, p. 579).

The campaigns were deeply divisive. An unprecedented motion of no confidence in Prime Minister Hughes was carried at a meeting of the parliamentary Labor party in Melbourne on 16 November 1916. Hughes walked out with twenty-four of his sympathisers, remained prime minister with the support of the opposition, and subsequently formed the Nationalist party. Buoyed up by electoral victory in May 1917, Hughes again pushed conscription to a popular referendum on 20 December 1917. This time the question was simpler and again rather misleading: 'Are you in favour of the proposal of the Commonwealth Government for reinforcing the Australian imperial force overseas?' The negative vote was more decisive the second time round, with Victoria now joining the previous three no states (Scott 1933, p. 582). Conscription had been defeated but at a political price. This first great party split over conscription wrecked the Labor party and kept it in opposition until the early 1930s.

The other casualty of the Great War was Australia's national spirit that had been so resourceful in nation building two decades before. Now Australia was a grieving nation that had suffered terrible losses. From a small population of less than five million people, 416,809 volunteers had enlisted, 329,000 had served overseas, 60,000 were killed or died as a result of war service, and total casualties numbered in the hundreds of thousands (Gullett 1933, p. 546). A generation of Australian men had been killed or scarred and a generation of Australian women mourned or nursed them. Virtually every local community had suffered losses and many built their own war memorials. As Ken Inglis has eloquently shown, these were 'Sacred Places' that transformed the Australian landscape and signified respect and mourning for those who had died (Inglis 1998). The scale of death required sentiments deeper than the celebration of nation or empire. The Great War left Australia exhausted, mourning its dead and nursing its wounded; more independent within the British Empire, but deeply divided over the boundaries of service to nation and empire.

Australia's enormous commitment and losses in the war were used by Prime Minister Hughes in demanding an independent place for Australia in the peace talks at Versailles in 1919. In plenary sessions Australia's representatives, along with those from the other senior dominion countries, took part on an equal footing as representatives of the Allied and Associated Powers. Australia was a founding member of the League of Nations in 1919, and was an original member of the International Labour Organisation of the League, and represented at its annual meetings and conferences (Royal Commission on the Constitution 1929, pp. 113, 117). Some contemporary commentators argued that because Australia and the other dominions had signed the instrument establishing the League individually, but under a group heading of 'British Empire', they had somehow been accorded an inferior status. However, most agreed that this was not the case, particularly as it was a system of international law among individual and equal states that the League covenant was establishing (Baker 1929, pp. 67–80).

Imperial and Dominion Transition

Formal recognition by Great Britain that members of the Empire had the right to make treaties with other nations was acknowledged by the Imperial Conference of 1923. This right was subject to consideration of the possible effect upon other members of the Empire, and with taking steps to inform appropriate governments of such intentions (Latham 1929, p. 51). The 1926 Balfour Declaration and resolutions of the 1926 Imperial Conference finessed this new equality of status in terms that implied the end of both Empire and dominion status. The Balfour Declaration had one foot in the past and one in the future, proclaiming that the dominions were both equal in status within the British Empire and free associates of the British Commonwealth:

> *They are autonomous Communities within the British Empire, equal in status, in no way subordinate one to another in any aspect of their domestic or external affairs, though united by a common allegiance to the Crown, and freely associated as members of the British Commonwealth of Nations* (In Baker 1929, p. 386. Emphasis in original).

The British Empire was in the process of untidy transition to becoming an innocuous Commonwealth of independent nations. 'Equality of status', the Balfour Declaration explained, 'so far as Great Britain and the Dominions are concerned, is thus the root-principle governing our inter-imperial relations.' The effect, according to Hancock, was to exorcise 'the inequality-complex'. That was only for the select club of self-governing dominions that were white, or white-ruled countries – Australia, Canada, New Zealand, South Africa and the Irish Free State. India was, in the main, excluded from the resolutions of the Inter-Imperial Relations Committee of the Imperial Conference of 1926, but was said to be maintaining its 'special' and 'important' position in the British Commonwealth. The Report admitted its unlikely conclusions:

> A foreigner endeavouring to understand the true character of the British Empire by the aid of this formula alone would be tempted to think that it was devised rather to make mutual interference impossible than to make mutual co-operation easy (Baker 1929, pp. 386–87).

The devil was in the detail: numerous clauses detailed the extensive consultation and negotiation procedures with other potentially affected members of the Empire that the dominions were to follow in concluding treaties on their own behalf. However, treaties negotiated under the auspices of the League of Nations were to continue to be made in the name of the King, with the 'British units on behalf of which the treaty is signed' to be grouped in a similar order to that appearing on the Covenant of the League of Nations. The Report reached no conclusion on how this new 'equal status' in the Empire would alter existing imperial legislation and constitutional practice. It did recommend that the principles of the Colonial Laws Validity Act 1865, the convention of reserving certain dominion legislation for the Crown's assent, and the competence of dominion parliaments to give their legislation extra-territorial operation, be investigated further by a special committee. Concerns over the jurisdiction of British Merchant Shipping legislation was also referred to an expert committee (Baker 1929, pp. 388–98).

As if exhausted by its earlier efforts, Australia was not one of the drivers for increased dominion autonomy. It went along with the Balfour Declaration but had not demanded it. Rather Canada, South Africa and Ireland forced the pace as each of these countries addressed more serious issues in their domestic politics. Canada was busy with national unity and forging its place in North America where external relations with the United States were now more important. Quebec nationalism and prairie continentalism were also absorbing issues that required national responses: of healing in the aftermath of forced conscription that Quebeckers resented, and of trans-Canada nation building to satisfy the prairie provinces. South Africa was controlled by the old Boer leaders and steered an increasingly independent course. The Irish Free State was in the process of becoming a completely independent republic. In contrast to these countries, Australia slumped back into an imperial torpor.

Following the Balfour Report in 1926, but before the Statute of Westminster was passed in 1931, there was further desultory debate over the status of the dominions. But the tide of informed opinion had turned to recognise that the dominions were equal in status and entitled to participate independently in international affairs. Harrison Moore claimed that signing the League of Nations Covenant in their own right, as well as members of the Empire, signalled that the dominions had attained full international personality (Moore 1926). In Harrison Moore's view, the dominions' formal membership of the League of Nations made all the difference. Before the First World War the dominions had been members of international associations for particular economic and social purposes, rather than political purposes. Membership of the League of Nations was quite different, Harrison Moore argued:

> the scope of the League of Nations extends to every possible subject of international relation or dispute, so that it is concerned with the first and last things of state life. Members of a society which deals with the issues of peace and war, the Dominions have entered upon relations which differ not merely in degree but in kind from those which arise from the Membership of international administrative unions (Moore 1926, p. 36).

Harrison Moore's view on equal status for the dominions was endorsed by other leading British constitutional authorities of the day. A qualified independence in treaty making was also being asserted by Australia during the 1920s. The 1929 Commonwealth Royal Commission on the Constitution observed that it had been common practice, well before the 1926 Report, for commercial and technical treaties concluded by the Imperial Government not to be binding on dominions unless they had expressly adhered to the treaty. In some instances provision was made for a dominion to exclude itself from such treaties. Australia had done so 'in relation to a great number of treaties which were thought to be inconsistent with national policy, and has not acceded to a number of commercial treaties concluded by the Imperial Government since the War' (Royal Commission on the Constitution 1929, p. 114). The Royal Commission reiterated the view that, following the Balfour Committee Report of 1926, the 'right of a Dominion to make political treaties with a foreign country is the same as that of the government of the United Kingdom'. It noted, however, that the Australian government had not yet exercised that right. Nevertheless, by 1928 Latham felt confident that '[t]he Commonwealth ... has full treaty-making powers in its own hands already – as a matter of law'. There was of course the qualification of adhering to agreed imperial procedures as laid down in the 1923 and 1926 Imperial Conferences (Latham 1929, p. 55). The resolutions of these various Imperial Conferences were formalised in the Statute of Westminster enacted by the British parliament in 1931. Most significantly, the Statute of Westminster provided that British laws no longer extended to the dominions, including the Commonwealth of Australia, unless the dominion requested and consented to the law. It repealed the Colonial Laws Validity Act (1865), and explicitly stated that no law passed by a dominion government would be void or inoperative on the ground that it was repugnant to the law of England. Importantly for the development of Australia's external affairs capacity, dominion parliaments were given 'full power to make laws having extra-territorial operation' by section 3. Since the Act only applied to the legislative power of the Australian Commonwealth Government and not the states, it would take the belated passing of the Australia Act in 1986 to tidy up this anomaly.

While the Statute of Westminster may now appear innocuous and a natural development of the independence of Australia and the other dominions, its 1931 enactment was controversial among Australian leaders. H. V. Evatt and Robert Menzies, who would be key players in Australia's politics during subsequent decades, gave contrasting views on the new Statute at a legal convention in Adelaide in 1936.[4] Evatt was then a prominent Justice of the High Court and an exponent of the Commonwealth's external affairs power who, subsequently as Attorney-General in the Curtin Labor government, would engineer Australia's adoption of the Statute in 1942. Evatt asserted that the Statute merely brought legal relationships between the dominions and the Imperial Government into line with existing political ones, and put into effect recent Imperial Conference resolutions.

Menzies who was then Commonwealth Attorney-General and would be the leader of the opposition in the 1940s took a different view. He was more guarded and deferential towards Britain, although giving qualified support for the Statute's adoption:

> [I]t should be adopted ... in circumstances which do not give rise to any suggestion this is an anti-British movement ... [W]hen Australia comes into line with [the other dominions]

she is not doing it because she desires to hasten the process of disintegration, but because she desires harmony between the various parts of the British world (Menzies 1936, p. 108).

Menzies was at pains to distinguish loyal Australia from the other more obstreperous members of the Empire, South Africa, Canada and the Irish Free State. Australia was merely doing its duty to 'fall in line with what appears to be a uniform feeling in the British Empire', whereas they had become 'unduly obsessed with notions of status and independence'. Menzies was sensitive to Whitehall's 'remarkable tenderness about the feelings of the Dominions', but concerned that the Statute had taken the 'loose and flexible and strong' tenets of the Balfour agreement, and made them 'unduly crystallised and brittle' (Menzies 1936, p. 108).

Menzies' view characterised the Australian position in the interwar decades and remained the dominant one until the Second World War when there was a sea-change in attitude to favour the Evatt position. The matter came to a head on the issue of the Commonwealth's authority over its naval forces and foreign ships in Australian ports (Wheare 1953, p. 216). The Curtin Labor government finally adopted the Statute in 1942 and made its effect retrospective to the start of the Second World War on 3 September 1939. The government's action was provoked by a 1942 High Court case that determined Australian servicemen were still subject to British naval law in war time.[5] The reasons for the change were set out in the preamble to the new legislation:

> Whereas certain legal difficulties exist which have created doubts and caused delays in relation to certain Commonwealth legislation, and to certain regulations made thereunder, particularly in relation to the legislation enacted and regulations made for securing the public safety and defence of the Commonwealth of Australia, and for the more effectual prosecution of the war in which His Majesty the King is engaged.

Adoption of the Statute of Westminster in 1942 was part of a broader assertion of Australian autonomy required by war in the Pacific and orchestrated by Evatt and a nationalist Labor government. Throughout the 1920s and 1930s, however, Australia was ruled by conservative politicians, except during the Great Depression when Labor was briefly in office. During the interwar years, Australia had little interest or energy in charting an independent course in national defence or world affairs. Politics was focused on pragmatic issues of soldier resettlement, rural and manufacturing development, industrial relations and trade. Conservative leaders savoured the dregs of British imperialism and the afterglow of victory in the Great War. Labor was briefly in office during the Great Depression but not in control of either economic policy that was dictated by the collapse of world markets and financial orthodoxy, or even domestic politics because of a hostile Senate. As in 1916 over conscription, the Labor party split over economic policy for dealing with the Depression, with its ablest leaders leaving the party and combining with conservative forces on the other side. The party that might have charted a more independent course for the Australian nation was again sidelined, and would sit out the 1930s on the opposition benches. During that period, Australia showed little inclination to pursue its own course in international affairs. It took the shock of the Second World War and a change of government to dislodge Australia from the British imperial nest.

Second World War: From Dominion to Pacific Nation

The Second World War began as a repetition of much of the same response as Australia had made in the First World War. Prime Minister Menzies told Australians in a radio broadcast on 3 September 1939: 'It is my melancholy duty to inform you officially that … Great Britain has declared war upon [Germany], and that, as a result Australia is also at war'. There was no question in Menzies' mind of Australia pursuing a different strategic course from that of Britain, or even making the declaration of war in its own name.

Australian volunteers in large numbers were soon fighting in the Battle of Britain, in Bomber Command that took the war to German cities from bases in the North and East of England, and at Tobruk in North Africa. But that was soon to change with Japan's dramatic entry into the war. The bombing of Pearl Harbor, the surrender of Singapore, the easy conquest of the Philippines, the Dutch East Indies and most of Papua-New Guinea brought the Japanese army to Australia's doorstep. Darwin was bombed and the Japanese navy controlled the Asia Pacific. Australia was called upon to defend itself as best it could, to switch its military alliance mainly to the United States, and to forge a new understanding of nationhood in the crucible of war.

Fighting for national survival was both a novel and a desperate task. Australians were used to fighting all over the world and thought of 'war as an expedition; as a campaign … fought thousands of miles away from home' (Macmahon Ball in Evatt 1945, p. *v*). The struggle for national survival required a new strategic and foreign policy of the most fundamental kind for, as Macmahon Ball pointed out in introducing Evatt's ministerial speeches of the time, 'a nation must survive before it can have a foreign policy'. National survival required that Australia break away from its traditional dependency on Britain and chart its own course in the Pacific. Macmahon Ball explained why in terms that are as valid today as in the early 1940s:

> Britain is a European Power, intimately involved in the fortunes
> of Europe. Her destiny lies mainly in Europe. Australia's destiny
> lies mainly in the Pacific. ... The world's lights and shadows often
> appear different in London and Canberra. To the British Govern-
> ment the problem of protecting Australia and New Zealand is the
> problem of protecting distant kinsmen. To us it is the problem of
> protecting our own homes (Macmahon Ball in Evatt 1945, p. *xi*).

Australia was ill-prepared for its new national role of self-defence against
a powerful Asian predator in the Pacific. It needed a government prepared
to pursue the war effort with great vigour, and it needed that government to
develop a foreign and defence policy to ensure national survival in the Asia
Pacific. The first occurred when the Curtin Labor government replaced the
fractious Menzies National-Country party coalition on 7 October 1941 after
two independent members of parliament switched their support. The second
was crafted by wartime Prime Minister John Curtin and Herbert Vere Evatt,
Australia's Minister of State for External Affairs from October 1941 until
December 1949. Evatt's was the official voice on Australian foreign policy
and Australia's place in the new world order. Through Curtin's leadership and
Evatt's actions and voluminous speeches during this formative period we can
observe Australia's emergence as an independent nation.

Evatt's first speech as Minister for External Affairs was made to the House
of Representatives on 27 November, only ten days before the Japanese attack
on Pearl Harbor. Most of it was concerned with reviewing the fortunes of war
in Europe where stubborn Russian resistance had slowed the advance of the
German armies. A major theme of Evatt's speech was the assertion of national
sovereignty and equal status of the dominions with Britain. The British
Commonwealth was 'in fact an association of free nations possessing equal
status in every respect of their internal and external affairs', Evatt reminded
members using the words of the Balfour Declaration. Exercise of the 'right of
legation' was 'a mark of sovereignty in international affairs', he insisted, and
Australia had exercised that by establishing full diplomatic representation
with the United States, Japan and China. Australia had a special concern
in the preservation of the 'complete political independence' of Portuguese
Timor, whose capital Dili had become a regular stopping place on the Empire
Airways route from Darwin to Singapore. Australia now had an official
representative in Dili and was negotiating to establish direct relations with
the Netherlands East Indies. Other than such fledgling diplomacy, Australia's
security depended on the good will of the United States and Britain's defence
cordon centred upon Singapore.

Less than three weeks later, Evatt was back in the House of Representatives
making a second ministerial statement. The Japanese had suddenly bombed

Pearl Harbor on 7 December 1941, destroying much of the American Pacific fleet, and a few days later sunk the British warships *Prince of Wales* and *Repulse* that were Singapore's main defence. By attacking while diplomatic negotiations with the Americans were still in progress the Japanese action was both infamous and treacherous. In response, the Australian cabinet met on 8 December and decided to make a declaration of war against Japan as from five o'clock on that day. Ironically, Evatt the constitutionalist spent most of his statement explaining and defending the novelty of Australia's making a declaration of war on its own behalf. He linked this discussion to authoritative declarations of Imperial Conferences that dominion countries enjoyed fully equal status with Britain in internal and external affairs. To avoid any legal controversy as to the power of the Governor-General to declare a state of war without specific authorisation of the King, the government had previously obtained from the King a special instrument assigning the power to declare war on the particular countries. Relying upon the principle that the King should act exclusively on the advice of the Australian prime minister and cabinet, the government had gone directly to the King via the High Commissioner in London and not through British ministers.

Technicalities aside, Australia was now in grave danger of invasion. The nation's forces were scattered all over the world: Australia's airmen were fighting in England and training in Canada, Australian sailors were 'in many of the seven seas', and Australian soldiers were fighting 'with indomitable courage on distant shores in Europe, in Africa, in Asia'. Meanwhile according to Evatt: 'the defence of our country has been treated as a subordinate and subsidiary part of the distant war. From now onwards we shall be thrown back more and more upon our own resources' (Evatt 1945, p. 21). Australia was put on a total war footing, and the Curtin government sought to have moderate forces diverted from Europe to the Pacific war, and Evatt was dispatched to the United States and Britain to plead for a more coordinated war effort and larger military supplies for the Allied campaign in the southwest Pacific.

Australia's situation was desperate, Evatt informed a British audience in a BBC broadcast from London in May 1942. 'If the danger of Japan had been fully appreciated,' he said, 'it is impossible to believe that so little aid could have been sent, and sent so slowly, to crucial points'. In less than five months Japan had acquired 'a new empire', including Singapore, Malaya, the Philippines, the Dutch East Indies, many Pacific islands and Burma. 'If we lose more', Evatt warned, 'we may lose all' (Evatt 1945, p. 58). With Japan already in possession of vital strategic points in and near New Guinea, Australia faced its equivalent of Dunkirk. Evatt reminded his British listeners of the generosity of Australians in the early war years. At the outbreak of war in 1939, Australia had sprung to Britain's assistance without counting the cost:

Without question, without thought of the cost involved, without
dwelling upon the fact that the first Great War cost us sixty
thousand lives and suffering and sacrifice beyond telling, the
Australians again rushed to the assistance of the Mother country.
We sent considerable land, sea and air forces into the thick
of the fighting elsewhere. As before, the cost was heavy; as
before, the cost was never counted. Many thousands of Australian
sailors and airmen have helped in the defence of Britain (Evatt
1945, p. 59).

In a subsequent article in *The Times* in May 1943 during a second visit to
Britain, Evatt again played upon the ties of kinship and the generosity of
Australians in rushing to Britain's aid in both wars. Australia was now in a fix
at home because of its cooperative dependence on Britain and the fact that its
defence policy had always been based upon Empire strategy. The establishment and development of the Australian Navy were 'governed by the
postulate of Imperial Conferences that, in the event of war in the Pacific, the
Singapore base would be held for sufficient time to enable the British Fleet to
engage the main enemy fleet' (Evatt 1945, p. 125). Despite the dismal failure
of that strategy, Evatt endorsed Churchill's guarantee of 'Britain's joint
responsibility and primary interest in safeguarding Australia's integrity',
and, once again reinforcing the ties of kinship, adding that '[a]s between
members of the same family it could not be otherwise' (Evatt 1945, p. 127).

It had long been clear to Australians, however, that Churchill's pledge was
one that Britain could not honour. Whatever the sentimental value of ties
of 'brotherhood and kinship' – that Australian leaders repeated when they
visited London – they were no safeguard for Australia facing the threat of
Japanese invasion in the Pacific. Realising that, the Australian government
had already turned to America as 'the paramount factor on the democracies'
side in the Pacific'. As Prime Minister Curtin emphasised in a broadcast to the
American people on the eve of Evatt's first special war mission in March 1942,
the Japanese onslaught and string of easy victories had forced a quick
reassessment of Australian defence strategy. Curtin presented the resultant
switch in primary allegiance from Britain to the United States as follows:

Who among us, contemplating the future on that day in December last when Japan struck like an assassin at Pearl Harbor, at
Manila, at Wake and Guam, would have hazarded a guess that by
March the enemy would be astride all the South-west Pacific
except General MacArthur's gallant men, and Australia and New
Zealand? But that is the case. And, realizing very swiftly that it
would be the case, the Australian Government sought a full and
proper recognition of the part the Pacific was playing in the general

strategic disposition of the world's warring forces. It was, therefore
but natural that, within twenty days after Japan's first treacherous
blow, I said on behalf of the Australian Government that we
looked to America as the paramount factor on the democracies'
side of the Pacific (Curtin in Evatt 1945, p. 43).

Australia pushed for the formation of a Pacific War Council to be headed
by President Roosevelt and located in Washington. After the fall of the
Philippines, Australia put all its armed forces under General MacArthur's
command.

Re-focusing upon national survival in the Pacific and relying upon America
to that end required a redefinition of national character as well as purpose.
Britishness continued to be affirmed, but increasingly as a minor theme.
While it was a key foundation ingredient, the Australian national character
had been shaped in a different domestic and international environment.
There was 'no belittling of the Old Country' in Australia's turning to America,
Curtin insisted, only the recognition that Britain could not 'go all out in
the Pacific'. According to Curtin, Australians were an English-speaking race
'committed heart and soul to total warfare'. 'There was no fifth column in this
country.' Australian fighting forces were 'born attackers' who had been 'tested
in the crucible of world wars and hallmarked as pure metal'. Australia would
use its 'great space' in fighting for every 'yard of our soil'. Curtin's speech
emphasised Australia's military toughness in battles all over the world:

> For, remember, we are the Anzac breed. Our men stormed
> Gallipoli; they swept through the Libyan desert; they were the
> "rats" of Tobruk; they were the men who fought ... down Malaya
> and were still fighting when the surrender of Singapore came.
> These men gave of their best in Greece and Crete; they will give
> more than their best on their own soil, when their hearths and
> homes lie under enemy threat (Ibid., p. 45).

Australia's greatest strength was 'the calibre of our national character', Curtin
said. That would survive and triumph even if the country were reduced to
ruins. 'There will always be an Australian Government and there will always
be an Australian people', Curtin promised. Even if all that had been built up
over one hundred and fifty years were to be swept away by war, there would
still be 'Australians fighting on Australian soil until the turning point be
reached'. Even if that should come about, Curtin concluded: 'we will advance
over blackened ruins, through blasted and fire-swept cities, across scorched
plains, until we drive the enemy into the sea. I give you the pledge of my
country' (Ibid., p. 46).

The Second World War was the crucible in which Australia's consciousness as a Pacific nation was forged. As Evatt explained to New York's

Overseas Press Club in April 1943 during his second special war mission to the United States:

> The civilization of the Australian community is based upon a long European tradition. But while our geographical position has developed local characteristics in our social and political outlook which differentiate us from our kinsmen in Britain and our Allies in the United States, it has needed the war to force upon the Australian people the full consciousness of the fact that their responsibility and their rights are primarily those of a key Pacific nation (Evatt 1945, pp. 113–14).

Many Australians had been compelled to turn their attention to the longer term problems of the Pacific that were 'many and infinitely complex'. War forced Australia to rethink its nationhood in a Pacific context. But it also provided an opportunity for affirmation and development of a new Australian nationalism. While acknowledging derivation from British stock, this new nationalism was based on greater independence and self-confidence in a new world order. Britain was literally now the 'Old Country' rather than the 'Mother Country'. Its future was in Europe whereas Australia's future was in the Asia Pacific. For leaders like Evatt, the prospect for Australia as a Pacific nation was expansive and exhilarating. In a ministerial statement in October 1943, Evatt declared that while Australia had an interest in the future of Europe, 'it is obvious that our predominant interest must lie in the Pacific regions. Australia has a leading part to play in those regions.' While acknowledging that the peace and prosperity of all nations were interlinked, Evatt emphasised Australia's new Asia-Pacific perspective: 'because of our special geographical position and our growing responsibility and power, we can and should make a very special contribution towards the establishment and maintenance of the peace settlement in South-east Asia and the Pacific' (Evatt 1945, pp. 141–42).

As the tide of war had turned in the Pacific, Evatt became more insistent on the right of 'middle powers' like Australia to have a say in Allied strategies for victory and peace. He pursued this vigorously but with only limited success in the formation of the United Nations. Australia had already experienced the lot of a smaller ally in pressing its claims with the United States, Australia's new liege lord and the emerging victorious giant of the Asia Pacific. Somewhat in pique, Evatt orchestrated the Australia-New Zealand Agreement, a cosy if rather ineffectual treaty arrangement with its own smaller ally. In explaining that agreement, Evatt called for 'a positive Australianism'. 'Australians are a great and virile people', Evatt said. They had proved themselves 'magnificent pioneers in many fields of human endeavour' and 'fought on many battlefields of this war and the last war with unexampled courage ... Let us cease being fearful of our destiny', he counselled (Evatt 1945, p. 178).

Increasingly, as victory in both Europe and the Pacific became more likely, the Australian government's attention was directed towards a new world order that would secure peace and prosperity. As Sir Frederic Eggleston wrote in the foreword to Evatt's second book of speeches covering the transitional period from March 1945 to March 1946, Evatt was 'an internationalist who felt that the security of Australia could at this stage be guaranteed only by an extension of her commitments and the establishment of a world order on firm foundations' (Eggleston 1946, p. vii). The world order that was to emerge was only partly in accord with Evatt's vision, and after 1949 Evatt would be on the sidelines of political power. Great power politics and the Cold War would overshadow the United Nations that Evatt put so much store upon. The new world order would be one of complex interdependency as we show in Chapter 6. Australia could play the role of a relatively independent nation in contributing to construction of a new international governance regime.

Australia's destiny would lie mainly in the Pacific, and not with Britain in Europe. At least this was Evatt's vision for postwar Australia put to the House of Representatives in a ministerial statement in early 1946:

> Australia stands to Asia, geographically and politically, in something of the same relationship as the United Kingdom to Europe ...
>
> By study of Pacific affairs, and through expansion of direct diplomatic and consular representation, Australia is setting out to make her own assessments of the problems of the Pacific. By so doing we may speak with a fresh, direct and independent voice in the councils of Pacific nations. It is our wish and intention to play a dynamic part in achieving, as a member of the British Commonwealth, a world comity. It is our destiny and duty to play that part in the Pacific (Evatt 1946, p. 171).

Evatt's vision of Australia as an independent nation whose future lay in the Asia Pacific would only be partly fulfilled during the second half-century of nationhood. National politics during the 1950s and 1960s would be dominated by Menzies and Liberal-Country Party Coalition governments who talked up British imperial sentiment as its substance drained away. Australian foreign policy and defence required security arrangements primarily with the United States and its economy depended on increasing trade links with Asia. But British links, British accents, British titles and British immigrants were preferred by a generation of Australian government leaders. So much so that the Labor party in opposition seemed to forget about the Curtin-Evatt reorientation of Australia as an Asia-Pacific nation. When Labor finally returned to office in 1972, Gough Whitlam had to rediscover Asia. Labor's most recent prime minister, Paul Keating, purported to do the same in the early 1990s.

Thus, Australia's dramatic reorientation as an independent nation in the Asia Pacific during the Second World War was temporary and partial. Australia would slip back into the more traditional habits of loyal British dominion for decades to come, or at least would keep alive its language and sentiment in public discourse because the old world of imperial motherland no longer existed. Typically, when Britain sought membership of the European Community in the 1960s, this was bitterly opposed by Menzies and Australia. But the die was long since cast: the old world of British Empire and dominion dependency had gone forever. Britain would join Europe, and Australia would be left to fend for itself in the Asia Pacific. In fact, if not always in national sentiment and rhetoric, that is what had been happening progressively since the 1940s, as subsequent chapters will document. Global forces would be recast and the experience of Australian citizenship would take on a different character.

Chapter 5

Australian Citizen Subjects

The formation of the Commonwealth of Australia as a nation-state at the close of the nineteenth century opened up a whole new sphere of democratic governance and citizenship. The immediate task of federation was to build institutions of national government while preserving, in somewhat modified form as member states, established colonial governments in a federal union. The larger purpose of federation was to extend democratic self-government and citizenship by means of national government that could better secure the safety of citizens and promote their general well being in a changing world. National independence and state sovereignty, usually considered to be hall-marks of nationhood, were not features of the Australian founding. As Chapter 4 has shown, Australia was founded and developed as a nation while remaining a dominion of the British Empire, dependent upon Great Britain for its foreign policy and defence until the 1940s. Citizenship arrangements were not too dissimilar, as this chapter shows. Australians remained formally British subjects, but in fact were Australian citizen subjects who developed an independent Australian nationalism that incorporated, in varying degrees, loyalty to Britain. The Australian nation and citizenship were grounded in British culture and political traditions that had been transported to the Aus-tralian colonies during the nineteenth century and become part of colonial culture and politics. The grand aspiration at federation was to create a new and better Britannica: a nation of 'Independent Australian Britons' (Hancock 1961) who would share a common ancestry, a homogeneous culture and unlimited prosperity. The new Australian nation extended and consolidated existing colonial and imperial political associations.

Achieving national prosperity and ensuring its equitable distribution required extensive government intervention in a political economy of regulated and protected markets (Capling & Galligan 1992). Racial and cultural homogeneity would be achieved through zealous promotion of British immigration and the imposition of the White Australia policy to exclude coloured immigrants and marginalise or assimilate Aboriginal peoples. This chapter examines nation building as the process of establishing and developing a national citizenry in which British elements played an important, but declining, part. Those who accept at face value a binary progression from 'British subject to Australian citizen' miss the wood for the trees and give a superficial and distorting account of the early character and development of Australian citizenship. While British elements were strong in early Australian citizenship, they were only one part of a complex and multi-layered set of political associations. Membership of the Australian federal nation, in its Commonwealth and state spheres, was the most important part.

As we saw in Chapter 3, Australian citizenship was not enshrined in the constitution but left to the Commonwealth and state parliaments to define and develop. Moreover, it was not literally Australian citizenship at all but British subjecthood. After a robust discussion of Australian citizenship, the founders had settled, rather conservatively, on using the term 'subject of the Queen' instead of 'citizen' in section 117 of the constitution. They and their constituents shared a political culture in which such formal shorthand was sufficient constitutional code for a richer, more complex and contested reality. This chapter takes up the story of Australian citizens as British subjects for the first half-century of federation, until passage of the Australian Citizenship Act in 1948 made Australians formally 'Australian citizens' from 26 January 1949. As we shall see, the nomenclature of British subject was not merely a formal title but had substantive richness and emotive appeal for many, but by no means all, Australians. This was reinforced by state policy and civic culture, especially during the Great War that diverted the young nation's energies into bloody defence of Britain's global interests that Australia shared.

Australian nationalism was repackaged in the deeply moving Gallipoli myth that celebrated heroism and defeat in the distant service of an incompetent superior. The war memorial in Canberra became the cathedral of the Australian spirit and was replicated in local memorials throughout the country, their sombreness lightened by the ubiquitous Diggers' clubs. Alignment with Britain and membership of the Empire provided a strategic international cushion for domestic nationhood, but came at a terrible price. Cultivation of British imperial preferences boosted immigration and investment in the growth of White Australia, but that was soured by periods of high unemployment and the accumulation of interest payments that crippled the national economy during the Depression. If British culture promoted sturdy self-independence of individuals and households and cultivation of a multiplicity of voluntary associations for the self-governance of communities, the adoption of British Australianness was as exclusive of some as it was inclusive of others. Monoculturalism, cramped by temperance reform and wartime censorship, bred narrowness and intolerance.

Pember Reeves, at the turn of the century, referred to the governments of New Zealand and Australia as socialist (Reeves 1969, 1902). They may have been relatively interventionist, but the agendas that were successfully pursued were those of progressive liberalism and state action rather than socialism. The White Australia policy was adopted to ban cheap, coloured labour, but assisted immigration schemes often brought unskilled people to an already unstable labour market. The economic dislocation of postwar adjustment and soldier repatriation and the deflationary spiral of depression resulted in widespread unemployment. The ill-conceived soldier settlement schemes following the First World War and the disastrous 'grow more wheat' campaign of the 1930s led to rural hardship and ruin. Massive business failure and retrenchment of workers during the Great Depression left many destitute when there was no adequate welfare net to cushion the blow. The 1930s crisis in capitalism was global in its cause and effect, but especially severe for Australia because of its dependence on international capital and markets. Australia's reactions to economic crisis were shaped by global ideas and movements, but constrained by international financial pressures and conservative orthodoxy. While at times democratic governance was challenged and communities polarised, civic coherence and political stability prevailed.

Being far away from the centre of empire, Australia was an antipodean backwater where secondhand Britishness was often touted as a preferred civic orthodoxy. At times, as during the Great War and royal visits, this was fanned into mass enthusiasm as a sort of surrogate nationalism. But it was also a dampener on the development of a distinctively Australian civic and political culture and resented by large sectors of the nation who were republican in sentiment and from Irish Catholic background. Australian nationalism had emerged in the nineteenth century with generations of native-born Australians and the establishment of colonial self-government. It took national prominence at federation with the creation of a new national framework of government. In this institutional hybrid and in Australian civic and political culture more generally, British traits and influences were prominent but, at the same time, were changed and modified. They had taken root in new national soil and would produce a different Australian variant, in combination with other indigenous and imported elements. During the 1920s and 1930s the promotion of a fading British imperialism constrained the development of a fresh Australian nationalism.

Our emphasis throughout the chapter is on the character and development of Australian civic culture during the first half-century of nationhood. Civil society and civic associations played a formative and sustaining role in shaping citizenship and welding together its multiple spheres of local community, regional state, nation and empire. While the overall process was harmonious, there was at times vigorous dissent and shameful discrimination against those who did not fit a narrow mould of white Anglo-Australian citizenship.

The earlier part of the chapter highlights the strong Britishness of Australians during the first decades of federation; the second part shows how this was progressively replaced by an Australianness that nevertheless incorporated British elements. The two themes are not separate entities, as Australian civic and political culture incorporated much that was British in origin. Nor was there a substantive break either at federation or with the adoption of Australian citizenship in 1949. One emerged from, and partly coexisted with, the other for generations. Australians remained British subjects as well as becoming formally Australian citizens in 1949. Indeed for some, including Menzies who was to dominate Australian politics as prime minister from late 1949 until his retirement in 1967, Britishness would continue to be boosted as the better part of being Australian. For most, however, it would have declining relevance.

The evolution of Australian citizenship was a complex process of civil and political change: it was developmental over time, variable among diverse groups, and uneven in its temper and progress. It included the subjective world of individual and group identity, as well as the more objective world of recognition and entitlement. Some Australians were ultra-British while others were anti-British. Amid all of this complexity, variability and flux, Australia's citizenry, partly consciously and partly unconsciously, did develop a more independent and distinctive Australianness, but an Australian identity that incorporated a good deal of the British. The formal change from subject to citizen during the first half-century of federation registered that development, while at the same time preserving the duality. When Australians formally became Australian citizens they remained British subjects as well.

Australian British Subjects

The act of federation by the Australian colonies did not immediately result in radical change. Indeed the continuities were to be more evident than the discontinuities. The colonies attained the newly won status of statehood and were zealous in their wish to retain their own powers and independence. There were strong reasons of international and domestic concern for establishing a nation-state. The colonies needed to present a united front on the international stage in such matters as immigration, trade, financial borrowing, quarantine and defence. On the domestic front, economic union would enhance trade and commerce by eliminating colonial tariff barriers and border customs houses. Australian federation was not part of a larger scheme of Imperial Federation, but neither was it an act of disaffiliation from the British Empire. The Australian Commonwealth built on a legacy of British endeavour and its future was aligned with that of the British Empire. The next fifty years would see two complementary processes: increased cultural homogenisation to give expression to Australian Britishness as British subjects and, increasingly in its place, the development and consolidation of a unique Australianness. The Commonwealth, States and local communities each combined self-government with continuing allegiance to the British Empire. There was widespread endorsement of British cultural ideals and practices in public life, and promotion of patriotic loyalty as civic virtue.

Australian citizens were not just formally British subjects: most had British ancestry and many identified with being British. Reared on stories of British history and British heroes and heroines, they admired the anglophone world and the glories of the British Empire. Many shared a patriotic loyalty to the British monarchy who played a figurehead role at leading public occasions. From 1905 Empire Day was celebrated as a national holiday on 24 May, the birthday of the late Queen Victoria. In 1901 the Duke and Duchess of Cornwall opened the first Commonwealth parliament in Melbourne. In 1920 Prince Edward, under the instruction of his father, George V, visited Australia as part of a world trip to thank the countries of the British Empire for their patriotic support during the Great War. In 1927 the Duke and Duchess of York opened the first session of the Commonwealth parliament in Canberra. Australian prime ministers made it their business to be present in London to celebrate Royal jubilees and coronations. In a more routine way, vice-regal surrogates hosted ceremonial gatherings and presided at occasions of state at both the Commonwealth and state levels. The monarch provided recognition for outstanding service, presenting Victory medals to all veterans at the end of the war in acknowledgment of their service to king and country. Heroic acts, whether in war or peace, were nominated for commendation by the monarch and rewarded with honours or medals. The British royal honours system, introduced in the colonial era, continued into the twentieth century and was broadened in 1917 through establishment of the Most Excellent Order of the British Empire.

Paradoxically, Australia's close alignment with Britain and the British Empire and the promotion of Australian Britishness led to a certain withdrawal and isolation from the rest of the world. As we saw in Chapter 4, the building of White Australia and protective state policies entailed selective closure to the non-British world, especially Asian cultures and countries, that produced a narrower monocultural identity. Populist ideals of egalitarianism were touted but were not translated into policies that made substantial impacts on economic and social realities. Australian democratic egalitarianism

was grafted onto a culture of hierarchical authority that cultivated strati-
fication. If Australia's strain of radical liberalism and egalitarian democracy
had a levelling political effect, its capitalist political economy and British
imperial connections produced and fostered inequality and hierarchy.
Inevitably, there were those who were marginalised and would register protest and flirt with ideas of revolution but these were always a minority.
Virtually all Australians, regardless of social rank or economic position,
however, wanted to maintain a White Australia.

Identity and entitlement are the two fundamental components of citizenship policy. Identity specifies those attributes that a citizen must have in order
to be a citizen and qualify for the benefits that citizenship provides.
Citizenship entails belonging to a particular political community so that the
individual attributes of membership are ones that also define the citizen body.
Australian citizenship was effectively based on being white, preferably of
British descent. As we saw in the previous chapter, non-whites were excluded
at national borders through discriminatory measures under the Immigration
Restriction Act. The White Australia policy was fundamental to the nation
and 'the indispensable condition of every other Australian policy', as Hancock
pointed out (Reeves 1969, p. 59). It was grounded in discriminatory assumptions of racial superiority and political considerations of ensuring an appropriate citizenry for a constitutional democracy. Alfred Deakin's justification
for White Australia blended the two:

> The unity of Australia means nothing if it does not imply a united
> race. A united race means not only that its members can inter-
> marry and associate without degradation on either side, but
> implies ... a people possessing the same general cast of character,
> tone of thought, the same constitutional training and traditions
> (Quoted in Reeves 1969, p. 61).

For the non-British, getting entry into Australia was only the first hurdle
in gaining citizenship. Persons who were not British subjects had to be
naturalised, and the Naturalization Act 1903 specifically excluded anyone
who was 'an aboriginal native of Asia, Africa, or the Islands of the Pacific,
excepting New Zealand' (section 5). New Zealand Maoris were exempted
from this and other prohibitions because they had political rights in New
Zealand and there was some expectation at federation that New Zealand
might join the Australian federation. Otherwise, Asian, African and Pacific
Islander migrants who slipped through the immigration cordon could be
denied naturalisation as well as other citizenship rights such as voting. There
was a sizeable group of such people living in Australia at federation, partly as
a result of the various colonies having different immigration practices. In
moving the amendment to exclude these people from naturalisation in the

1903 legislation, Senator Higgs from Queensland made clear that his purpose was 'to prevent any of the 80,000 coloured aliens who are not naturalized at present, but who may be naturalized, or desire to be naturalized, in the future, from applying for Commonwealth naturalization papers'.[1] The government had not intended to be so restrictive, and other senators advocated a more liberal regime. Senator Charleston from South Australia, for example, thought the amendment restrictive and unnecessary. 'We have put a fence right round Australia,' he reminded colleagues, 'and have said that certain races shall not come in unless they comply with certain conditions.' If people passed the dictation test and by their industry prospered, 'why should they not have the right of citizenship?' he asked.[2] Senator Glassey from Queensland gave Charleston, whom he dubbed as this 'strong stickler for coloured men being placed on the same footing politically in the Commonwealth with whites', the answer. He preferred to 'keep out the goods of these people, and also to keep out the coloured people themselves'; those who were already here should be treated kindly and humanely but not on terms of equality with whites.[3] The tougher line pushed by the Queensland senators was narrowly carried in the Senate and subsequently accepted.

While the Immigration Restriction and Naturalization Acts provided the legal and administrative foundation for restricting citizenship, some additional racial cleansing was also carried out. The worst breaches of White Australia had occurred in colonial North Queensland with Pacific Islanders being brought in to work sugar plantations. The Pacific Islanders Act of 1903 required enforced repatriation of Kanaka labourers, many of whom had been forcibly recruited to Queensland in the previous century. After federation, White Australia had no place for Kanaka sugar cane workers in its new political economy. Resident non-whites like the Chinese suffered various discriminatory practices. Most shamefully of all, indigenous Australians had the formal title of British subject and, after 1949, Australian citizens, but were effectively excluded from most benefits and entitlements of citizenship. Race and discrimination were at the core of Australian citizenship until the 1960s when normal citizenship rights and benefits were extended to indigenous Australians and the White Australia policy was dismantled.

Despite immigration restriction, migration was fundamental to Australia's future growth as a nation because at federation the population stood at a mere 3.8 million. Given the vastness of the continent, population increase was a priority in order to secure possession of the land and stimulate growth of the domestic market. It became clear that Australia could not simply rely on the natural increase of native-born Australians because the birthrate, as elsewhere in the anglophone world, was starting to fall. The New South Wales State government established the first public inquiry into population, a Royal Commission into the Decline in Birth Rate in 1903, that confirmed population growth needed to be augmented by immigration. This was to be done through an active policy of recruitment of, and assistance to, British migrants (Roe 1995). Such a policy reflected and consolidated British sentiment and British imperialism. The 1907 Imperial Conference in London agreed that it was 'desirable to encourage British emigrants to proceed to British colonies (rather) than to foreign countries'. Emigration to Australia, which had slumped following the 1890s Depression, rapidly revived. Between 1911 and 1914 almost 300,000 migrants arrived in Australia; most were British, and half of these received assisted passages.

Britain's support for emigration was premised on its own self-interest as well as that of its emigrating subjects. In 1917 the Dominions Royal Commission recommended emigration to the dominions as a way of developing overseas markets for British exports. After the First World War British migration was resumed with increased enthusiasm and included soldier settlers and their families who started arriving in Australia from 1919. Stanley Bruce, Australian prime minister from 1921 to 1929, who had strong personal connections with Britain dating from his school days, championed closer ties in the interrelated areas of 'Men, Money and Markets'. Bruce hardly needed to spell out that this slogan meant British Men, British Money and British Markets. During the decade when he was prime minister to 1929, more than 300,000 migrants arrived in Australia of whom roughly two-thirds were assisted British migrants.

Not all came freely. Large numbers of children were shipped out ostensibly to a better future as Australian British subjects (Gill 1997). Child 'rescue' work had been carried on in Britain since the 1830s and was given fresh impetus in the early decades of the twentieth century through renewed faith in environmental determinism. Children born in what were regarded as 'slums' were thought to be destined for lives of vagrancy unless given a new start. Such children were removed from their familial backgrounds and sent to Australia for placement in settlements that were deemed more salubrious. The Dreadnought Scheme shipped 7,000 boys to New South Wales between 1911 and 1930, and from 1912 The Kingsley Fairbridge's Child Emigration Society sent children to Western Australia and later to the eastern States. These were supplemented by Dr Barnardo's scheme from 1921[4] and 'The Big Brother Movement'[5] from 1925.

Not all migrants were British. Following the 1921 American restriction on immigration, increased numbers of southern European migrants, particularly Italians, migrated to Australia. Approximately 24,000 Italians had arrived by the end of the decade, and many of these settled in Queensland where they helped pioneer sugar cane and tobacco growing in the north of the state. Like the Chinese in the nineteenth century, European workers were subject to prejudice and discrimination. Participation of Italians in the sugar industry occasioned unrest and complaints by other sugar workers that led to a 1925 Royal Commission. Italians working through strike action on the Melbourne docks were subject to harassment and violence (Alafaci 1999).

Australian Political Economy

To attract migrants and ensure high standards of living for citizens, Australian governments took responsibility for creating jobs and setting wages. Australia's primary industries that provided the basis of its export trade were relatively capital intensive and efficient, and becoming progressively more so. While agriculture and mining provided opportunities for some migrants, rural industries and mining overall were shedding jobs as country Australia lost population to the cities throughout the century. In order to create sufficient jobs and fix higher than market wages, government had to mediate international market forces and rearrange the domestic economy. It did both in an elaborate system of political economy that protected Australian industry and redistributed part of the benefits to workers. Since Australia's 'protective state' has been documented and analysed elsewhere (Capling & Galligan 1992), it need only be briefly mentioned here in the context of attracting immigrants and building an Australian citizenry.

The three pillars of the protective state were extensive government provision of capital infrastructure and utilities, protection for industry and wage setting. These three policies were interlinked and had their origins in earlier colonial policies that have been dubbed as 'colonial socialism' (Butlin 1959). Colonial socialism survived federation and was expanded by the states that remained large providers of infrastructure and utilities until recent years (Alford & O'Neill 1994). The states provided railways, electricity generation and distribution, water supply for the city and irrigation in the country, and metropolitan transport systems. In some states, Labor governments added a curious range of goods and services such as insurance, saw-milling in Western Australia, and the catching and retailing of fish in New South Wales. Victoria consolidated 'State socialism' to such an extent that F. W. Eggleston, a ministerial exponent cum critic, could claim that Victoria in its heyday around 1930 had 'possibly the largest and most comprehensive use of State power outside Russia' (Eggleston 1932, p. 1).

The States used their giant public utilities for provision of community service obligations, public employment and the provision of economic infrastructure to assist industry in providing jobs to support individuals and households. All the States blatantly used infrastructure provision to attract industry that would generate jobs and so attract migrants, while some like South Australia provided cheap public housing as an added incentive for industry and migrants to locate there. Symbolically, if not in overall terms, the baton of public provision of infrastructure passed to the Commonwealth Government in the postwar Snowy Hydro-electric Scheme.

Infrastructure provision was only one aspect of Australian political economy; the others were tariff protection for industry and wage setting for workers. The two were interlinked with the Tariff Board protecting industry and the Arbitration Commission setting industry wages. Both policies spread to other sectors of industry: protection was extended to weak rural industries like dried fruits and dairying, while wage fixing (as it was officially termed) became a national way of industrial life. Each policy had its origins in colonial government, in wages boards that set wages in most colonies and in tariffs used by the State of Victoria to protect its manufacturing industry or Western Australia to protect its wine industry. Linking the two policies originated in the Deakinite settlement of 'New Protection' during the first decade of federation. This extended the uniform tariff imposed by the first Commonwealth parliament in the Customs Act of 1902 that, according to Prime Minister Barton, provided 'revenue without destruction'. Sufficient revenue was needed to fund the fiscal requirements of the new government as well as compensate the states for loss of their main tax base, while preserving established industries that relied on protection. To satisfy both objectives, the tariff rate was set on the high side.

Besides boosting Australian industrial development, the purpose of the national policy was also to expand jobs and pay higher wages. The Commonwealth's arbitration power provided the constitutional base for a national system of wage fixing that would increasingly dominate, although not displace, the state systems. Arbitration was the complementary pillar to tariff protection in supporting Australia's political economy of manufacturing industry. Its origins were in Deakin's 'New Protection' that extended the protective purpose of the tariff but tied its benefit to the granting of 'fair and reasonable wages' and working conditions. It underpinned a political alliance between Protectionist Liberals led by Deakin and the Labor party. New Protection was legislated in the 1906 Excise Tariff Act that levied an excise tax, equivalent to the protective tariff, on agricultural machinery made in Australia. This was waived if the manufacturer paid workers wages set at a rate higher than the unregulated market would have paid. This scheme was overturned by the High Court on the grounds that it regulated business that was a matter of State jurisdiction. That did not matter, however, as wages and conditions could be set by the Commonwealth Arbitration Commission that was only too willing to pass on to wage earners a proportion of the benefit from tariff protection. Moreover, national unions were able to escalate industrial disputes beyond State boundaries and so bring them within the jurisdiction of the Commonwealth body.

Tariff protection linked to industrial arbitration became the core of Australian industry policy until the 1970s. Tariff levels were raised in 1908, again in 1921 and to record levels as a Depression measure by the Scullin Labor government in 1930. 'Effective Protection', as it was later called, emphasised the linked goals of national development through industry promotion, as well as fair and reasonable wages for workers and, rather implausibly, fair prices for consumers. As we have seen, the tariff served broader purposes of national citizenship by providing additional jobs at higher wages than the market would have delivered. This underpinned immigration and ensured a modest level of economic sufficiency for workers and their families. Last, but not least, imperial links with Britain and the British Empire were preserved through reciprocal preference margins from 1919 and in the 1932 Ottawa Agreement. The multifarious purposes of tariff protection were nicely summed up by F. A. Bland in 1923:

> It has been used as a weapon to further the interests of manufacturers, to improve the standard of living of employees, to maintain the policy of White Australia, and to foster closer trade relations with the United Kingdom and the various dominions (Quoted in Capling & Galligan 1992, p. 78).

Protectionism was to be rigorously pursued until the 1970s, with Australia along with New Zealand eventually having among the highest levels of protection in the world. Protection had bipartisan and virtually unanimous support. Perhaps most surprising of all, Australia's leading economists championed the cause. The Brigden committee of inquiry, appointed by the Bruce government in 1927 and staffed by such giants of the profession as J. B. Brigden, L. F. Giblin and Douglas Copland, found strongly in favour of the tariff (Brigden 1929). Protection had been as beneficial to Australian as free trade had been to Britain, it was claimed. Free trade could not have supported the same population at the same level of income; agriculture was an inferior alternative owing to the marginal quality of uncultivated land and the adverse effect of increased exports on international markets. Tariff protection received the official imprimatur of early generations of Australian economists for supporting a larger population at higher average incomes than would have otherwise been the case. Established public policy was also good economic policy.

Whatever the virtues of protection for shaping a distinctive domestic political economy, Australia's wealth and prosperity still depended crucially on foreign investment and international trade. Federation enabled the establishment of national bodies for fiscal management including loan raising and debt management. The Premiers Conference and Loan Council became fixtures of Australian federalism. State and Commonwealth borrowing was coordinated and an orderly procedure adopted for accessing the London and New York capital markets for government borrowing. Federation produced no immediate economic bonanza, but enabled more orderly overseas borrowing for public purposes as well as enhanced opportunities for private capital investment. Economic growth was modest, with relatively lower rates achieved in the first decades of federation than had been evident prior to 1890. This growth was arrested by the war and dislocation of postwar reconstruction, but by the 1920s British capital was financing public infrastructure development in the dizzy way that it had in the 1880s boom. In 1925 a 34 million pound agreement was entered into with Britain to finance development schemes seen as complementing British immigration. Accumulated public indebtedness combined with the vulnerability of its export economy to collapsed international commodity markets contributed to Australia's being one of the hardest hit countries in the Great Depression. This was a salutary reminder of its dependency on global capitalism and the limited power of the national government to mediate its adverse consequences for Australian citizens. Whatever their limitations, however, national government and national political economy are only part of a more complex system of Australian governance.

State Governments and Local Governance

The years to the jubilee of federation, despite the global disruptions of the wars and the Depression, were predominantly inward looking. If national emphasis was on Australia's finding its place in the world, the domestic corollary was promoting a distinctive way of life. In this endeavour, the States were considered to be the primary political communities and, constitutionally, they retained the full panoply of domestic powers. Although many of the ablest politicians switched to the Commonwealth Government after federation, State parliaments provided an established institutional base for zealous leaders intent upon retaining crucial powers over a broad spectrum of economic and social life. With State populations becoming less geographically mobile than in the colonial era, primary allegiance was given to the State. As Hancock pointed out in 1930:

> The average citizen looks more frequently to the Government which sits in Melbourne or Adelaide than to the Government which sits in Canberra. It is this closer, more intimate Government which protects him from the wicked, educates him, watches over his health, develops roads and railways and water supplies so that he may find permanent employment as a farmer or temporary employment as a navvy, regulates his local trade conditions, inspects his factory – performs, in short, all those functions which seem to affect most nearly his economic and social well-being (Hancock 1961, p. 58).

If British imperial sentiment and national pride were enhanced by war, state loyalties and civic pride remained strong. Referendums to increase centralised constitutional powers for peacetime governance were resisted. Despite the consolidation and growth of the Commonwealth Government and Australian nation, separate State identities remained firmly established and interstate rivalries were strong. The States had the longer heritage of history and, in this period, were looking to celebrate the centenaries of their foundation. Different State identities were reflected in a set of affectionately coined appellations that dated from the 1890s: such as Crow-eaters, Sand-gropers and Banana-benders for South Australians, Western Australians and Queenslanders respectively. During the decades after federation, there was greater government involvement in domestic economic and social affairs, especially in widening opportunities for property ownership and education that were traditionally associated with the privileges of citizenship.

More intensive land settlement had been a popular cause since early colonial times but had always met with limited success, partly due to the harshness of the land. Although Australia was already highly urbanised by the turn of the century, there was strong political commitment to fostering small farms and rural settlements. During the nineteenth century, the struggle to wrest the large pastoral holdings from squatters and establish self-sufficient small 'cocky' farmers had only mixed success. In the early twentieth century, there was a comparable passion for closer rural settlement. In 1893, the South Australian government had fostered village settlements, especially along the Upper Murray, and at the turn of the century invested in rail infrastructure for the development of wheat farming. The following year, the Queensland Agricultural Lands Purchase Act provided landmark legislation for the resumption of large stations and their subdivision for closer settlement. The same year Victoria launched a policy of fostering village settlements that numbered 88 by 1919. From 1903 Tasmania progressively opened land which led to the development of dairy farming, while in 1906 New South Wales passed legislation for opening up irrigation along the Murrumbidgee. After the First World War, there was renewed emphasis on rural settlement for repatriating returned soldiers. New South Wales set up soldier settlement schemes in the Riverina, and South Australia opened up wheat growing areas for closer settlement. The Western Australia government developed dairy farming in the south-west, sponsoring the first of 40 group settlements from 1921, and opened up wheat growing areas for farming. It also agreed under the Empire Settlement Act to make available 6,000 new dairy farms to assist repatriation of British soldiers. Victoria spent over 13 million pounds to make available 12,000 blocks for dairying, market gardening and wheat growing. Despite all the good intentions, inexperience, smallness of holdings, marginal lands and falling commodity prices led to substantial personal suffering and public debt.

Rural hardship prompted political activism and mobilisation of the rural sector through the Country Party, that became a powerful coalition partner in Liberal/conservative governments and won political concessions for rural regions. In addition, progressive city dwellers founded voluntary organisations to improve rural life, taking advantage of new technologies of radio, car and air travel. These included a movement for the development of bush nursing and hospitals. Established in Melbourne in 1909 by the then Governor-General's wife, the bush nursing movement was always strongest in Victoria but also spread to the other states. The Australian Inland Mission was established in 1912 by the Presbyterian Church on the initiative of the Rev. John Flynn to serve the needs of those living in isolated outback areas. Health and education services in the outback were improved through radio and an aerial medical service from 1928. State education departments established special rural correspondence courses supplemented by Schools and Kindergartens of the Air.

Education policy and reform were given prominence. In 1902 Victoria introduced its New Syllabus for elementary schooling and New South Wales followed several years later. The emphasis was on reducing rote learning and broadening the curriculum to include greater focus on aesthetics and civics. All the states extended educational opportunity by establishing a State system of secondary schooling, often with a strongly technical focus. The kindergarten movement flourished and by 1916, Kindergarten Training Colleges and Free Kindergarten Unions had been formed in most States. Technical and further education were also promoted. In 1913 Albert Mansbridge, who had established the Workers' Educational Association (WEA) in Britain, toured Australia and stimulated formation of State branches.

During these early decades of the twentieth century, there was less emphasis on other aspects of social policy. The carry over of the prevailing ethos from the Victorian era assumed individuals and households had primary responsibility for their own self-sufficiency and welfare, and that provision of assistance would encourage welfare dependency. The Depression highlighted the plight of the most vulnerable. New South Wales, Victoria and South Australia all established commissions of inquiry into pensions for the old and infirm who could not earn a living. One of the few direct powers granted to the Commonwealth was that over pensions for the aged and infirm. New South Wales and Victoria had pioneered the principle of means-tested, non-contributory schemes that the Federal Government incorporated into its own scheme in 1908, rather than that of insurance. Despite the periodic attraction of a comprehensive pensions system paid for by contributory insurance, plans for introducing such a scheme were aborted by the First World War, then by the Depression and subsequently by the Second World War.[6] Apart from the Commonwealth setting up the Repatriation Commission in 1919 for public assistance to disabled ex-servicemen and their families, matters of social welfare rested with the States. New South Wales, which had pioneered public housing, also pioneered a widows pension scheme in 1926. During the Depression, as the Commonwealth lowered its payments to aged and invalid pensioners, all the States, led by Victoria, initiated financial payments for stringently administered unemployment relief. Apart from responsibilities in child welfare that dated back to the previous century, most social welfare work was carried out not by the state but by a plethora of voluntary organisations, albeit subsidised by the States. In 1935 the New South Wales Council of Social Services was formed, being replicated in other states and, eventually, at a national level. These Councils, or COSSs as they were known, co-ordinated local voluntary groups and became powerful lobbying forces for further government intervention or funding.

Well into the twentieth century, provision of social benefits and welfare relied heavily on voluntary effort and charity workers, based in the communities of urban suburbs, regional townships and country towns. Governments at a national and state level set the framework for policy development, but implementation relied mainly upon the efforts of ordinary people actively engaged in civic affairs and public life. Although Prime Minister and Treasurer, Ben Chifley was an active councillor in his home shire in New South Wales where he attended meetings, putting aside matters of national interest to participate in local affairs.

A Citizen Soldiery

Citizenship entails responsibilities as well as rights, including that most fundamental duty of fighting for and, if necessary, dying for one's country. As has been seen in the previous chapter, Australia was a major participant in both world wars through its affiliation with the British Empire, and relied for the most part on volunteer forces.

The most notable, and controversial, feature of the new nation's defence strategy was the adoption of 'a citizen soldiery inspired by patriotism', as Alfred Deakin termed it in 1907, rather than a standing professional army. The 1904 Defence Act enabled the establishment of Citizen Military Forces that relied on voluntary enlistment. The following year an Australian National Defence League was formed whose bulletin *The Call* encouraged militarism and the establishment of universal compulsory training. New defence legislation enacted in 1909 and implemented in 1911 provided for both voluntary and compulsory military service. School cadets and a senior cadet system were established, as well as paid compulsory military training on a part-time basis for eight years for men aged 18 to 26 years. In requiring this sort of training, Australia became the first anglophone country to introduce conscription in peace time. While some acclaimed the legislation for providing moral training for young men as well as military preparedness for the nation, others opposed it vehemently. A campaign of opposition and civil disobedience was promoted by the Australian Freedom League and thousands of young men refused to enlist. Between January 1912 and June 1914 there were some 30,000 prosecutions for evasions that resulted in imprisonment and fines for thousands of conscientious objectors.

Local communities and associations were the source of manpower and patriotic motivation, as well as dissent. Councils held receptions for volunteer soldiers who had served in the Boer War. On the other side, miners in Broken Hill gave a medal to a young man who had been imprisoned on a diet of bread and water for two weeks as punishment for failure to enlist. When Australia went to war in 1914 after the British Government's declaration, communities across Australia responded with patriotic fervour. Labor leader Andrew Fisher narrowly won a war election by pledging that 'Australians will stand beside the Mother Country to help and defend her to our last man and last shilling'. As young men rushed to enlist, many expected a short war with soldiers being repatriated in a few months. The war dragged on and by June 1915 voluntary enlistments were dwindling. The Commonwealth Government set up State War Councils to boost recruitment, hoping that State efforts and rivalries would be harnessed to stimulate enlistment. Long recruitment marches were staged from country areas to the city in New South Wales and Queensland that gathered locals along the way. In each of the States, local communities pushed recruitment through band playing marches, soapbox oratory and the exhortations of young women. Councils canvassed the intentions of eligible men about enlistment and organised visits of persuasion to those whose written responses were suspect. By 1916 war weariness was replacing enthusiasm as news of the bloody stalemate of Flanders filtered home. Communities resorted to shaming with clubs and associations using social ostracism and mocking dissident families and individuals with white feathers.

Local communities mobilised around the war effort while schools raised funds and sent patriotic hampers. Women knitted balaclavas and baked Anzac biscuits as well as supporting branches of the Australian Red Cross. Ceremonial farewells and presentations were organised for new recruits, and condolences and sympathy were extended to the families of those whose names appeared in the columns in local newspapers entitled 'In Memoriam'. Honour Boards were placed in schools, churches and work places to record the names of those from the district who had enlisted and those who had fallen. At war's end, war memorials were erected in most communities and became shrines of remembrance. After the war, however, extravagant promises of compensation for patriotic service were largely forgotten by governments that faced the difficulty of demobilisation and postwar reconstruction. Branches of the Returned Services League, set up as a federal body in 1916 to press the interests of veterans, became social clubs. From the mid-1920s Legacy societies, founded by local veterans, helped dependants of their deceased comrades.

The patriotic support for military duty that united loyalist communities sparked division in others. People of German descent, who constituted the second largest non-English-speaking group of colonial immigrants and had pioneered settlement in various regions, became an easy target for excesses of local patriotism and discriminatory treatment by authorities. Some Slavic miners from Western Australia who were only technically Austrians were included in the round up as a consequence of a campaign by the mine workers' union over 'enemy labour' (Fischer 1989, pp. 77–8). As was also happening in Canada, German place names were changed to Anglo-Australian ones – for example, Weinberg Road in Hawthorn, Victoria, was changed to Wattle Road. The teaching of the German language and the observance of German cultural practices and traditions were stopped. Almost 7,000 people of German and Austrian descent were interned during the First World War, of whom about 4,500 were Australian residents. Of these German-Australian internees, about 700 were naturalised British subjects and 70 were native-born Australians. These were 'subjects of Australia' who had 'secured their citizenship by birth in this Country'. Yet, they were being 'kept in close confinement for periods of 12 to 20 months, during which time their personal and business interests [were] completely ignored'. The President of the Association of Australian Born Subjects pointed this out in a letter to the Minister for Home Affairs in October 1917. He asked 'whether we are still citizens of Australia, and, if so, to what degree we retain its privileges'. The official response reassured him that 'no doubt arises regarding your citizenship. You are citizens of Australia, who are confined, according to the laws of Australia' (quoted in Chesterman & Galligan 1999, pp. 27–28). During the Second World War there was similar persecution of Italians who, following substantial immigration in the 1920s, formed the largest group of non-British immigrants at the 1933 Census. Much of this migration was intensely regional and Italian settlers formed their own local networks that made them prone to prejudice and discrimination.

Women and Civic Education

Pressures for conformity to accepted standards of public behaviour and upright respectability were intense in Australian society. First-wave feminism, with roots that stretched back to the nineteenth-century global movements of temperance reform and suffragism, added political force to such causes. The Woman's Christian Temperance Union had championed women's franchise so that they might purify and reform public life, and were gratified that this was granted under the Commonwealth Franchise Act 1902. Most of the first-wave feminists were educated middle-class women who wished to train young women, especially those from poorer backgrounds, in maternal skills and proficiency in domestic science to make them better housekeepers. They influenced State bureaucracies to include in the secondary school curriculum training in parenting skills and the rudiments of cooking and housekeeping. Women activists supported the development of kindergartens and the establishment of maternal and child health clinics. Housewives Associations were formed in every State during the First World War to lobby on matters of consumerism, while the Country Women's Association was formed in the 1920s to champion the interests of country women and children.

People were less on the move than had been the case in the nineteenth century and local communities became quieter and more orderly places to live. Life settled into the peaceful insularity of suburban and rural respectability. The drunken and disorderly behaviour and insulting words cases (that had earlier reflected a good deal of civil strife and chaos) were no longer common. Local courts of petty sessions were without work and closed shop. Vicarious pleasure in the adventures of others was now to be enjoyed, not on the streets, but in the local picture theatres. Schoolchildren were socialised in the dual loyalties of nationalism and Empire and inducted into civic culture. This included the cultivation of charitable behaviour, such as collections for the children's hospitals and the Red Cross. Patriotic loyalty was fostered through the singing of the royal anthem, patriotic fundraising during the wars and observance of Empire Day. National appreciation of native flora and fauna was cultivated through the growth of Gould League clubs. Imported from abroad, the New Education movement at the turn of the century inspired curriculum reform in all the States that included the introduction of civics courses to prepare children for active citizenship in their communities (Murdoch 1911). These civics courses included liberal components of British and imperial history and emphasised moral values that underpinned civic virtue. Church and Sunday school reinforced the public virtues of industriousness, honesty, punctuality, courtesy, respect for property, duty to others and patriotism. Stories of imperial and Christian valour vividly illustrated the courage and fortitude of heroes and heroines whose deeds children were urged to emulate.

Civil society groups extended the nurturing of moral behaviour in young people to support the development of virtues and habits conducive to citizenship. The Young Men's Christian Association and the Young Women's Christian Association, that had spread from Britain throughout the colonies in the nineteenth century, fostered Christian virtues among young men and women. A new wave of organisations in the early twentieth century had broader secular appeal and from a younger age. The Boy Scout movement founded in Britain in 1908 and the Girl Guide movement founded in 1910 quickly spread to suburbs and towns where branches of Cubs or Brownies were drilled in obedience, discipline, self-respect and service. Popular media reinforced civic culture with special women's magazines such as *The Australian Women's Weekly* appearing on news stands, alongside the British *Women's Weekly*, from 1926.

Cracks in the Edifice

Indigenous Australians were subjected to the same process of enculturation. The original colonial policy had been one of protection in settlements removed from white settler habitation. If full-blood Aborigines died out, as was thought, increasing numbers of mixed race people, called 'half-castes', provided a challenge for a White Australia. From the 1930s, the official policy was one of assimilating Aborigines from mixed descent into mainstream culture. The original colonial policy of assimilating tribal Aborigines had failed, but it was hoped that those with European ancestry would be more readily socialised. Just as children from impoverished British and British-Australian households were removed to be educated in more respectable ways, so children from European-Aboriginal households were also forcibly taken from their families to be subjected to a process of assimilation. Meanwhile, indigenous Australians remained marginalised from community life and civic engagement, effectively citizens without rights in their own country (Chesterman & Galligan 1997). The long fight for proper citizenship rights began in the 1930s. Aborigines and Torres Strait Islanders had served in the First World War. On the assumption that parliamentary representation would help their cause, the King was petitioned in 1930 and again in 1938 to have an Aboriginal representative in the Commonwealth parliament, but to no avail. On the sesquicentennial of British colonialism in Australia, while British Australians engaged in ceremonial festivities, indigenous Australians in Sydney declared a Day of Mourning.

Indigenous Australians were not the only ones who fell outside the narrow confines of racial and cultural homogeneity that defined Australian citizenship. Others were effectively marginalised because they lacked the material means to participate in any meaningful way. Despite extensive state action in economic affairs and the rhetoric of egalitarianism, there remained considerable inequities in the distribution of income and wealth. There may have been less inequality of wealth in Australia than other comparable industrial societies during this period, but that was partly because there were fewer wealthy Australians and a narrower spread of incomes. At the poorer end of the scale many ordinary men and women possessed no assets and had precarious incomes.

For many, state regulation of wages and conditions backed by strong union demands did ensure a moderately comfortable standard of living. The extremes of a more laissez-faire market economy of the nineteenth century, particularly the effects of a casualised labour market on the family life of employees, were alleviated. Progressive political leaders supported the labour movement's demands for greater government regulation of employer–employee relations and work conditions. Radicals and conservatives alike were aware of the cost of extended strike action. The Commonwealth established the Arbitration and Conciliation Court in 1904 to deal with industries, such as railways and maritime shipping, where there were strong national unions or whose work stretched beyond state boundaries.

Nevertheless, reform to the work place was slow in coming and the States were variable in having wages boards and livable wage setting. The famous

Harvester Judgment made by Justice Higgins in the Commonwealth Court in 1907, establishing a 'basic wage' having regard for 'the normal needs of the average employee regarded as a human being in a civilised community', was a radical departure. It would be five years before state jurisdictions such as Western Australia enshrined the concept of a 'family wage' in legislation, and South Australia incorporated the notion of 'a living wage' in its industrial legislation. It was another decade before Queensland's Court in 1916 had the power to declare a minimum wage, and New South Wales in 1918 gave legislative recognition to the principle of a basic wage. Moreover, workers continued to work long hours despite union claims. At the turn of the century, the average hours worked were 48 per week and long hours of labour were still the norm in some industries. In 1905, New South Wales carters argued against employers' claims for a 64-hour week and succeeded in obtaining 57. In 1920, shearing shed hands still worked a 52-hour week. Although there were awards made in the 1920s to shorten the working week to 44 hours, the Depression restored the 48-hour week and turned the clock back to the status quo at the turn of the century.

In the period from federation to the outbreak of the Second World War there was very limited economic growth, despite diversification of the economy to include more manufactured goods and a wider variety of primary produce. Recovery from the 1890s Depression was slow and growth in gross domestic product until the outbreak of the First World War was less than one per cent per year. The arbitration system had difficulties in establishing appropriate indices and there were inevitable lags in making awards. Recognition of the principle of a minimum wage did not ensure liberality. A Royal Commission in 1920 chaired by A. B. Piddington found that the basic wage was well below what was required for a minimum decent standard of living. The Commission's recommendation for automatic quarterly adjustment of the basic wage was ignored. During the Depression wages fell and the principle of 'a living wage' was eroded.

While trade unionism was extensive, the proliferation of unions undermined their effectiveness. By 1910, Australia was the most highly unionised country in the industrial world. But union strength was dissipated by the proliferation of small unions, rather than a small number of large unions. In any case, only those employed benefited from arbitrated work conditions and minimum wages and there were significant numbers of unemployed. Militating against full employment and depressing wage levels for unskilled work was the national pursuit of increased immigration. Although the government had been at pains to enforce the White Australia policy to prevent exploitation of cheap imported labour, the 1920s program of British immigration was not so dissimilar in increasing the supply of labour and dampening its price. In March 1911 the Victorian Women Workers' Union protested at the State's proposal to encourage the migration of British female domestic workers. Following the cessation of hostilities in 1918, the dislocation of repatriation and the worldwide economic downturn in 1920–21 exacerbated demobilisation. The 1930s Depression, together with the deflationary policies adopted by the Commonwealth in association with the States, led to massive unemployment of between 20 and 30 per cent of the workforce.

In view of such sluggish economic performance punctuated by major dislocations of war and depression, it is hardly surprising that class divisions from the nineteenth century should continue into the twentieth century. Disaffected workers and intellectuals turned to international industrial movements and socialism. As nation-states were developing in the nineteenth century, Marxism offered a heady brew of ideological prescription and practical prognosis based on a critique of capitalist modes and relations of production. International socialist movements sought global linking of the dispossessed in an international brotherhood. In the first wave of twentieth-century international socialism to reach Australian shores, a branch of The International Workers of the World (IWW), founded in Chicago in 1905, was established in Australia in 1907 (Burgmann 1995). Dedicated to establishing One Big Union, the IWW appealed for union amalgamation and militant action among unionists soured by the limited reformism of Labor. Their campaign to disrupt the war effort during the First World War foundered on tough government measures and the climate of patriotism they reflected and engendered. Empowered by the War Precautions Act, the Commonwealth Government prosecuted the activities of the IWW, charging its leaders with sedition and jailing the editor of its mouthpiece, *Direct Action*.

Fresh impetus was given to socialism by the success of the Bolshevik revolution in Russia in 1917 that gave rise to the second international movement. The Communist party was formed in Australia in 1920, amid the social dislocation of demobilisation and economic recession. Vehemently opposed to reformism, it advocated militant industrial action and was successful in radicalising leadership and membership of key trade unions such as transport, metal, mining and waterfront industries. The unemployment of the Depression and the work of the Communist party in organising the unemployed gave fresh impetus to membership, which increased to roughly 4,000 in the 1930s. In 1939, the Communist party's doctrinal affiliation to Moscow dictated its initial opposition to the war effort and resulted in its being banned between 1940 and 1942 under the War Precautions Act. Following the Soviet Union's switch to fighting Hitler after his attack on Russia, the party gained legitimation and its membership increased to 20,000 by the end of 1944. Menzies' belated attempt to ban the Communist party in the early 1950s was to be overturned by the High Court and defeated at referendum.

The conscription battles of 1916 and 1917 exposed fault lines in Australia's complex amalgam of Empire loyalty and Australian nationalism.

Prime Minister Hughes' campaigns for the introduction of conscription aggravated religious and political divisions that were never far from the surface of early Australian politics. British colonisation of Ireland and centuries of repressive rule had left a residual resentment among Irish immigrants and those of Irish descent. A historic sense of injustice and anti-authoritarianism was strong among Catholic Irish who were also predominantly Labor supporters. Their commitment to religious education meant separate schooling in Catholic schools, and their eschewal of freemasonry meant severance from key networks of local power and influence. Repression of the Easter 1916 uprising in Dublin signalled the continuing imposition of British rule that many Australian Irish found repugnant. Melbourne's Irish Catholic Archbishop, Daniel Mannix, became a national champion in leading the successful campaign against support of conscription. Others were socialists and pacifists, while many supported the ideal of a citizen soldiery of volunteers rather than a conscripted army of those compelled to fight.

On the other side, declining fortunes of war and the sectarian and socialist opposition to conscription provoked counter loyalist movements, such as the Citizens' Loyalist Committee founded by leading Melbourne citizens. Others who were marginalised by failure of the group settlement schemes and the 'grow more wheat' campaign, or who despised socialism and communists, joined fringe fascist groups. The New Guard in New South Wales styled itself as a movement representing the 'decent citizens' of the state against Jack Lang's policies of British debt repudiation. The White Army in Victoria took root in various towns and suburbs, its membership pledged to putting down the insurrection of red flaggers. The most significant counter offensive to communism in the trade union movement was mounted by Bob Santamaria and The Movement. This was a semi-secret organisation of Catholic trade unionists, backed by the Catholic Church in Victoria but not in New South Wales, that was established to counter communist infiltration of trade union leadership and the Labor party.

Australian Citizens

A milestone in the developmental process of Australian citizenship formation was the Nationality and Citizenship Act of 1948 that came into effect on 26 January 1949. This made Australians formally 'Australian citizens' for the first time. There was no switch from subject to citizen, however, because Australian citizens 'by virtue of that citizenship' also remained British subjects. Moreover, as we have seen throughout this chapter and in Chapter 3, Australians had been citizens since federation but chose to retain the nomenclature of British subject. Nor did the switch in terminology sever the continuity of the British connection because Australians remained British subjects as Australian citizens. The change signalled that Australian identity was paramount and the British connection of diminished significance.

The Citizenship Act was introduced by Arthur Calwell, Minister for Immigration in the Chifley Labor government and architect of postwar migration. Calwell was considered one of the more radical ministers at the time, but his explanation of the design and purpose of the new Act was balanced in the extreme. This was an historic occasion in the life of the nation, he told the House of Representatives on 30 September 1948. The proposed legislation would 'establish for the first time the principle of Australian citizenship, while maintaining between the component parts of the British Commonwealth of Nations the common bond of British nationality'. It marked 'another step forward in the development of Australian nationhood', Calwell said, rather than a break with its past. That step was the logical consequence of decisions made by successive Imperial Conferences, culminating in the passage of the Statute of Westminster. That Act had established the dominions as equal partners with Great Britain, 'independent of each other and joined together in a legal sense by the bond of a common allegiance to His Majesty the King'.[7]

For the conservative side of Australian politics, uncomfortable with the rhetoric of equal partnership and national independence, this change was a significant break with Britain and past tradition. Conservative Australian governments in the 1920s had not pushed for the Balfour Declaration of equality between Britain and its senior dominions, nor had they bothered to adopt the Statute of Westminster in the 1930s. That had been done by the Curtin Labor government in 1942 as part of Australia's assertion of independent nationhood in the Pacific, as we saw in Chapter 4. The assertion of Australian citizenship was a further recognition of national maturity and independence from Britain reflected in the parallel transition from British Empire to Commonwealth. This was emphasised by Calwell who said that the bill was designed to help Australians express 'pride in citizenship of this great country'. The time had come for Australians 'to recognize officially and legally their maturity as members of the British Commonwealth by the passage of separate citizenship laws'.[8] Nevertheless, the British connection was preserved by the continuation of British subjecthood as part of the new Australian citizenship. It was also evident in the privileged treatment extended to British subjects who were not Australian citizens. They would be free of the disabilities and restrictions applying to aliens and would enjoy the rights and privileges available to Australian citizens, such as the franchise and being able to stand for parliament and join the public service.

The generous treatment for non-Australian British subjects under the new Citizenship Act was in sharp contrast to the continuing treatment of indigenous Australians. They were effectively 'British Subjects without Rights' before 1949 and would become 'Citizens without Rights' until the

1960s. Things might have been different if the old radical Jack Lang, sitting out his final years of public life in Federal parliament, had been listened to. Lang complained that the new legislation gave 'nothing except the title' of Australian citizenship. 'Every Australian citizen should have certain basic rights and privileges', Lang urged, 'and they should be stated explicitly'. Given the deficiency of the constitution in this respect, Lang claimed there was 'an overriding obligation upon the Parliament to provide a real definition of Australian citizenship'.[9] But Jack Lang was not listened to, partly because the Labor government had no desire to overturn the half-century of exclusion of indigenous Australians from effective citizenship. The fact that British subjects could be included in the benefits of Australian citizenship and Australian indigenous people excluded reflected the continuing cultural homogeneity of the citizenry.

Citizenship was formally Australianised in 1949 but without cutting off British permeability. While preference for British migrants and cultural traditions would continue to be touted into the 1960s, the Australian citizenry was already being transformed by a massive program of more diverse European migration that Minister Calwell had also put in place. That plus finding its place in the world as a more independent nation in the Asia-Pacific region during the long period of the Cold War would change the character and dynamics of Australian nationhood and citizenship in ways that are analysed in the following two chapters. Those changes would transform Australia and its place in the world, but in ways that build upon its dominant British heritage of civil society, governance and citizenship.

Chapter 6

New World Orders

At the beginning of the twentieth century, when Australia was taking its place in the world as a newly fledged nation-state, barriers were erected at its boundaries to preserve a distinctive way of life. By mid-century there were already profound shifts in Australia's nation building that would affect both its citizen body and its orientation to the world. At the end of the Second World War, Australia adopted a massive immigration policy to expand its population as it had done at the turn of the century and again after the First World War. The imperative was populate or perish. Whereas previously Australia had looked solely to Britain for immigrants, after the Second World War there was a dramatic shift in recruitment to include European refugees and southern European migrants. Two decades later the White Australia policy was abandoned and the immigration policy broadened to include migrants from all countries of the world. During the 1970s following the end of the Vietnam War, Indo-Chinese refugees including some who came as 'boat people' to Australian shores boosted the proportion of Asians. Australia's political and social institutions that had been used for generations in monocultural nation building now had to cope with a more multicultural population whose familial ties and ancestry stretched to every part of the globe. While Australian political and civil institutions proved robust, the old Australian nationalism was abandoned.

As Australia and the world have changed, so have the prominence of the nation-state and the role of government in mediating global forces and shaping the citizen body. Since the 1970s Australia has been less inwardly focused on being self-contained and distinctive as a nation-state. It has been more oriented to the global and to demolishing national barriers of protection. If for the middle years of the twentieth century Australia was in the foreground and the world in the background, that has been reversed. For contemporary Australians, the world has become more the foreground and the nation-state but a part, albeit an important part, of the larger whole. Australia's orientation to the world has been deeply influenced by its alliance with the United States. Postwar American hegemony and world leadership have also shaped Australia's world, although Australia has played a significant role for a 'middle power' in that process. America in the immediate postwar period abandoned isolationism and provided leadership for the establishment of a new trading paradigm: one that sought to remove protective barriers and return to principles of free market competition on a global basis. Australia was a strong initial advocate of institutions for liberalising world trade but only adopted competition policy in concert when it was revived globally in the mid- to late-1980s.

The outside world is more accessible to contemporary Australians. The advent of television, satellite communication and computerised email has opened up a large public space that national governments have trouble in regulating. The concern in the 1950s was that mass communication had the potential to lead to totalitarianism. On the contrary, the ascendancy of neo-liberalism and expansion of new technologies have created a proliferation of divergent paths and invigorated global politics. Global competition has broken down national boundaries and opened up regional trading blocs. Old certainties have dissolved as economic opportunism has created new rivalries and alignments, and produced greater fragmentation and complexity. Accompanying the trade and capital flows that have been liberalised, especially following the collapse of the Soviet Union, there have been marked increases in transnational population flows. However, nation-states which have put in place rigorous boundaries to restrict displaced people from becoming citizens have created a global problem. By the 1980s, refugees displaced from their homelands by civil wars have been treated as 'illegal immigrants' in Australia as elsewhere and subjected to the humiliation of detention and denied basic civil rights. For better and worse nation-states still retain the dominant role in determining those who have citizenship and what their rights and entitlements are.

Global governance at the same time has become more pronounced. At the end of the Second World War there was greater determination to establish international government organisations. Sensitivities around respect for national sovereignty have been tempered by international regimes that have focused on the upholding of human rights by nation-states. The witnessing of human rights abuses in Nazi Germany and Stalinist Russia strengthened a determination to hold political communities accountable to the international community for their domestic policies. Particularly from the 1980s there has been a strengthening of human rights regimes to protect civil and political liberties associated with national citizenships. Parallel with the proliferation of international government organisations has been a vast increase in non-government organisations and issue movements dedicated to political lobbying and other human and environmental purposes.

Since the collapse of the Soviet Union and the end of the Cold War, Australia's need for direct security reliance on the United States has diminished. Nevertheless, Australian foreign policy continues to be dominated by the search for security in the Pacific (Meaney 1985, p. 38). Geo-economics has not so much superseded geo-politics as been superimposed upon geo-politics. With the floating of the Australian dollar and the deregulation of Australian financial markets, economic policy set in Washington directly affects Australia. The new world order of global capitalism is in part an extension of American capitalism and certainly congenial to it. If, as Whitlam observed in the early 1970s, it is 'better business for the US to have cooperative partners rather than resentful allies' (Quoted in Higgott 1989, p. 165), Australia has been a cooperative partner and ally in both the strategic and economic spheres. Although Australia has become more of an independent actor on the world stage in matters of multilateral international trade and security, it must still follow or react to the agenda set by the larger powers.

Today, Australia's security, trade and political alliances encompass a complex web of associations and treaties. These include regional arrangements such as Asia Pacific Economic Cooperation (APEC); sectoral affiliations, such as the Cairns Group of agricultural exporting nations, and membership of the major international economic and political organisations. Apart from being a signatory to most of the key multilateral agreements on human rights and the environment, many more significant links with individual nations are maintained through a myriad of bilateral agreements. These cover areas as diverse as trade, security, the environment, diplomatic relations, technical mutual assistance and development of standards, financial cooperation, information technology and scientific and medical research and development.

The first part of this chapter analyses the change in Australia's strategic and trade alliances over the last fifty years. The second part of the chapter examines Australia's interaction with the postwar global order, particularly the United Nations and its specialised agencies. It assesses the development of Australia's international treaty obligations over the past half-century, focusing on the controversial area of human rights. This example illustrates the increasing globalisation of major policy questions because of the more integrated and informed global community and the spillover of issues beyond national borders. Information technology has a significant impact especially in the media and information fields. Cable and free-to-air broadcasting, the Internet, the World Wide Web and newly developing technologies such as broadband make access to information and events global and immediate, and challenge the traditional regulatory, legislative and policy-making role of national governments. Government is not made redundant; if anything its regulatory role is expanded in attempting to coordinate, monitor and regulate global movements of intellectual property, legal and illegal money, in cooperation with international agencies and other states (Williams 2000*b*). It is also called upon to respond to an increasing number of international standards.

Strategic and Trade Alliances

The Second World War had forced Australia to become more independent from Britain and oriented towards the Asia Pacific. This process would continue during the postwar decades as Australia's nearest northern neighbours broke the shackles of European colonialism and the United States became the dominant superpower in the region. The relationship with Britain and the Commonwealth would continue to be important for some time, but decreasingly so as Britain declined and retreated into Europe. The geo-political landscape changed dramatically as the erstwhile allied victors of the Second World War, the United States and Russia, confronted each other as enemies in the escalating Cold War. This had critical security implications for Australia and the region, and hampered the effectiveness of the United Nations for decades to come.

Communism was the new enemy that threatened Asia as well as Europe, and the containment of communism was the main objective of American foreign policy around the world. Australia and New Zealand formed the strategic ANZUS pact with the US in 1951 although the Americans were somewhat reluctant about the agreement. Support for American intervention in Korea and the persistence of the Australian Minister for External Affairs, Percy Spender, sealed Washington's resolve to form the alliance (Ravenhill 1989, pp. 3–4). The tripartite pact effectively disintegrated in the mid-1980s in response to New Zealand's decision to ban US nuclear-armed or powered warships in New Zealand waters. This left Australia in the awkward position of maintaining its links with the USA and New Zealand, neither of whom was cooperating with the other. The Australian-American substitute, AUSMIN, a series of bilateral ministerial talks, has never assumed the prestige and significance of its predecessor (Smith, Cox & Burchill 1996, pp. 75–76).

In 1950, Australian troops formed part of the UN force defending South Korea from the communist North in what was really a show of support for the US. The resolution supporting a UN force in Korea had been passed by the UN Security Council without veto only because the Russian representative had boycotted the UN. It was the last time such a boycott was made. Following the French defeat by the communist Viet-Minh in 1954, SEATO (South East Asian Treaty Organisation) was established as a defensive alliance that further linked Australia with the United States, and aimed to stem the domino effect of communism sweeping through Asia. The alliance also included Britain, New Zealand, France, Thailand, the Philippines and Pakistan. It was a weaker South East Asian equivalent of NATO (North Atlantic Treaty Organisation), that linked 11 of America's trans-Atlantic allies in 1949 against communist Eastern Europe and the Soviet Union.

Although Australia supported British troops against communist insurgency in Malaya in 1955, its alliance with the United States increasingly dominated Australian foreign policy during the second half of the twentieth century. The Suez Crisis in 1956, and Britain's formal announcement in 1967 to withdraw its military presence 'east of Suez', provided further impetus towards alignment with the USA and the military strategy of forward defence. Menzies also committed Australian troops to fight in Vietnam to reinforce the relationship with the US even though no British troops were involved. By 1966, national controversy raged over the justice of the war and Australia's commitment to sending conscripts. Undeterred, Menzies' successor, Harold Holt, promised to go 'all the way with LBJ' and invited the US President, Lyndon Johnson, to visit Australia at the height of the Vietnam War in 1966. American defence installations established in Australia, at North West Cape (1967), Pine Gap (1969) and Nurrungar (1970), were significant but controversial embodiments of the US-Australian military relationship, and 'tied Australia much more closely to American global nuclear strategy' than the ANZUS treaty ever did (McDougall 1998, pp. 53, 57).

Australia's reliance on Washington rather than Whitehall for its foreign policy increased as the Cold War escalated during the 1960s. The Whitlam Labor government in the early 1970s attempted a more distinctively Australian foreign policy with less dependence on the US. While still in opposition, Whitlam visited China in 1971 and met with Chinese Premier Zhouenlai, signalling that Australian foreign policy would take a different direction under a Labor government (Meaney 1985, pp. 724–27). The Liberal Coalition government had refused to recognise the communist government of the People's Republic of China, in line with American policy. Liberal Prime Minister McMahon publicly condemned Whitlam's historic visit to Peking as an exercise in 'instant coffee' diplomacy, and argued that recognising China would 'isolate Australia from our friends and allies not only in South-East Asia and the Pacific, but the Western world as well' (Meaney 1985, pp. 728–29). Whitlam proved to be more in tune with the changing world order than McMahon. The US National Security Adviser Henry Kissinger had held secret talks in Peking with the Chinese Premier within days of the Whitlam meeting and President Richard Nixon announced that he would accept an invitation to visit China (Meaney 1985, p. 72).

Trade policy is typically more pragmatic and fluid than strategic policy that has crystallised around treaty alliances. That was certainly the case for

Australia's trade and economic alliances after the Second World War. Changes have reflected the shift in Australia's earlier status from British dominion to a more independent nation with a greater focus by Australia on the Asia-Pacific region. Australian trade has been shaped by or in response to globalisation with Australia becoming a member of key trading organisations at the sectoral, regional and global levels. Australia is also party to many more specific bilateral trade agreements with other nations. Globalisation of world markets is reflected in the changing composition of Australia's trade: agricultural exports, that once dominated Australia's exports, now comprise 20 per cent which is roughly equivalent to the share of both services and manufactured goods as a proportion of the export market.

Australia's traditional political economy of 'protection all round' peaked in the postwar decades under McEwen who was Deputy Prime Minister in the Menzies era and the powerful Minister for Trade and Industry. By 1970 Australia, along with New Zealand, had the highest tariff rates on manufacturing industries in the industrialised world as well as protective schemes for weaker rural industries such as dairying and dried fruits. Although one of the original signatories to the General Agreement on Tariffs and Trade (GATT), established in 1947 to liberalise global trade, Australia refused to take part in any GATT negotiations during the 1950s and 1960s (Capling & Galligan 1992, pp. 106–7). All of that changed with the dismantling of Australia's protective policies in the 1980s and its championing of free trade in global forums. From being an outrider, Australia became a champion of liberal trade orthodoxy and a fervent member of its international organisations.

This has not always been greeted with such enthusiasm at home. Domestically, the reform of industry, the push to lower tariff barriers and reforms to rural subsidies and assistance have met with resistance from farming groups, unions, especially in industries which were previously heavily subsidised, and other rural and regional community groups who have experienced the negative consequences of economic globalisation: the closing of businesses, industries and farms and the economic and social inequalities which flow from that. The vigorous display of opposition to the World Trade Meeting at Melbourne in September 2000, like the earlier Seattle protests, showed the strength of anti-globalisation sentiments among well organised groups of Australian citizens linked to international protest movements. The consensus among international and Australian economic elites and governments in favour of freer world trade is contested by a growing backlash globally and within Australia. This tension has complicated the Australian government's 'two level game' of negotiating Australia's interests in international forums and having the deals that it brokers accepted domestically within Australia (Galligan & Rimmer 1997). Through international agreements and treaties the Commonwealth increases its own policy jurisdiction at the expense of the states, although it limits its independence by so binding itself to international standards. There are sensitive political as well as jurisdictional aspects, however, as the Commonwealth has to win domestic support for its international forays and demonstrate the benefits of agreement to domestic constituencies. In this it has been far from successful particularly in rural electorates where people feel disadvantaged by globalisation.

OECD policies have also proved contentious. A notable recent example was the Multilateral Agreement on Investment (MAI) that foundered in Australia and globally because of public opposition to the perceived evils of liberalising foreign investment regulations.[1] In Australia, the newly formed Joint Standing Committee on Treaties tabled an extensive Final Report in Parliament in March 1999. Out of more than 900 submissions received by the Committee, 86 per cent opposed ratification of the agreement and 36 per cent were concerned that it would infringe Australia's sovereignty (Commonwealth Parliament, Joint Standing Committee on Treaties 1999). The agreement was roundly criticised by state and local governments, industry and conservation and community groups. The criticisms were twofold: first, that the government, and particularly Treasury, had been unduly secretive in conducting negotiations; and second, that increased foreign investment under the MAI would severely circumscribe the Australian governments' independent policy-making capacity. Defeat of the MAI demonstrated the effectiveness of a well organised global campaign by committed opponents who mobilised public opinion in many countries.

Nonetheless Australia has become a promoter as well as a joiner of international bodies, playing a key role in establishing the regional organisation for Asia Pacific Economic Cooperation (APEC) in 1989. Aimed at developing regional free trade and economic cooperation, the original proposal made by Australian Prime Minister Bob Hawke did not include the USA and Canada (Ravenhill 1994, p. 88). The Department of Foreign Affairs and Trade describes APEC as the 'key component of Australia's regional trade policy' and boasts that the combined output of APEC members accounts for almost half of world exports and more than half of world GDP. But that also means that APEC is diverse and relatively weak. Nevertheless, APEC achieved a high point of aspiration in the Bogor Declaration signed in November 1994 under the auspices of the ailing Indonesian dictator, General Suharto. APEC leaders committed their countries to the goal of free and open trade and investment in the Asia Pacific to be achieved by industrialised countries by 2010 and by developing countries by 2020. This was a 'tip-top result' for Australia's Prime Minister Keating who placed great store by his special relationship with Suharto and had worked hard for such an outcome. He boasted to the House of Representatives:

> With Bogor ... Australians can say for the first time that the region around us is truly 'our region'. We know its shape; we have an agreed institutional structure; we share with its other members

a common agenda for change. Just as the Bretton Woods agreements after the Second World War established structures in the IMF and the World Bank, which enabled the world to grow and prosper, so in APEC we have established a model, which will serve the interests of the post-Cold War world (Keating 2000, pp. 116–17).

Subsequent events soon deflated such hopes. President Clinton did not bother attending the next APEC meeting in Osaka the following year, favouring, in Keating's terms, 'presentation in domestic politics over substance in international affairs' (Keating 2000, p. 120). APEC has languished with the Asian countries of the region shaken by the 1997 financial crisis and Indonesia weakened in its transition to democracy and strife over East Timor.

Less ambitious but probably more effective has been the establishment of the Cairns Group, a ginger group of primary-producing nations in world trade forums named for its inaugural meeting in Cairns, Queensland. Australia played a key role in forming the group and getting agriculture included in the Uruguay Round of the GATT in 1986 where some concessions were won. The failure of the Uruguay Round to reach consensus led to the establishment of a new organisation, the World Trade Organisation (WTO), in 1995 that now conducts the multilateral negotiations aimed at liberalising world trade. The WTO has been no more successful with its 'Millennium Round' of trade talks. The WTO's 1999 Seattle meeting was disrupted by vigorous protests from anti-globalisation campaigners, and the EU remains intransigent against lowering trade barriers, particularly on agricultural products.

Finding a Place in the Modern World

Australia's ties with Britain were not severed after the Second World War but gradually watered down in the British Commonwealth of Nations. The creation of two new Commonwealth nations immediately after the war, India in 1947 and Ceylon (now Sri Lanka) in 1948, signalled that the Commonwealth itself was becoming less British. In 1957, the first African member, Ghana, gained independence and joined the Commonwealth; as did Malaya that was later incorporated as Malaysia in 1963. As the British Empire dissolved, most former colonies of Africa, Asia, the Caribbean, Mediterranean and Pacific joined the Commonwealth.

While not bound by any formal legal constitution or framework, the modern Commonwealth operates on the principles of the Singapore Declaration (1971) and the Harare Declaration (1991). These declarations were the outcome of the Commonwealth Heads of Government Meetings (CHOGM), a regular forum in which views are exchanged, agendas set and policy developed and endorsed. The modern Commonwealth actively supports the broader UN objectives of international peace and security, and the promotion of human rights. The Singapore Declaration reinforced the aims of the UN Charter and the UN Declaration on Human Rights by seeking to promote institutions and guarantees for personal freedom under law; to combat racial prejudice and colonialism; and to overcome poverty, ignorance and disease. The Harare Declaration reaffirmed the pre-eminence of human rights in Commonwealth nations, and specifically pledged Commonwealth nations 'to continue action to bring about the end of apartheid and establish a democratic, non-racial and prosperous South Africa'. Australia has at times been an active player in the Commonwealth forum and used it effectively for international purposes, as did Prime Minister Malcolm Fraser in his crusade against apartheid in South Africa.

After the Second World War, and more particularly after the 1970s, Australia has become increasingly independent from Britain and more integrated economically and politically into the new international order. Finding a place and a national role with which Australians are comfortable has proved rather more difficult. Underlying the heightened attention to national identity and the challenges of globalisation is a curious blend of uncertainty and exhilaration about the changes that are transforming Australia and its place in the world. There have been both optimistic and pessimistic responses. An energetic internationalist, Gareth Evans, Minister for External Affairs in the Hawke and Keating Labor governments, saw that Australia could 'box above its weight' as a decent middle power in the international arena. While Evans relished the encounters, perhaps inevitably given the complexity of international affairs in a fluid post-Cold War world, he often seemed removed from Australian public opinion and sentiment. Keating, Labor Prime Minister from 1993 to 1996, was a brilliant simplifier who cast the options as breaking with Britain and turning to Asia, both of which had mainly occurred. An alternative response is to revive simpler nostrums of old Australia: no coloured immigration or pandering to Aboriginal people, and return to a protective state economy. This was popularised by Pauline Hanson's One Nation party in the late 1990s and finds support among those marginalised by economic changes.

Coming to office in 1996, the Howard Coalition government defined its foreign policy stance as that of 'practical diplomacy'. Pragmatism is a traditional attribute of Australia's domestic politics and international relations. While the Howard government and its Minister for Foreign Affairs Alexander Downer called themselves 'realists', their policy approach acknowledged the complex interrelationships between Australia's economic, strategic and political interests, and the diverse bilateral and multilateral treaties which underpin these relationships (Downer 1999). The government's 1997

White Paper on Australia's Foreign and Trade Policy, *In the National Interest*, called for a 'whole of nation approach' that involved linking foreign and trade policies with domestic policies. Such an integrated approach, although obviously required, was somewhat novel for Australia as Richard Higgott pointed out a decade ago:

> The search for national economic well-being in the international order for a state such as Australia is as significant as the search for national security (traditionally defined in politico-strategic terms) as we head toward the last decade of the century (Higgott 1989, p. 132).

Despite its sense, there had been 'an overall reluctance to treat the economic relationship as a political phenomenon' (Higgott 1989, p. 163).

Despite distancing itself rhetorically from its Labor predecessor, the Howard government continued with the main components of Australian foreign policy that Labor had pursued. These are a primary commitment to the Asia Pacific, particularly East Asia; continuing strategic defence alliance with the United States; sustaining links with key trading partners, such as the USA, Japan, Indonesia and China; and supporting trade liberalisation through forums such as the WTO and APEC. These are cast as 'the important elements of continuity in the Government's policy framework'. The difference is a preference for bilateral over multilateral relationships as the 'basic building block' upon which regional and global foreign and trade policy are to be built (DFAT 1997, p. *iii*). This is in reaction to the robust internationalist approach pursued by Labor and its Minister for External Affairs, Gareth Evans, who was a firm supporter of the UN and its many specialised agencies in the mould of Evatt (Hudson 1993; Evans & Grant 1993). Evans proliferated Australia's accession to international multilateral agreements and was criticised for sacrificing Australia's sovereignty at the altar of globalisation and being out of touch with the Australian public. In contrast, Alexander Downer has focused on bilateral relations and 'a selective approach to the multilateral agenda' and issues 'where its national interests are closely engaged' (DFAT 1997, p. *iii*).

The Howard government was jaundiced about internationalism and 'realistic about what multilateral institutions such as the United Nations can deliver'. In similar pragmatic fashion, its advice to the UN was to 'focus on practical outcomes' that matched its aspirations with its capability. The Howard government recognised that globalisation and the economic rise of East Asia would continue to be the two major foreign and trade policy influences on Australia during the next 15 years. The Asia Pacific would clearly remain the focus of Australia's foreign and trade policy because Australia's 'most substantial interests' lay with the region's three major powers and largest economies, the USA, Japan, and China, and with Australia's largest neighbour, Indonesia. Not far behind Australia has 'significant interests' in the Republic of Korea, other ASEAN states and New Zealand and Papua New Guinea, in the South Pacific (DFAT 1997, p. *vi*). The government sought to diffuse anxiety about globalisation and Asianisation by emphasising the job growth and higher standards of living that it produced. Australia could have the best of both worlds. Familiar and historic links to Europe and America did not need to be jettisoned to accommodate the new economic and strategic order. Nor did closer engagement with Asia require 'reinventing Australia's identity or abandoning the values and traditions which define Australian society'.

One obvious difficulty for Australia is its relative isolation adjacent to Asia in the Pacific. It does not fit easily into any strong regional trade association, such as the European Union (EU) or the North American Free Trade Association (NAFTA). Being a footloose middle power has anxieties as well as opportunities. The categorisation of Australia as a 'middle power' has been a recurring theme in postwar decades. The label – and the international political power or lack of power it represents – has been seen as both a strength and a weakness. At international forums from Versailles to San Francisco, and in world trade organisations since the Uruguay Round of the General Agreement on Tariffs and Trade (GATT),[2] Australian leaders used middle power status in advancing their claims. Between a superpower with enormous responsibilities and vested interests and small countries with little means, Australia's being a middle power conferred benefits of credibility, independence and integrity. Australia's middle power diplomacy boasted some notable successes such as promoting freer agricultural trade through the Cairns Group, and brokering a UN peace-keeping force and free elections in Cambodia. APEC is another instance where Australia's credibility, because of its 'domestic commitment to internationalising the economy', and the lack of an ulterior political motive as a middle power, compared with the USA or Japan, contributed to its successful creation (Evans & Grant 1993, pp. 323, 325).

The downside of middle power status is the inability to determine outcomes that affect the global economic, political, trade or security agenda. A middle power might help set the agenda but is unlikely to carry the day; its main contribution to international affairs is facilitating alternative avenues of resolution for larger powers caught in otherwise intransigent positions (Cooper, Higgott & Nossal, 1993). The Cairns Group in the Uruguay Round 'provided an alternative middle ground upon which the major actors could meet'. In the post-Cold War world where bipolar rivalry has diminished and 'there are no longer any guarantees that larger allies will always take care of a junior partner's interests' middle powers must 'engage in more creative diplomacy ... to fill the obvious gaps left'. Reflecting on recent Australian and Canadian experience, Cooper, Higgott and Nossal suggest an enhanced role for middle powers in world affairs:

> [T]he technical innovation and entrepreneurship in the inter-
> national diplomacy of middle powers could, if effectively co-
> ordinated, play an important role in shaping the future. To be
> sure, the major powers will continue to play the principal role in
> the structuring of the global order ... Yet, Australia and Canada
> are two states, differences notwithstanding, that have sufficient
> common interests and international status and credit to make an
> important contribution to shaping that future (Cooper, Higgott
> & Nossal, 1993, p. 180).

Successive Australian governments have claimed that Australia is already
playing that role.

Compared with Canada, there is much more at stake because of Australia's
relative isolation from an adjacent powerful friend: 'Australia was not protected by a long, open frontier and the Monroe Doctrine', as Hancock
observed in the 1930s. That did not seem to matter while the British Empire
was strong and engaged in Asia. Hancock could also observe that 'in Australia
we are as a rule hardly conscious that we have a foreign policy' (Hancock
1961, pp. 51, 204). Indeed, Australia barely had a foreign policy, having entrusted it to Britain. Nevertheless, distance and isolation were often sobering
considerations for those who thought about Australia's geographic and
strategic place in the world. For Frederick Eggleston, who had an extensive
personal knowledge of Asia, Australia in the 1950s was 'a small nation in an
alien sea', being a 'democracy with a way of life and political ideas practically
identical with those of the United States or of Britain and other Western
democracies' (Eggleston 1957, p. 1). From the mid-twentieth century onwards, Australia's challenge has been to integrate its British heritage and
Western culture with its Asia-Pacific geography. Writing in the late 1960s,
historian Geoffrey Blainey captured the historic tension between Australia's
history and geography in the expression 'the tyranny of distance', which
reflected the impact of both the distance between Australia and the rest of the
world, as well as the vast distances within it (Blainey 1968). For the optimists
at least, Australia is uniquely poised to capitalise on its enduring links with
Europe and the USA and its location adjacent to Asia (DFAT 1997, p. *iv*).

One obvious consequence as well as a cause of globalisation is that
distance and location are no longer barriers to international participation,
nor bulwarks protecting national attitudes and practices. Human rights
protection is an outstanding instance of a global issue movement. As well as
being affected by the human rights movement in domestic politics and law,
Australia has also championed human rights internationally. Australia took a
strong international stand against South Africa's apartheid policy, capitalising
on links among British Commonwealth nations and the Commonwealth
Heads of Government Meeting (CHOGM) forum to galvanise international

action including trade sanctions. Australia's human rights advocacy has not always coincided with its strategic and trade interests. Examples include its sanctioning of Indonesia's annexation and treatment of East Timor until 1999 and silence on China's human rights record.[3] Australia supported China's membership of the WTO and signed a trade agreement with China to give Australia better access to the Chinese market. Australia has been justifiably criticised for being 'Janus-faced' on the issue of human rights – vigilant abroad but reluctant and complacent about the protection of those rights at home (Charlesworth 1994, pp. 21–53). The treatment of Australia's indigenous people and so-called 'illegal immigrants' have been two striking examples of charity not beginning at home. At the same time, Australia has become more enmeshed in international accords for protecting human rights, as the next section shows.

UN Rights Protection and Australia

The proliferation of international human rights following the birth of the United Nations (UN) in 1945 has influenced Australian domestic governance, law and citizenship practice. The way in which this has occurred has been mediated by the Commonwealth Government and shaped by Australia's constitutional system, particularly the politics of federalism and the interpretation of the external affairs power by the High Court. The international human rights regime and web of UN agencies challenge formalist notions of the sovereignty of the nation-state. Participation in an international organisation that sets norms and standards that affect domestic practice is not novel for Australia because of its history as a colony and dominion within the British Empire. The UN's new world order was rather different from the British Empire, however, and international human rights law and practice markedly different from the common law that Australia traditionally relied upon for human rights protection.

In creating the United Nations, the central objective of the victors in the Second World War was to avoid the possibility of such devastation occurring again. That purpose was expressed in the Charter's preamble:

> We the Peoples of the United Nations
>
> Determined to save succeeding generations from the scourge of war, which twice in our lifetime has brought untold sorrow to mankind ...

The UN Charter reaffirmed 'faith in fundamental human rights, in the dignity and worth of the human person, in the equal rights of men and women and of nations large and small'. For the first time, individuals' rights and freedoms were explicitly recognised in international law (Charlesworth 1997, p. 281). This set up a tension between state sovereignty, hitherto the immutable basis of the law of nations, and human rights, which had the potential to open up to international scrutiny states' treatment of their own citizens. The Charter's human rights were drafted in general terms but imposed a legal obligation on states (Charlesworth 1997, p. 281). There was a built-in escape-hatch, however, that allowed critics to argue that the General Assembly's human rights powers 'boil down to discussion, exhortation, and the drafting of treaties' (Cassese 1992, p. 27). These powers are also subjected to Article 2 (7), aptly described by the Italian international jurist, Antonio Cassese, as 'that sword of Damocles' that excludes the UN's intervention on matters 'essentially within the domestic jurisdiction of any state'. Despite indications in the preparatory works for the Charter that the UN could intervene where violations of rights were 'grievously outraged' to an extent that would threaten peace or obstruct the application of the Charter (Cassese 1992, p. 28), the line between state sovereignty and UN jurisdiction remains a hotly contested area.

Fundamental human rights and freedoms were articulated at length in the Universal Declaration of Human Rights adopted unanimously by the United Nations General Assembly in 1948. Its thirty articles cover a range of traditional civil and political rights including the right to life, liberty and security of the person; equality before the law; freedom from arbitrary arrest and fair trial; freedom of thought, conscience and religion; freedom of expression and opinion; and freedom from slavery and torture. The Declaration also includes the 'second generation' economic, social and cultural rights, such as the right to a nationality; the right to marry and found a family; the right to work and to an adequate standard of living; and the right to education, social security and health care.

Twenty years later – and after much international debate – the UN adopted in 1966 the International Covenant on Civil and Political Rights (ICCPR) and the International Covenant on Economic, Social and Cultural Rights (ICESCR). Australia ratified these covenants in 1980 and 1975 respectively. From the outset, tension existed between civil and political rights, given primacy by the developed powers, and economic and social rights, supported by the developing and smaller nations. Insistence upon the observance of civil and political rights was criticised as a form of cultural imperialism by the less developed nations, and ideologically opposed by communist states during the Cold War. The UN is also weakened because of its disparate and inclusive membership and the fact that the General Assembly reflects the prevailing views of its member states.

Nevertheless the UN has been instrumental in formalising an ambitious human rights regime that is constituted by its Charter and the Covenants which together are known as the International Bill of Rights. Given their wide international acceptance, the principles contained in the three instruments are generally considered to have the weight of customary international law.[4] This is only one part of the broader international human rights regime, which includes UN agencies such as the International Labour Organisation (ILO), and the United Nations Educational, Scientific and Cultural Organization (UNESCO); and the various regional human rights organisations such as the Council of Europe, the Organization of American States, and the Organisation of American Unity. To this list could also be added the international norms, processes and institutional arrangements, as well as the activities of domestic and international pressure groups, which also promote human rights (Alston 1992, pp. 1–11).

The UN system itself is a complex one of promotion and implementation of human rights. Its Charter-based organs include the 'inner circle' of the International Court of Justice (ICJ), the Trusteeship Council, the General Assembly, the Economic and Social Council (ECOSOC), the Security Council and the Secretariat. Power politics, however, presides at the apex of the system with a veto power vested in each of the five Permanent Members (the allied victors of the Second World War, the United States, Britain, France, the USSR and China). The veto was frequently relied upon by the East and West during the Cold War and did much to cripple the UN. Other significant UN organs include the Commission on Human Rights and the Commission on the Status of Women. The main treaty-based organisations are the Committee on the Rights of the Child (1991), the Committee on the Elimination of Racial Discrimination (1970), the Committee on Elimination of Discrimination against Women (1982), the Human Rights Committee (1976), the Committee against Torture (1988), the Committee on Migrant Workers, and the Committee on Economic, Social and Cultural Rights. These committees monitor the compliance of states parties under each corresponding treaty.

Despite its cumbersome and costly administrative structure and processes, the UN has managed to place human rights squarely on the international agenda. A number of recent successes, such as the trials against perpetrators of genocide in Bosnia and Cambodia, indicate 'the level of development of international ethical norms on human rights in the 1990s' (Gyngell & Wesley 2000, p. 208). In recent years, the UN Security Council has taken action against human rights violations by authorising enforcement measures under the powers of Chapter VII of the UN Charter. The Council's decisions in favour of 'collective humanitarian intervention' have extended to the Kurds in Iraq, to Somalia, the former Yugoslavia and Haiti. In this current phase of development in UN rights protection, there is an emphasis on individual criminal responsibility and minority rights as well as collective humanitarian responsibility. As the leading American international jurist, Thomas Buergenthal, concludes:

> The idea that the protection of human rights knows no inter-
> national boundaries and that the international community has an
> obligation to ensure that governments guarantee and protect
> human rights has gradually captured the imagination of mankind
> (Buergenthal 1997, pp. 703–4).

While many governments still violate human rights on a massive scale, they are being forced to give an account of their actions to the international community. This prospect together with some high profile prosecutions of leading offenders has contributed to an improved human rights situation.

Australian domestic politics and law are affected by this evolving international human rights regime. Australia has been a party to all of the key UN human rights treaties. These are the Convention on the Prevention and Punishment of the Crime of Genocide (1948),[5] the UN Convention on the Political Rights of Women (1953), the Standard Minimum Rules for the Treatment of Prisoners (1957), the International Convention on the Elimination of All Forms of Racial Discrimination (CERD) (1965), the Convention on the Elimination of All Forms of Discrimination against Women (CEDAW) (1979), the Convention Against Torture and Other Cruel, Inhuman or Degrading Treatment or Punishment (1984), the Convention on the Rights of the Child (CORC) (1989), the Second Optional Protocol to the ICCPR against the Death Penalty (1989), the Protection of the Rights of All Migrant Workers and Members of their Families (1990). The ILO and UNESCO and other UN agencies also administer many other human rights instruments (Charlesworth 1997, p. 282).

UN human rights norms are affecting Australian domestic governance in various ways. A recent instance that erupted in March 2000 concerned the Northern Territory's mandatory sentencing laws. Opponents claimed that such tough legislation that prescribed fixed sentences for often minor crimes and denied the tempering discretion of magistrates and judges was in breach of UN standards and used criticisms by members of the UN Human Rights Committee as ammunition (*The Australian*, 14 July 2000, p. 3). Aboriginal groups that were affected attracted international attention by hiring Cherie Blair QC, wife of the British Prime Minister, to argue their case before the UN Human Rights Committee in Geneva. The Northern Territory's mandatory sentencing law was challenged on the grounds that it removed judicial discretion, breached the right of a defendant to a fair hearing, and discriminated against Aboriginal people who were most likely to be affected. The Howard government took the controversial stance of rejecting the UN Committee's legitimacy and capacity to review Australian domestic policy.

This was surprising because, from its inception, Australia has been an active and supportive UN member. Evatt was an early and enthusiastic promoter of the inclusion of economic and social rights in the UN Charter,

arguing that without economic and social security there could be no enjoyment of civil and political rights by a nation's citizens. Evatt made an
enthusiastic beginning to Australia's engagement with the UN and its commitment to multilateral human rights treaties (Russell 1992, p. 18). Australia
signed the Convention on the Elimination of All Forms of Racial Discrimination in 1966, but it was not ratified until 1975, during the final months
of the Whitlam government. The Whitlam Labor government elected in 1972
renewed Australia's commitment to human rights and a fuller participation in
the UN regime. Australia's shameful treatment of its own indigenous people
had drawn increasing fire from critics abroad, including Soviet leader
Khrushchev in his infamous shoe-banging address to the General Assembly.
Addressing the UN General Assembly in 1974, Prime Minister Whitlam
admitted:

> We must be unremitting in the efforts sanctioned by the Assembly
> to break the illegal regime in Rhodesia, to end South Africa's
> unlawful control over Namibia and to end apartheid ... My
> government – conscious that Australia's own record is seriously
> flawed – is determined to remove all forms of racial discrimin-
> ation within our own shores, notably now, as notoriously in the
> past, against our own Aborigines (Whitlam 1974, p. 583).

This new trajectory of identification with international rights standards both
at home and abroad continued with the Fraser Liberal Coalition elected in
late 1975. Prime Minister Fraser took a strong stance on apartheid and finally
achieved ratification of the ICCPR and the ICESCR. His government also
passed the Northern Territory Land Rights Act that has been effective in
returning half the land mass of the Northern Territory to traditional owners.
Although less committed to indigenous land rights until the landmark *Mabo*
decision of 1992 triggered a national response by the Keating government,
successive Labor governments of Bob Hawke and Paul Keating stepped up
Australia's commitment to the UN. Foreign Minister Bill Hayden echoed
Evatt in re-emphasising the importance of economic and social rights and the
place of international human rights in the domestic agenda:

> The platform of my party recognises human rights as a legitimate
> international concern, as well as a domestic one, transcending
> national boundaries. It accepts the right to food, shelter, health,
> education and economic security as fundamental; that freedom
> from such degrading treatment as discrimination and torture is
> indispensable (Hayden 1986).

In view of Australia's record of close identification with UN human rights
standards, the Howard Liberal Coalition government's criticism of the UN

committee system monitoring compliance with human rights treaty obligations was something of an about face. In contention were the reporting
mechanisms set up under such UN human rights treaties as the International
Covenant on Civil and Political Rights, the Convention on the Rights of the
Child, and the Convention on the Elimination of Racial Discrimination. The
Howard government charged that the CERD Committee's decisions in March
and August 1999 and its concluding observations in March 2000 that
were critical of the government's handling of Aboriginal policy were not well
founded or reasoned. According to Attorney-General Williams, the Committee failed to 'engage seriously with the extensive material put before it by
the Government'; it 'failed to deliver well-founded criticism, strayed well
beyond its mandate and made recommendations of a political nature'. In
response, the government announced 'a whole of government review of
Australia's interaction with the UN Treaty Committee system' to 'ensure that
such interaction is constructive and worthwhile' (Williams 2000b). In April
2001, the Howard government announced a series of measures to improve
the quality of work of the UN committees and human rights monitoring.
These include strengthening the system and getting Australians on UN treaty
bodies. Curiously for a country under criticism itself, Australia is proposing
to encourage other countries in the region to sign and ratify the six core
human rights instruments and will provide practical assistance to help them
comply with reporting obligations. Criticisms of the reviewer and its monitoring process, even if well grounded, suggest a government overly defensive
of domestic practices that many Australians also find offensive.

International Law: Mediation and Impact

The growth of international law and treaties has posed significant challenges
to successive Australian governments and Australian courts of law. In
recent times UN international instruments and standards have become the
dominant influence on domestic practice. Among High Court judges, Kirby
is a strong advocate of using international law in construing ambiguous
domestic statutes or common law precedents, and Brennan did this
brilliantly in the *Mabo* case.

The main institutional means for mediating international influences are
the executive and legislative power of the Commonwealth Government over
external affairs. The treaties power was used sparingly by the Commonwealth
during the first half-century of federation and mainly for routine matters
because diplomacy and security were mainly entrusted to the British Imperial
Government and international affairs were less dense. In the High Court's
first case regarding external affairs, the *Burgess* case (1936),[6] the Court both
predicted, and laid foundations for, its future expansion. The case concerned
the Commonwealth's ability to make aviation laws implementing Australia's

international treaty obligations in the new field of aviation. Sensibly, the Court did not attempt to define the scope of the power. Indeed, Chief Justice Latham pointed out its potential for expansion. The Commonwealth had already implemented a multitude of international treaties to which Australia was a party; by the end of 1935 the list of such treaties ran to over 18 pages. Latham concluded that it was 'impossible to say *a priori* that any subject is necessarily such that it could never properly be dealt with by international agreement' (Ibid., pp. 640–41). The only limitations on the Commonwealth's power were those contained in the Australian Constitution itself, such as section 116 that prohibited the Commonwealth from making laws establishing a religion or section 113 that controlled the use of intoxicating liquor. Otherwise, Latham insisted: 'Australia was established as a new political entity and Australia was to be given control of her own external affairs' (Ibid., pp. 643–44). Evatt and McTiernan were similarly expansive, asserting that no subject matter could be excluded from 'international negotiation, international dispute or international agreement'. This was a 'consequence of the closer connection between the nations of the world' and combined with 'recognition by the nations of a common interest in any matters affecting the social welfare of their peoples' (Ibid., pp. 680–81). In this landmark case, Dixon was more restrained, although he too conceded that air navigation would fall under the 'external affairs' power, no matter how it was defined. He rejected as 'an extreme view' that parliament could effectively make laws over any subject matter, that was otherwise not an 'external affair', merely because Australia had entered into an international treaty. Somewhat ambiguously, Dixon argued that domestic legislation must entail a 'faithful pursuit of the purpose' of the treaty being implemented, where the Commonwealth would otherwise not have the power to make law in a particular subject area (Ibid., p. 674). Rather than speculate as to how this field could be confined, Dixon preferred to allow the limits of the power to be determined by future courts 'in which the application of general statements is illustrated by example' (Ibid., p. 669).

Subsequent cases reinforced the power of the Commonwealth to implement international treaties into domestic law relying on the external affairs power. The High Court was not always unanimous with different judges giving different weight to the power. In a mid-1960s case regarding the validity of Commonwealth airline regulations, only some judges held that the external affairs power could be used for such a purpose; others found it was the Commonwealth's trade and commerce power; while a third group favoured both (*Airlines* case 1964–65).[7]

Within less than a decade, however, Chief Justice Barwick was asserting the 'plenary power given by s. 51 (xxix)' in the *Offshore* case (1975).[8] This plenary legislative power over external affairs complemented the Commonwealth's full executive power under section 61 to allow 'the prospect of independent nationhood which the enactment of the Constitution provided'. Barwick and the Court were in a phase of bullish nationalism. His rhetoric of independent nationhood mirrored that of his fellow judge Windeyer in the 1971 *Payroll Tax* case that nationhood had been 'consolidated in war, by economic and commercial integration, by the unifying influence of Federal law, by the decline of dependence upon British naval and military power and by a recognition and acceptance of external interests and obligations'. The consequence that has become the leitmotif of federal jurisprudence was that 'the position of the Commonwealth, the Federal Government, has waxed; and that of the States has waned' (*Payroll Tax* case 1971, pp. 395–96).[9]

During the 1980s and 1990s, the 'extreme view' staked out by Evatt and McTiernan in 1936, that no subject matter could be excluded from external affairs, became dominant on the High Court. Reflecting on the scope of the power Sir Anthony Mason, one of the prime architects of its extension and chief justice at the time, said: 'the power must be interpreted generously so that Australia is fully equipped to play its part on the international stage' (Mason 1988, p. 755). Judicial interpretation of the external affairs power was generous indeed, with Mason and Brennan leading the High Court in affirming and reaffirming a full and plenary power of the Commonwealth. The groundwork was laid in two leading cases in the early 1980s concerning the two key policy areas where international treaties and norms have been most significant and controversial – human rights concerning Aboriginal people and the environment. In the *Koowarta* case (1982),[10] the Court upheld the validity of the Commonwealth Racial Discrimination Act, passed by the Whitlam government in 1975 and implementing the UN Convention on the Elimination of Racial Discrimination. At issue was a discriminatory Queensland law preventing the transfer of pastoral land to an Aboriginal purchaser. The decision was a close call, however, with only three of the four judges in the majority allowing that any matter that became the subject of an international treaty qualified as an 'external affair'. The fourth required some inherent attribute of 'international concern' as a qualifier.

After two changes to the High Court bench, a new majority of four consolidated and expanded the broad view of the Commonwealth's external affairs power, as well as its corporations power, in the *Tasmanian Dam* case (1983).[11] According to the Court, any subject of a bona fide treaty could be brought under Commonwealth jurisdiction, and even a treaty might not be necessary for matters that were of genuine international concern for the national government. At issue in the case was legislation of the Hawke Labor government, elected in early 1983 with strong support from environmentalists, preventing Tasmania from building a hydro-electric dam on the Gordon-below-Franklin, a wild river in a restricted heritage area. The area had been listed on the World Heritage List maintained under the UN World Heritage Convention to which Australia was a party. In his opinion, Mason claimed 'there are virtually no limits to the topics which may hereafter become the subject of international cooperation and international treaties or conventions' (*Tasmanian Dam* case 1983, p. 486). The dynamics of globalisation and such an open-ended Commonwealth power would inevitably change the federal system, expanding the Commonwealth's jurisdiction and eroding that of the states. This was affirmed with approval by Brennan who repeated Windeyer's earlier prognostication that the position of the Commonwealth has waxed and that of the states has waned (Ibid., p. 528). It was also affirmed, although deeply resented, by the dissenters. Chief Justice Gibbs claimed that the federal division of powers 'could be rendered quite meaningless if the Federal Government could, by entering into treaties with foreign governments on matters of domestic concern, enlarge the legislative powers of the Parliament so that they embraced literally all fields of activity' (Ibid., p. 475). Wilson complained that the expansive reading of the section 51 (xxix) external affairs power so as to bring the implementation of any treaty within Commonwealth legislative power posed 'a threat to the basic federal polity of the Constitution. Such an interpretation, if adopted, would result in the Commonwealth Parliament acquiring power over practically the whole range of domestic concerns within Australia' (Ibid., p. 517). The expansive interpretation was adopted and consolidated in subsequent environmental[12] and human rights cases.[13]

While this did not spell the end of federalism, the Hawke and Keating Labor governments between 1983 and 1996 took full advantage of the Commonwealth's power to make and implement treaties. The Federal Government used its expanded jurisdiction to dominate domestic environmental policy, protecting rainforests in northern Queensland and blocking a huge pulp mill in Tasmania (Lynch & Galligan 1996). Even more controversially, it extended Australia's reliance upon international human rights norms and UN monitoring committees. The consequences are that domestic rights issues are increasingly influenced by international practice and domestic controversies are readily escalated to international forums. Two notable instances have already been discussed: the challenge to the Northern Territory's mandatory sentencing laws before the UN Human Rights Committee in Geneva and the Howard government's rejection of adverse findings by the UN monitoring Committee of the Convention on the Elimination of Racial Discrimination. Both these cases concern the treatment of Aboriginal people that is Australia's Achilles heel in rights protection, and an area in which the Howard government has been niggling and regressive. In both of these instances the Commonwealth could have fixed the matter: by changing its own policy on Aboriginal affairs, especially native title, and by overriding the Northern Territory that is constitutionally a legislative creature of Canberra. In choosing to do neither, it has to defend itself in the international UN forums.

The previous Keating Labor government took the opposite tack in another sensitive area of domestic and state policy, that of sexual practice. The Toonen case was a cameo instance of the practical operation of international human rights norms in trumping discriminatory domestic practice. On behalf of the gay and lesbian reform group in Tasmania, Nicholas Toonen mounted a complaint to the UN Human Rights Committee against Tasmanian criminal law forbidding homosexual conduct between adult males. While Tasmania did not enforce the law, it refused to repeal it. The UN Committee found in favour of Toonen (*Toonen* case 1994; Tenbensel 1996) and, when the Tasmanian government refused to act, the Commonwealth Government passed legislation overriding the Tasmanian law.[14] In turn, Tasmania repealed its offending law and replaced it with non-discriminatory provisions. The Toonen case shows how determined individuals and groups can now take their human rights grievances to international bodies and use their favourable advisory decisions to leverage political change through the Australian federal system. This alternative is particularly significant for Australia in the absence of a domestic Bill of Rights, as Justice Kirby has noted:

> As we do not have a general constitutional Bill of Rights in Australia and as there is no regional human rights court or commission for Asia or the Pacific, the importance of the ICCPR could not be over-stated. Indeed, the significance of the Toonen decision runs far from Tasmania and Australia ... It brings hope to people in countries where individuals are still oppressed by reason of their sexuality (Kirby 2000, p. 18).

Kirby is a staunch advocate of the 'Bangalore Principles', adopted by a conference of judges mainly from British Commonwealth countries meeting in India in 1988, that judges of the common law tradition may properly use international rules in construing ambiguous statutes or filling in gaps in common law precedents (Kirby 2000, pp. 21–22). While other judges may not be so forthright in principle, they have been more radical in practice. A notable example was Justice Brennan's appeal to international standards in overturning established common law that denied any Aboriginal title to land. In this instance there was no ambiguity or gap, but a long-established law based on the principle of *terra nullius* that denied Aboriginal native title had ever existed to Australian land. According to Brennan's leading opinion in the *Mabo* case:

> Whatever the justification advanced in earlier days for refusing to recognise the rights and interests in land of the indigenous inhabitants of settled colonies, an unjust and discriminatory doctrine of the kind can no longer be accepted. The expectations of the international community accord in this respect with the contemporary values of the Australian people. The opening up of

the international remedies to individuals pursuant to Australia's accession to the Optional Protocol to the International Covenant on Civil and Political Rights brings to bear on the common law the powerful influence of the Covenant and the international standards it imports. The common law does not necessarily conform with international law, but international law is a legitimate and important influence on the development of the common law, especially when international law declares the existence of universal human rights.

A common law founded on unjust discrimination in the enjoyment of civil and political rights demands reconsideration. It is contrary both to international standards and to the fundamental values of our common law to entrench a discriminatory rule, which, because of supposed position on the scale of social organisation of the indigenous inhabitants of a settled colony, denies them a right to occupy traditional lands (*Mabo* case 1992, p. 42).[15]

The *Mabo* case revolutionised Australian property law by acknowledging the existence of native title. It shows how the line of demarcation between international and domestic law is being blurred through Australian judges' incorporating international norms into their decision making (Kirby 1995; Patapan 1996).

Also contentious has been the issue of the impact of international law in the absence of domestic legislation implementing it. The basic principle that international law does not have effect unless it is incorporated into domestic law was challenged by the *Teoh* case (1995).[16] The Court found that by entering into a treaty the Australian government creates a 'legitimate expectation' in administrative law that the executive and its agencies will act in accordance with the terms of the treaty, even when the treaty has not been incorporated into Australian law. The case involved the deportation by the Immigration Department of Mr Teoh, a non-citizen father of young children convicted of possession and trafficking in heroin. Australia had entered into the United Nations Convention on the Rights of the Child that makes the best interests of the child a primary consideration in cases involving separation from their parents. However, it had not implemented the provisions of the Convention into domestic law, and the Immigration officials had not taken it into account. The High Court's innovative finding was summed up by Mason and Deane:

[R]atification (by Australia) of a convention is a positive statement by the executive government of this country to the world and the Australian people that the executive government and its agencies will act in accordance with the Convention. That positive statement is an adequate foundation for a legitimate expectation, absent statutory or executive indications to the contrary, that administrative decision-makers will act in conformity with the Convention (*Teoh* case 1995, p. 291).

For Gaudron the paramount consideration was that the children concerned were all Australian citizens:

> What is significant is the status of the children as Australian citizens. Citizenship involves more than obligations on the part of the individual to the community constituting the body politic of which he or she is a member. It involves obligations on the part of the body politic to the individual, especially if the individual is in a position of vulnerability. ... [C]itizenship carries with it a common law right on the part of children and their parents to have a child's best interests taken into account ... in all discretionary decisions by governments and government agencies which directly affect that child's individual welfare ... (*Teoh* case 1995, p. 304).

Both sides of politics were aghast at the decision. The Labor Minister for Foreign Affairs and the Attorney-General immediately issued a joint statement denying any such legitimate expectation and promising to introduce legislation to that effect.[17] The Court had also made it clear that a legitimate expectation cannot arise where there is a statutory or executive indication to the contrary. The government changed before legislation could be passed, and the new Liberal-National Coalition government made a similar declaration in 1997. Their proposed legislation also lapsed with the calling of the 1999 election, and a new bill has been subsequently introduced but not yet passed by the Senate. The *Teoh* case shows the High Court's increased privileging of international treaty obligations and the objection of government, regardless of political stripe, to broadening the impact of treaty standards before they are passed by parliament into domestic law.

Despite their reservations with *Teoh*, the Labor government and its forceful Minister for Foreign Affairs, Gareth Evans, exploited the untrammelled treaty-making power with little concern for parliamentary scrutiny or public accountability. The practice of bulk tabling of treaties every six months developed and, by the 1990s, between 30 and 50 treaties per year were being tabled in parliament. In about two-thirds of cases, Australia had already ratified or acceded to the treaties before tabling and was obliged to comply under international law (Twomey 1995, p. 8). Such contempt for parliament, combined with concern about the High Court's open-ended interpretation of the external affairs power that favoured the Commonwealth over the states, caused a political backlash. A Senate Committee called for greater public scrutiny and public accountability (Commonwealth Parliament, Australia, Senate Legal and Constitutional References Committee 1995), and its key recommendations were adopted by the incoming Howard Coalition government in 1996. The 1996 overhaul of the treaty-making process included: mandatory tabling of treaties 15 sitting days before the government takes action to bring them into force; provision of an accompanying National Interest Analysis explaining the reasons for Australia's becoming a party; scrutiny by a Parliamentary Joint Standing Committee on Treaties; establishment of a Treaties Council under the auspices of the Council of Australian Governments (COAG); and public access to treaty-making information via the Internet. Since 1996, the Joint Standing Committee on Treaties has issued 34 Reports covering 185 treaty actions (Williams 2000*a*).

Some have been concerned by Australia's 'loss of sovereignty' in the recent proliferation of treaties. The Department of Foreign Affairs and Trade estimates that the current Australian Treaty List contains 2920 entries as at 31 December 1999. The entries break down to 1669 bilateral, and 1251 multilateral agreements. The figures themselves, however, can be very misleading. For example, although this appears to be an increase of 902 entries since 1989, in fact only 400 entries represent Australia's signature, ratification or acceptance of new treaties. Of the 400 entries generated by new treaties, many are terminations or replacements of existing treaties. Most of the other new entries concern measures for improving the availability of treaty information. A key point, and one which is often overlooked, however, is that Australia is a member of all of the international organisations which oversee the treaties it has ratified. In that way, Australia has, subject to the usual caveats of the disparities of power in international relations, as much or as little influence over the terms, implementation and enforcement of treaties as any other nation. As a member of all the key international bodies, and particularly in the case of the UN, Australia has been involved in the long negotiations leading up to the drafting of many major human rights and other treaties. Most importantly, Australia can choose not to support or ratify a particular treaty, and has done so, as the MAI case shows. Finally, it remains for Australia and Australia alone to implement treaties domestically. Unlike some other jurisdictions, such as the United States, treaties are not self-executing in Australia: that is, they do not become part of domestic law unless legislation is passed for such purposes.

Numbers aside, Australia is party to a wide range of international instruments touching on almost all areas of domestic policy: environment, health, education, food production and land use. Many treaties spring from Australia's traditional relations with other nations: bilateral treaties cover diplomacy, medical treatment of another nation's citizens, mutuality of telecommunications, postal and other forms of media. Treaties also cover environmental, military and other security and criminal concerns. Examples include agreements banning nuclear testing, land mines and chemical testing, as well as those on organised crime and drug smuggling. Treaties that have come into force in the past five years include the 1993 Chemical Weapons Convention, the 1997 Land Mines Convention and the 1995 Blinding Laser Weapons Protocol. The 1996 Comprehensive Nuclear-Test-Ban Treaty has been concluded but is not yet in force. Environmental standards have also been a focus of international agreements: for example, the 1997 Kyoto Protocol to the Climate Change Convention, and controls over the international movement of hazardous substances incorporated into the 1998 Rotterdam Convention on Prior Informed Consent. On the international crime front, the 1990 European Money Laundering Convention and the 1997 OECD Bribery Convention have recently come into force for Australia. Treaties that have drawn particular criticism are in sensitive policy areas of human rights, labour relations and the environment. Examples include the Convention on the Rights of the Child, the ILO Convention 158 on Termination of Employment, the World Heritage Convention, the Climate Change Convention, the Basel Convention on Hazardous Waste and the Desertification Convention.

A recurring theme has been the States' complaint of lack of consultation in areas they claim to be of vital concern for their jurisdiction. Key sectoral groups have also criticised the Commonwealth for failing to consult about the domestic implications of treaties in Australia. Examples include mandatory sentencing of juvenile offenders under the CORC; agreements on desertification that have a critical impact on land use and development; and listing sites as World Heritage. It has been claimed that complying with the Kyoto Climate Change Convention would reduce national output by up to 1.5 per cent or nearly $7 billion annually and the Howard government, like the Bush administration in America, has refused ratification. The COAG Treaties Council is designed to provide a regular forum for the prime minister and the premiers and first ministers from the States and Territories to meet to discuss such matters. As well, States like Victoria have implemented their own State parliamentary scrutiny of treaties that affect them.

Treaties do matter. The UN monitoring committees provide an international outlet for aggrieved Australian parties whose rights are not adequately protected in domestic law and practice. The UN's Human Rights Committee has recently turned the spotlight of international censure on a number of key outstanding human rights issues that Australia is currently facing. Most of these concern Aboriginal people: mandatory sentencing in the Northern Territory and Western Australia, compensation for the 'stolen generation', and a greater say in land title issues. The Committee has also criticised 'mandatory imprisonment' of 'illegal immigrants' and recommended the adoption of alternative mechanisms for maintaining an orderly immigration process.[18] Australia's participation in international treaties, especially in the human rights area, has proved to be a 'dangerous liaison', as Hilary Charlesworth has argued: it unsettles and challenges many of the rigidities and limitations of Australian law (Charlesworth 1998, p. 57).

Globalisation is having a significant impact on Australian law and public policy at both the Commonwealth and State and Territory levels. The Australian system of federal government and its domestic law are being challenged and transformed in the process. While the extent and intensity of change have increased dramatically in recent decades, it has been an ongoing phenomenon throughout the second half of the twentieth century. Menzies reflected in 1967 after he left politics:

> [W]hen the draftsmen of the constitution wrote down the magic words 'external affairs' there did not leap into their minds any vision of the complex and novel things that were to come many years later. Least of all could they have imagined a comprehensive world organisation of which Australia would be a member, that there would be an International Labour Organisation, or that the political stuff of 19th century treaties would largely have substituted for it the bargaining of merchants, of exporters and importers, agreements in the fields of health and science, the literally hundreds of matters engaging our attention and turning our eyes out to other lands and other peoples (Menzies 1967, p. 116).

The international stage is profoundly different from what it was at federation, and even the late 1960s when Menzies wrote these words. Developments in information technology ensure that the decisions of the UN Human Rights Committee are the stuff of evening television news both domestically and globally. Australian laws and practices are exposed to the glare of international media attention, and domestic governments are forced to defend and explain their policies at home and abroad. In defending Australia's system of parliamentary responsible government and the common law system for protecting rights, Menzies proudly appealed to its venerable British heritage. But that too has come under critical review with the European Court of Human Rights criticising the protection of fundamental civil and political rights in the UK (Nash 2000, pp. 859–60). However Australian governments respond to challenges from globalisation of its human rights regime, they will be subject to scrutiny from the world community. At the start of the twenty-first century, there is a new permeability of the domestic by the global. Australian citizenship has a new international dimension in human rights treaties that affects domestic law and practice. The changing shape of Australian citizenship has brought opportunities as well as contestations, as the following chapter documents.

Chapter 7

Citizenship in a Global Nation

As John Stuart Mill observed, representative government works most easily and smoothly where there is homogeneity (Mill 1972, 1861). Homogeneity eliminates ethnic, religious and cultural differences that so often provide the ground or pretext for civil strife and political conflict. Some like Jean-Jacques Rousseau have gone further in claiming that democracy required homogeneity in economic circumstances as well as political culture. Otherwise those with greater means would have greater political power and the resources to participate more effectively in politics. Hence Rousseau thought that democracy was only possible in small city-states or republics where there was uniform culture and moderate means. Personal wealth and largeness of domain bred inequality and difference that was antithetical to true democracy where citizens should participate equally in politics (Rousseau 1968, 1762). The downside of homogeneity is sameness that narrows civic life and limits creativity and enterprise. Australia has had both the advantages and disadvantages of homogeneity: civic harmony and stable democratic politics on the one hand and monotonous cultural conformity on the other.

Australia's global links have always been important in leavening its civic and political culture, and in expanding the collective and individual aspirations of its citizenry. New waves of global influence, immigration and social movements have combined with domestic initiatives in reshaping Australian civic culture and citizenship practice during the second half of the twentieth century. In responding to increasingly diverse migration from non-English-speaking backgrounds, Australia has been progressively transformed from an anglophone nation of transplanted Britons and Irish into multicultural Australia. With the severing of British ties and the popular demise of

the monarchy, Australia's disguised republicanism of independent constitutional government based on popular sovereignty has become more overt
and formal monarchism challenged. Indigenous Australians have finally
achieved substantial citizenship rights and residual entitlement to land,
although the legacy of dispossession and exclusion from effective citizenship
for generations remains. Aboriginal culture and art have become prominent
in representing modern Australian identity, as was evident in the opening
ceremonies of the 2000 Sydney Olympics that were broadcast worldwide.
However, many Aboriginal people still live in poverty and dependency at the
margins of Australian society.

These transformations are making Australia a more richly diverse and
mature nation, yet so far at least all have been partial and contested.
Multiculturalism is more appropriately a cultural policy for facilitating the
incorporation of non-English-speaking migrants into Australian civic life
than a citizenship policy. Whereas some embrace it as the essence or ideal of
modern Australian identity, others resent it as a distortion of dominant
Australian culture. The republican push for an Australian head of state was
abortive and divisive, with the 1999 referendum to republicanise the head
of state foundering on disagreement over the structure of the new office.
The referendum failed not because of the strength of the monarchists but
because of deep divisions among republicans. The reconciliation movement
has stalled because the Australian government is unsympathetic towards
Aboriginal claims and rejects the need to say 'Sorry' for past wrongs. Truth
about the past and the morality of removing part-Aboriginal children from
their Aboriginal mothers and placing them in assimilationist institutions and
white families have become divisive public issues.[1] Aboriginal activists have
used global forums very effectively to publicise their grievances, and the
Australian government has reacted angrily to criticisms of the United Nations
Human Rights Committee.

Apart from these changes, Australian society and citizenship are being
transformed by the changed role of governments. The pillars of post-
federation political economy – tariff protection for industry, wage fixing to
ensure fair compensation for workers, and extensive government provision of
services and infrastructure – have been dismantled or undermined. During
the 1980s and 1990s both Commonwealth and state governments embraced
neo-liberal policies of deregulation, exposing the nation and its citizens to
volatile world markets and rapid technological change. The mediating role
of governments has switched from protective cushioning or providing a
buffer to global forces to one of promoter and facilitator of market solutions.
The benefits and costs of being joined up more directly with this new world
order are both considerable, and are spread differentially among sectors,
regions, classes and individuals. While liberating and lucrative for some,
without adequate domestic compensation policies provided by governments,

the result has been to increase the burden of structural inequalities and regional disparities on others. The political revolt of regional and rural Australia and the emergence of Pauline Hanson's One Nation party are sharp reminders of this.

This chapter examines Australia's changing civic culture and citizenship practice during the latter half of the twentieth century. It shows the complex interrelationship of global and domestic influences in stimulating and shaping these changes. One hundred years after its founding, the Australian nation is more independent and diverse and its people more assured, if somewhat anxious about their collective ability to cope with the rapidly changing world that now impacts more directly upon them. There are sharp political disagreements about the role of government in mediating global-isation and about multiculturalism, republicanism and Aboriginal recon-ciliation, all of which are important for the future shape of Australian civil society and citizenship but none of which are resolved at this point. That these issues are the key ones on the current agenda illustrates just how far Australia has changed from being a loyal British dominion obsessed with creating a White Australia behind protective state barriers. In this chapter, we examine some of those changes that have made Australians more distinctive and modern Australia more diverse.

It is worth emphasising that modern Australia is built upon the earlier foundations of Anglo-Celtic civic and political culture that have enabled the subsequent diversification of the national citizenry. We reject the superficial finding of the Australian Citizenship Council (2000, pp. 11–15) that there is 'no particular answer' to the question 'What is distinctive about Australian political life?' The answer is to be found in its unique history spanning several centuries and the idiosyncratic development of an increasingly distinct Australian polity and citizenry. The Council's claim that diversity and difference are what unites Australians today is equally implausible. As we pointed out in Chapter 1, the Citizenship Council was not looking in the right place to find the basis of Australian national identity and citizenship. As we have tried to show throughout this book and continue in this chapter, Australian citizenship is grounded in a rich and evolving civil society and political culture. It is not simply based upon abstract core values such as tolerance, acceptance of diversity and the rule of law, although they are part of its more formal articulation. Australian representative democracy and democratic citizenship were grounded in a relatively homogeneous society that, despite the development of greater complexity and diversity during the second half-century of nationhood, provides its foundational base.

One of the findings of this chapter is, as modern globalisation theory predicts, that national government is playing a less significant role in medi-ating the global and shaping the domestic. In Australia's case this is due partly to structural changes in global political economy and partly to choice, with the national government's choosing to jettison protective state policies and expose the national economy directly to global market forces. This obviously affects Australian citizenship, especially its social and economic aspects in the absence of adequate domestic adjustment and compensation policies. All is not lost, however, because citizenship has always been complex and multi-layered with membership in global and local associations. As Australia becomes more a global nation, there will likely be greater reliance on global and local organisations, but nor should the nation-state be written off. Given the current political climate in Australia and worldwide, there is likely to be a swing back to greater national assertiveness, albeit of a kind that is attuned to a more globalised world.

The Australian Way: Assimilation

Exclusive colonisation of the Australian continent by the British had resulted in the superimposition of anglophone culture. It established set patterns for getting on in the world, defining the common good and determining membership in local communities. Distinctive colonial settlements developed their own citizenship heritages that were variations of a transplanted Britishness. This common British-Australian civil and political culture was paramount and in its colonial variant underpinned federation and nation building. The purpose of national government was to extend and complement the common interests of the colonial governments in the national and international spheres. Increasingly, the national government would become more prominent, partly through constitutional change and partly through practical expansion of its policy responsibilities and fiscal base. Despite periods and issues of conflict, such as the Commonwealth's takeover of income tax during the Second World War, federal-state relations were con-sensual and relatively harmonious. On the key issue of anglophone culture and White Australia there was unanimity for the first two-thirds of the twentieth century. The mission of the Commonwealth, like that of the state and local governments, was to preserve that common culture and racial homogeneity. To this end, a restrictive immigration policy was complemented domestically by a relatively closed society that bred cultural uniformity.

Around federation, Australia's population switched from a preponderance of immigrants to a preponderance of native born. Until the closing quarter of the nineteenth century, most of the residents of the colonies had been born overseas and retained experiential links to another older nation. The new generations of native Australians had no personal knowledge of the immi-gration experience and no interest in what lay beyond the parochial par-ticularities of their time and place. The exception was wealthy families who could afford travel and education in Britain, and cultivated these as marks of superiority in the local establishment. Settlement entailed its own degree of cultural isolationism and parochialism. While governments continued to foster new immigrants to populate and develop the land, these New Australians were selected because of their cultural and racial compatibility. Being white was essential and being British was best, but in any case migrants were expected to assimilate and adopt the Australian way of life.

In homogeneous Australia there was limited tolerance of difference even when postwar migration was broadened to include refugees from non-English-speaking backgrounds and southern Europeans. The strictures of Anglo-conformism could be excruciating, depriving individual migrants of their personal and cultural identity by stripping the nomenclature of birth and replacing it with crudities of common appellation. This was consistent with the assimilation of indigenous Australians whose tribal names were typically replaced by dismissive epithets. This homogeneity was tinged with the vestiges of British overlordship in which its commoner Australian proponents had been schooled down through the generations. In the same way that servants had been referred to by a common name, or simply their gender, immigration officials and employees exerted their own superiority by screening out distinctive foreign names and substituting 'plain English' ones instead.

Prejudice against foreignness was evident in the rites of passage at arrival and initial containment. Given serious postwar housing shortages, the 170,000 displaced persons who arrived in the Australian states between 1947 and 1952 were initially accommodated in regional military camps. In this way European refugees were marginalised from mainstream Australian settlements, in a way comparable to indigenous Australians in reserves on the fringes of town, and the Chinese in compounds away from the main encampments in the goldfields. Many of these refugees were directed to work on the Snowy Mountains Scheme where they were accommodated in communal quarters apart from the dwellings erected for Australian staff employed in project management (Kobal 1999). In the cities, assisted passage migrants from Italy, Greece and Malta were often concentrated in old inner suburbs that had deteriorated with the spread of factories and were considered undesirable by aspirant native Australians. Novices to acculturation, these newly arrived immigrants were highly visible because of their foreign language, distinctive dress, their unusual food and customs, and were pejoratively referred to as 'Balts', 'Reffos', 'Dagos' or 'Wogs' (Kunz 1988; Panich 1988). Given the personal hostilities and group prejudices that could be encountered in the wider community, recent migrants naturally sought refuge in the social company of their own compatriots. This was not so different from a century earlier, when the massive influx of Anglo-British to the goldfields led to the establishment of regional associations for the Irish, Scots, Welsh and Manx. Social clubs flourished and helped provide informal networks of support. The darker side of such compatriotism was at times exploitation in finding jobs or housing for the newly arrived.

Assimilation into the mainstream, however, inexorably undercut local ethnic concentration and association. This process was assisted by general government policy that promoted full employment and included specific policy measures for migrants' learning English. Migrant employment in the cities was provided by the manufacturing industry, the expansion of which was deliberately fostered by protective tariff policy. Migrants could aspire to join in the Australian way of life and register success through the acquisition of suburban property that signalled success in getting on in the world. Learning English was an important factor in assimilation. Substantial resources were allocated for face-to-face classes, while radio programs of conversational English such as 'Let's join in' became a daily feature of ABC broadcasting. Existing qualifications for technical and professional skills were usually not recognised, so that improvements in material circumstances were usually the result of physical work, small business acumen and stringent savings. Between 1947 and 1961, immigrants provided an estimated 73 per cent of the increase in the workforce that contributed to general rising standards of living. Migrants shared with other Australians in full employment and rising consumerism that enabled home ownership and purchase of white goods. Initial prejudice against New Australians was followed by overall acceptance that was often only the civility of indifference, although Good Neighbour Councils encouraged native Australians to lend a hand in local communities (Winter 1993).

Citizenship was encouraged as part of embracing The Australian Way of Life. Many European migrants, having suffered from Soviet expansionism, were virulently anti-communist and eager to give their allegiance to a country that provided genuine freedom and civil liberties. Political institutions proved democratically robust in Australia. When the Menzies government enacted legislation to outlaw the Communist party, the High Court found the federal legislation to be unconstitutional and a subsequent referendum to amend the constitution was lost. While anti-communist sentiment was widespread and cleverly manipulated by Menzies in keeping his Liberal Coalition government in office during the 1950s and 1960s, there was not the same hysteria as in America (Macintyre 1999). Nevertheless, the Labor party was split by the warring pro- and anti-communist groups fighting for control of the trade unions and relegated to the opposition benches for three decades.

On the heels of war weariness, assertion of traditional family values struck a chord in the Menzies era. After separation and uncertainty, nothing seemed more desirable than settling down on a quarter-acre block in a newer suburb, building a modern house and raising a family. In these new communities, growing levels of property ownership coupled with the wartime memory of common endeavour and enhanced skills of civic competence resulted in a broadened base for civic participation. Local schools were supported by Parents and Citizens Associations. Activities for adolescents were established through Police and Citizens Clubs. Civic projects were sponsored through service clubs such as Rotary, Apex and Lions. Children might attend Brownies or Cubs, the Guides or the Scouts. Real estate agents, property developers and businessmen stood for office in local councils. Women who had been required for military and civil defence during the war became citizen wives and mothers at home in postwar prosperity.

The development of commercial telecommunications and air travel extended Australia's global links and broadened the access of Australians to world affairs, American pop culture and travel. In January 1958, Qantas Empire Airways inaugurated a world air service to 26 countries on five continents. Sports continued to link Australia with the globe, through participation in the modern Olympics and the British Empire Games. Australia played a prominent part in the new globalisation of sport, hosting the 1956 Melbourne Olympic Games and the 1962 Perth Commonwealth Games. By the 1960s Australian cultural activities were also being put on an international footing. Adelaide held its first international arts festival in 1960 and other capital cities soon followed suit. In 1962 the Australian Ballet had its inaugural season and three years later made its international debut at Covent Garden, the same year that the Sydney Symphony Orchestra embarked on its first major overseas tour. The scholarly community continued its tradition of internationalism and participated in extended opportunities for undergraduate and postgraduate study. In 1949 the United States Congress established the foundation which would administer a mutual exchange program to be known as the Fulbright Scheme; Britain instituted Churchill fellowships and Australia was a party in south-east Asia to the Colombo Plan studentships.

Australian citizenship was being defined increasingly by membership in the national political community and less in terms of separate State political communities. Following the war in 1946, January the 26th was renamed Australia Day, rather than Foundation Day. That same year, Arthur Calwell, then Minister for Information, was successful in gaining approval for the proceedings of the House of Representatives in Canberra to be broadcast by the Australian Broadcasting Commission, arguing that it would strengthen democratic citizenship. Five years later on 10 May 1951, Australian nationhood was celebrated with the Jubilee of Federation at ceremonial and sporting events across the continent. This quickening of national public life paralleled the formal acknowledgment of Australians as citizens in the Australian Citizenship Act that came into force on Australia Day 1949.

The national political community had come of age after fifty years. The war effort and postwar negotiations had raised the profile of Australia globally and stimulated new national alliances that shaped domestic political culture. Buttressed by Keynesian economic theory and funded by the Commonwealth's income tax monopoly, the role of national government expanded in macro-economic management and provision of welfare benefits for the needy. Government was pledged to provide full employment and redress inequalities, and to ensure that material, cultural and intellectual opportunities were available for all in the interests of securing greater civic inclusiveness, national cohesion and social harmony. Partly the outcome of postwar euphoria, this commitment to using the institutions of government to build an inclusive political community, responsive to the needs of all citizens, was to exert a more profound and lasting effect than had been the case following the First World War. The locus of political culture globally had moved leftwards, towards empowering ordinary citizens, albeit with markedly different political prescriptions. The Soviet Union and Eastern bloc countries relied upon Marxist principles and a command economy to improve conditions for all. The nations of the Western world endorsed liberal capitalism, confident that Keynesian techniques enabled national governments to correct its worst excesses through active intervention to ensure stability and redistribute resources to ensure greater equity for ordinary citizens. Government intervention and demand management through fiscal and monetary policy combined with government spending could smooth market fluctuations and maintain full employment while extending welfare benefits. This became the dominant Canberra orthodoxy that reinforced an enhanced role for national government and boosted the significance of national citizenship.

As we have seen, since federation Australia had a venerable tradition of government intervention to promote physical infrastructure development and assist land settlement and manufacturing industries. Although the 1944 referendum to greatly expand the Commonwealth's limited constitutional powers was lost, the important 1946 social services amendment was carried. This gave the national government the specific powers necessary for the creation of a welfare state while its lucrative income tax monopoly gave it ample financial means (Kewley 1980). National government and citizenship, particularly its economic and social aspects, became increasingly important. National government occupied its own distinctive place of residence in Canberra from 1927 with the inauguration of the Australian Capital Territory, but most of the associated bureaucracy had stayed in Melbourne. The expanded sense of national government mission in the postwar decades produced a transfer and burgeoning of the Commonwealth public service in Canberra. So great was its growth that the National Capital Development Corporation (NCDC) was established to plan for this new city. The home of federal politicians and the Commonwealth public service, Canberra became an ordered city of bureaucrats and affluent suburbs.

The era of expansive government was based on the assumptions that rational inquiry could direct public policy and government could manage the capitalist economy to ensure full employment and growth. Core components of the post-federation political economy were embellished. The provision of infrastructure, including public ownership of major utilities, centralised wage fixation and national wage standards, and protection for manufacturing and weaker rural industries were all continued. To these were added the new national goals of ensuring full employment and providing national social security and health systems. There were significant new policy directions for housing and education that empowered a broader citizenry through enhanced access to material and intellectual property. Low-cost housing was built with the assistance of Commonwealth money provided through Commonwealth State Housing Agreements and home ownership was encouraged. Even more important would be a national policy of increasing access to tertiary education. From 1951 a Commonwealth University Scholarship Scheme was introduced and, following the 1957 report of the British authority, Sir Keith Murray, the Universities Commission was established to oversee the development of more Australian universities with the injection of significant Commonwealth funds. This complemented a large rise in white-collar occupations, in management and the professions. Public services expanded and recruited officers with technical skills and professional knowledge. The middle classes no longer had jobs: they had careers. Political life, too, would be increasingly seen as a professional career option (Brett 1998).

National Diversification

As has been documented in Chapter 6, Australia keenly supported the formation of the United Nations and became party to various of the international organisations and instruments established to set new standards of global practice in protecting human rights. The various declarations and covenants inspired social movements struggling on behalf of disadvantaged groups. National minorities and groups gained solidarity and leverage in local politics by joining international movements: 'think globally, act locally' became the catch-cry for glocalised agendas. New grass roots movements mobilised individuals in what became known as 'people power' (Burgmann 1993). The earliest of these postwar movements were the peace movements protesting against the manufacture and testing of atomic bombs in the wake of the Cold War (Saunders 1986). Although nuclear capability rested only with the super-powers, Australia became a British testing ground from November 1946. Its vast spaces were deemed the best sites in the British Empire and, from the early 1950s, testing went ahead at Maralinga, South Australia, and on the Monte Bello islands off the north-west coast. Uranium deposits were also discovered in Australia and, from the mid-1950s, uranium was exported to the British Atomic Energy Commission. In spirited reaction the Australian peace movement campaigned to ban nuclear testing: by March

1958, 350 societies had petitioned the Commonwealth Government to stop nuclear testing and, in November 1959, 5,000 opponents gathered at an Australian and New Zealand Congress of International Cooperation and Disarmament in Melbourne. The campaign had some success when, in August 1963, the Commonwealth Government became the first nation to endorse the International Nuclear Test Ban Treaty and five years later signed the Nuclear Non-proliferation Treaty. The next generation of peace activists focused opposition against Australia's commitment of troops to support its American ally in Vietnam. From the mid-1960s, a moratorium movement against the Vietnam War paralleled a similar movement in the United States with thousands taking to the streets in nationwide protest meetings that peaked in May 1970 with a crowd of 100,000 in Melbourne.

In the 1970s the Whitlam Labor government orchestrated a move to the left in domestic policy, initiated by the campaign 'It's Time' for a change. Australian national awareness was heightened and the government's agenda shaped by the incorporation of United Nations and other international norms and standards in domestic policy. State intervention was legitimised to enhance 'quality of life' that reflected a renewed emphasis on enhancing citizenship through extending social amenities and cultural activities. The huge increase in the national population since the end of the war was concentrated in the sprawling metropolises with their endless suburbs. Whereas in 1933 roughly a third of Australia's citizens lived in rural areas, by 1966 this had fallen to 14 per cent of which only 8 per cent lived on farms. Enhanced levels of attendance at secondary school and at universities created a more youthful involvement in political issues. Amendments to electoral arrangements in national and state polities reflected these changes: redistributing seats from rural to urban areas and lowering the voting age to 18. Citizens became increasingly questioning, demanding and vociferous in advocating issues of social reform. The trend was to eschew traditional political representation in favour of direct action and group mobilisation. The conservative conformism of two decades was replaced by post-modern diversity, with the rhetoric of a 'fair go' and 'equal opportunity' supporting positive discrimination for those considered to be disadvantaged. A new tide of social reformism used campaigns of social activism and media manipulation to bring pressure to bear on formal political decision making. Although these campaigns drew on traditions of civil disobedience, their purpose was civil enhancement. These new trends in social globalisation spread from the United States and were often buttressed by appeal to benchmarks set for international best practice through the treaties and conventions of the United Nations.

Indigenous Australians worked through the Aboriginal Advancement League in the 1950s to claim the International Labour Organisation principle of equal pay for equal work and to press for civil rights that had been denied despite their citizenship. Under pressure from the United Nations, the right to vote was extended to all Aboriginal people in 1962. In 1963 the Yirrkala people presented a bark petition to the House of Representatives requesting that no excision of land be made from traditional areas in Arnhem Land without their permission. American-inspired freedom rides were mounted from the mid-1960s to draw attention to the social and economic deprivation of Aboriginal communities. Dispossession of tribal lands continued with the mining boom in Western Australia, Queensland and the Northern Territory in the 1950s and 1960s. The land rights movement was initiated in a dramatic way in 1966 when Gurinji stockmen at Wave Hill walked off the cattle station to fight for title to the land as well as fair wages in the cattle industry. They launched an unsuccessful appeal to the United Nations for better working and living conditions. The states with the highest percentage of indigenous Australians were the most recalcitrant in addressing social issues; indeed, the *Queensland Aborigines Act* 1971 reaffirmed paternalistic and authoritarian regimes. On the other hand, significant advances for indigenous citizenship were made in South Australia where landmark legislation in 1966 made discrimination unlawful, and enabled compensation for land dispossession.[2]

At the national level, the 1967 referendum deleting from the constitution the two sections that excluded indigenous Australians was a symbolic watershed. In an unprecedented show of unanimity, just over 90 per cent of Australians voted to support the changes that enabled indigenous Australians to be included in the census and the Commonwealth to legislate with respect to indigenous Australians. Unfortunately, however, the government failed to capitalise on the groundswell of support for improving the conditions of Aboriginal communities and made little use of its new power.

With indigenous Australians remaining the most deprived group of Australians, indigenous leaders became more militant in the early 1970s, inspired in part by the American black power movement. Self-help agencies became sites for leadership social action with the establishment of the Aboriginal Medical Service and Aboriginal Legal Services. The Tent Embassy was set up in the grounds of Parliament House in Canberra in January 1972 to publicise land claims. When the Whitlam Labor government came to power towards the end of 1972 it endorsed a policy of 'self-determination', upgraded the Office of Aboriginal Affairs that had been established in 1967 to full departmental status and established a National Aboriginal Consultative Council.

Second-wave international feminism was in the ascendancy from the 1970s (Oldfield 1992). From the turn of the century an International Alliance of Women, through standing committees, had campaigned first for the enfranchisement of women and then for equal civil and political rights, economic rights, educational rights and peace. The United Nations formed a significant point of reference for this campaign and new saliency was given to the women's movement through its International Women's Year in 1975 and its Decade for Women, 1976–1985. Just as the indigenous movement adopted its own colours, the women's movement advanced its cause under the banner of the traditional colours of purple and green. As with the indigenous rights movement, leadership of older advocacy groups was taken over by a new generation of more radical and strident feminists. In addition, resort was made to an earlier grass roots movement of electoral campaigning with the establishment of the Women's Electoral Lobby to quiz candidates on their views on women's rights. Standards set by International Government Organisations were important in national campaigns. These included the right to equal pay for equal work established in 1951 by the International Labour Organisation, the 1948 Universal Declaration of Human Rights adopted by the General Assembly of the United Nations as well as the Assembly's 1966 International Covenant on Economic, Social and Cultural Rights which was ratified by Australia in 1975. The feminists pushed for equal opportunity legislation, the establishment of dedicated government bureaucracy and enhancement of funding for a multiplicity of specific services for women including birth control, health, and child care (Kaplan 1996).

Multiculturalism that was copied from Canada began to replace assimilation as official government policy in the 1970s. Whereas in Canada multiculturalism supplemented Canada's deeper commitment to preservation of its two founding cultures and nations, English and French, in Australia the policy addressed the twin issues of cultural identity and social justice for non-English-speaking migrant groups. Initiated by Labor's Al Grassby during the Whitlam years, it was consolidated by the Fraser Liberal Coalition government. It recognised the rights of different ethnic cultures to retain their own distinctive culture and receive government assistance in order to overcome social disadvantage. The fostering of distinct ethnic groups and the inauguration of the Migrant Resource Centres spelt the demise of the Good Neighbour Council movement that was alleged to be paternalistic and anachronistic. Catching 'the ethnic vote' became an important consideration in electoral politics. Multiculturalism, like the other social movements of the 1970s, resulted in the establishment of dedicated government machinery. Implementation of the Galbally Report in the late 1970s funded a raft of specific services such as telephone interpreter services and ethnic broadcasting.

In the push and pull of politics, government initiatives and policies that benefit some groups inevitably provoke a backlash from others. Multiculturalism benefited ethnic Australians but was resented by large pockets of older Australians. As a social policy that supported diversity and encouraged migrants from non-English-speaking backgrounds to retain their own cultural heritage, multiculturalism was a great success. While improving the lot of such migrants, it also enriched the Australian mainstream by adding diversity and difference. Multiculturalism enhanced the Australian polity but did not change its predominant culture that had been formed over two centuries by predominantly British and Irish migrants and was buttressed by the English language. Multiculturalism was inappropriate as a de facto citizenship policy despite being touted as such by some of its protagonists and accepted by others who were concerned at the vacuum in modern Australian citizenship.

Environmental policy has been more divisive since the 1970s with a populist social movement challenging state development initiatives and giant resource development projects. During the 1950s and 1960s, Australia's mining industry expanded enormously with the discovery of world class deposits of bauxite, uranium, iron ore and coking coal. This was supplemented by state provision of cheap power to smelting and other industries from hydro-electric generation in Tasmania and coal-fired electricity in New South Wales, Victoria and Queensland that exploited vast open-cut reserves of steaming coal. Australia was well placed to benefit from the mineral and energy booms of the 1960s and 1970s, and remains a leading supplier of uranium, alumina, iron ore, coal and natural gas to world markets. The supportive developmental policies of state governments were questioned, and contentious projects such as drilling for oil on the Great Barrier Reef and a giant pulp mill for northern Tasmania blocked. The first major conservation campaign in Australia was staged against the Tasmanian Hydro-electricity Commission plans to flood Lake Pedder, which ultimately led in 1972 to the formation of the United Tasmanian Group, a political party dedicated to 'the green cause'. Lake Pedder was flooded, but a decade later the tables had turned. Tasmanian attempts to dam the wild Franklin river in the south-west of the state were stalled by organised protests in the early 1980s that precipitated Commonwealth intervention. As we saw in Chapter 6, this was one of the first instances of the Commonwealth using its foreign affairs power to gain jurisdiction over what would otherwise have been a matter for state determination.

The Commonwealth was able to trump Tasmania in preventing construction of the Gordon-below-Franklin dam because Australia had become party to the World Heritage Convention of 1974 and the Franklin river had been listed as a world heritage site. Environmentalists relied upon international benchmarks set by other conventions such as the 1973 Convention on International Trade in Endangered Species of Wild Fauna and Flora. The Australian government was active in promoting global initiative for environmental protection and preservation of endangered species. It championed an international ban on whaling and was one of the 39 member nations of the International Whaling Commission that agreed to end commercial whaling in 1982. The world conservation strategy launched by the International Union for the Conservation of Nature and Natural Resources in 1980 was followed in 1984 by a National Conservation Strategy between the Commonwealth and state governments. The 1982 International Year of the Tree was endorsed in Australia by a national 'greening' program.

As more active citizenship was accepted and encouraged, the formal public domain was enlarged and reformed to accommodate and respond to strident and sometimes discordant views. Official government discourse embraced some of the ideals of enhanced citizen participation and improved quality of public service. Ideally, it was recognised that government should be less directed by elites in 'top town' decision making and more sensitised to the grass roots views of the many. A complementary ideal was that public policy should be based on rational planning and informed by directed research that relied on the collection of available evidence and the canvassing of a diverse spectrum of opinion (Edwards 2001). Another ideal was that processes of government should be open and transparent and that members of parliament and public servants were accountable to ordinary citizens. This precipitated major changes to public administration within the multiple Australian jurisdictions and a range of experimentation in public policy. Ombudsmen and auditors were appointed to examine the probity of government and administrative appeals tribunals to review government decision making. In addition freedom of information legislation was passed to make government documents and papers available to members of the public. Even more significantly, the role of the judiciary as an avenue of reform and redress was elevated through the institution of law reform commissions, the funding of legal aid services and a new cadre of lawyers committed to citizen rights and class action.

Growth in government administration was complemented by a revival of support for community involvement in public issues at the local level. The public sector took the lead in encouraging and supporting the formation and politicisation of the interests of specific groups. Neighbourhood centres and community centres were funded to employ outreach workers who co-ordinated local populations to determine needs and gain resources for new services. It was an era of collective consciousness raising and activism. The women's movement watchword, 'the personal is the political', and the environmental movement's slogan, 'think global, act local', reflected a breakdown of traditional categories that constrained political action. Multiple specific-purpose funding grants were made available to encourage, by subsidy, personalised services such as meals on wheels for the disabled and elderly, and the home tutor scheme for migrants. Resident action groups in the metropolitan cities formed coalitions with trade unionists to protest 'slum redevelopment' in inner areas and the destruction of green spaces in cities during the early 1970s. By the start of 1975, there were roughly 50 green bans in place in Sydney, and about two-thirds that number in Melbourne (Burgmann & Burgmann 1995).

The significance of governance and citizenship was reflected in other ways. In the academy there was a renewed interest in public administration, public policy and policy studies as well as the study of identity politics and social movements. A lobbying industry developed to promote particular interests and causes, staffed in many instances by journalists who had for years been required to cultivate networks of association with politicians in order to obtain copy. The news industry itself, supported by general commercial prosperity, was able to capitalise on the groundswell of interest in debate on contested matters on the public agenda. Problems and challenges were increasingly seen as national ones requiring national solutions, or at least had national aspects that required joint responses from the national government in collaboration with the states and local governments. Australian news and public affairs received national coverage by a new genre of national newspapers, *The Australian, The Australian Financial Review* and *Nation Review*.

The national dimensions of Australian citizenship were expanded by the growth of national power and consciousness. The Commonwealth expanded the universal system of income security, introduced a universal health scheme, provided subsidies to disadvantaged schools and abolished university fees. There was a newfound pride in national identity that had been emerging since the late 1960s as Australia opened itself to the world. In 1966 a new decimal currency was introduced with Australian fauna on the coins and figures from Australian history on the banknotes. In 1968 an Australia Council was formed and in the early 1970s this was endowed with generous grants to the arts. There was a renaissance of Australian film, painting and writing that gave voice to Australian memories, dreams and reflections. No longer did Australian artists seek expression for their talents in exile; rather they became local folk heroes expressing contemporary mythology of the land, its cities and its peoples. Australian film directors gained box office success at foreign film festivals and Patrick White received the 1973 Nobel Prize for literature. In 1974 'Advance Australia Fair' replaced 'God Save our Queen' as the national anthem. The Australian title for the monarch was changed to 'Queen of Australia', and the federal government was to be known as the Australian Government rather than the Commonwealth Government. Grander new buildings were commissioned for the national capital: a new parliament house, a national gallery and a new High Court. The opening of the Sydney Opera House in 1973 epitomised the achievement of something exotic that would become an Australian icon. Australia became fashionable on the world stage with Australian culture being recognised in its own right. The paintings, dance and song of indigenous Australians together with images of the Australian landscape made Australia a preferred destination for tourists and especially young backpackers from around the world.

The celebration of the Bicentenary of the British settlement in New South Wales in 1988 and the sesquicentennials in other states provided the occasion for celebration of Australia's British cultural heritage and its colonial history (King 1989). Apart from official ceremonies, the occasions generated widespread populist interest in Australian social history. A focus on the costume, eating habits and demeanour of ordinary men and women of the past recovered some of the detailed experience of earlier Australian lives. There was a renewed interest in folk music and the initiation of 'bush dances'. Official histories were commissioned by the national and state governments, as well as by municipalities and townships. Some explicitly recognised the more lamentable episodes in colonisation, most notably the dispossession of indigenous Australians alongside the heroism of European pioneering. Australians became interested in researching their family histories, most for the first time, some tracing their genealogies back to early settlers and convicts. This very celebration of the Anglo-Celtic origins of Australian citizenship was nonetheless alienating for some. Looking at the past highlighted the fact that it was not necessarily a shared past. Descendants of migrants from non-English-speaking backgrounds were moved to write their own histories of involvement as minority groups in Australian colonisation, while indigenous Australians continued their struggle for recognition of distinctive rights.

Transforming the Role of Government

In the 1970s and early 1980s it seemed that Australian government was being rejuvenated in its traditional role of economic development and infrastructure provision while taking on new social, urban and quality of life functions at the Commonwealth and state spheres. Then the role of government was seriously questioned by a resurgent neo-liberal ethos that championed economic rather than government solutions and endorsed private enterprise strategies for running the democratic state. 'Managerialism', as it was dubbed in Australia, had captured the imagination of senior government officials and politicians and was implemented in various waves of reformist initiatives with bipartisan support and at both state and Commonwealth levels.

This was seen as an alternative way of achieving effective and efficient governance once the Keynesian prescriptions of interventionist government had been discredited. As a consequence of the retreat of government and the increased exposure of the Australian economy to global market forces, the economic conditions of homogeneity were starting to unravel. At the core were unemployment, continued high levels of immigration, and a systemic decline in rural areas as economic restructuring was pursued by Australian governments, anxious to commit to a new orthodoxy of political economy that were being re-established globally. The classic liberal principles of international free trade and domestic laissez-faire government that were dominant in the nineteenth century resurfaced as the new orthodoxy among political leaders and their advisers. Economists invented 'public choice' theory as a conceptual vehicle for applying economic methods and market principles to government decision making and the public sector. Whereas market failure had provided the stimulus for justifying Keynesian intervention by the state in the economy, now government failure and inefficiency became foundational assumptions for the public choice economists.

Applied to Australia, the new economic ideology radically questioned Australia's traditional government interventions to shape economic outcomes by protecting industries, fixing wages, providing infrastructure and subsidising particular companies and projects that brought investment capital and jobs. The legitimacy of these venerable Australian practices was undermined by the new ideology that government was more prone to failure than markets and prosperity better achieved through market supply and demand. Spreading from Thatcher's Britain and Reagan's US, the ideology of neo-liberalism had gained ascendancy by the 1990s. The state of Victoria under the Kennett Liberal Coalition went further than any other regime in Australia, jettisoning 'state socialism' for 'the Contract State' (Alford & O'Neill 1994). Osborne and Gaebler's American bestseller, *Reinventing Government* (Osborne & Gaebler 1992), became the favourite reference of Victorian leaders and officials who parroted its slick private sector prescriptions for streamlining government. The Commonwealth Government had changed its role from mediating global forces and blocking their more detrimental effects on the domestic economy to facilitating their impact through dismantling barriers to trade and levelling the playing field of business. According to national competition policy, state provision of utilities and services could no longer be privileged over private provision.

Governments have looked to partnerships with the business sector, and to not-for-profit associations of civil society to deliver services under contract. Management practices of private enterprise have been incorporated into the public service so that government is run along business lines with an emphasis on efficiency. Government is now run like a business with heads of government departments no longer being permanent secretaries but contract chief executive officers. Public services are no longer run by a cadre who rose through the ranks knowledgeable of the substantive aspects of the services they managed, familiar with those who staffed them and able to offer the advice of grounded expertise. The traditional notion of a servant of the public has been ousted by public sector management reforms that have fostered a new elite of senior executives recruited as generalist managers to manage any administrative unit. Salaries of the senior executive service have been greatly increased, far in excess of their political masters and commensurate with those offered by the private sector, with bonuses paid for management achievements on individualised contracts. Rewards are allocated for restructuring administration to accomplish budget management, reducing staff numbers, and privatising services as well as selling off public utilities.

In this process of public sector restructuring, citizenship has been devalued with people becoming clients or customers of government agencies. The government bureaucracy of the 1970s had proliferated into a complex web of service units, with considerable policy development capacity and a broad spread that allowed permeability and accessibility to members of the public. Twenty years later, the public sector has much less a public service focus or capacity. The restructuring has resulted in pared down bureaucracies managed according to bottom-line figures rather than public responsiveness, despite a rhetoric of 'customer service'. The emphasis has been on reining in expenditure, resuming centralised control by Cabinet, and privatising and corporatising delivery of services. Governments should be in the business of 'steering' not 'rowing' according to the popular metaphor of Osborne and Gaebler (King 1989). Public consultation has been replaced by telemarketing and opinion poll surveys, refined by focus group surveys. In this way government responses and policy agendas are devised, administered and monitored.

The political forums of government have also suffered an erosion of robust involvement on the part of constituent citizens. In federal and state parliaments, executive power has been growing at the expense of the legislature. Good government is seen as getting results, achieving efficiencies and generally achieving micro-economic reform. Those with reform agendas have often shown a lack of interest in the views of the public, preferring to mount their campaign through targeted advertising and direct lobbying of strategic ministers and officials. This distancing has also been accelerated by the ascendancy of the professional politician, who has little or no experience outside the corridors of power on the streets with ordinary citizens. The technologies of media releases, advertising, telemarketing and the Internet have reinforced a convention of impersonal mass communication. Electoral office staff buffer face-to-face inquiries from local constituents. Even local governments, hitherto the governments 'closest to the people', have been restructured in the interests of efficiency. Victoria led the way with the wholesale restructuring of its local government sector to create larger economic units with more streamlined management structures (Galligan 1995, pp. 43–55). Highly paid administrators manage larger territories with fewer staff who tender and regulate service contracts. In the neo-liberal world view there is little room for public debate in political forums. The task of governments is to achieve low-cost law and order for individual citizens to go about their personal business of getting on and getting ahead.

The political economy of immigration restriction, government intervention and protection was designed to achieve homogeneity and a certain equality among people. But it also encouraged parochialism, government paternalism and economic inefficiency. In jettisoning its restrictive immigration policy, scrapping the protective state and opening up its economy to world market forces as it did in the nineteenth century, Australia in the early twenty-first century has to cope with greater heterogeneity, diversity, inequality and potential conflict. Social globalisation brings together peoples of different race, ethnicity and culture. Economic globalisation without compensatory government policies has increased disparities in life chances and generated economic inequality. Deregulation of banking combined with the introduction of regressive broad based taxes, together with increasingly deregulated labour markets, have enhanced the profitability of investments that reward entrepreneurs and investors. Some have become very wealthy, those with marketable skills are doing better than ever, but a rump of blue-collar, rural and casualised workers have become relatively impoverished.

The implementation of global neo-liberalism in Australia since the 1980s was followed by high levels of economic growth in the 1990s but the benefits have been differentially distributed. Unprecedentedly high earnings for corporate executives have also been accompanied by sustained unemployment, an increasingly casualised workforce, a return to the working poor and the rise of the black economy. Housing prices have risen, but with it, homelessness. Metropolitan growth has been at the expense of regional hinterlands and regional centres at the expense of outlying country districts. There has been a hollowing out among Australia's hitherto homogenised middle ranks (Gregory 1995). The winners have been taking the largest share, while the losers are left with next to nothing. Desperation has spawned beggars, drug pushers, prostitutes and gamblers. There has been a return of pawnshops including a globalised syndicate of Cash Converters.

Whereas the polity has institutionalised acceptance of cultural diversity, it has failed to address economic advantage and deprivation. Australians have great difficulty in acknowledging the existence of class. At the turn of the century the nation was founded by progressives who, having lived through the worst excesses of nineteenth-century free-market capitalism, wanted to modify it and tame it. Part of the mythology of national identity has been pride in a tradition of a fair go. A return to survival of the fittest is not something that can be readily acknowledged in public discourse. The true picture of the fracturing of the nation into increasingly divergent socio-economic populations is blurred by national averages that take no account of the distribution of benefits within the population. When homogeneity is declining and heterogeneity increasing, the validity of per capita measurements is spurious and their use misleading.

Part of the explanation for the apparent complacency by governments at increasing inequality lies in the nature of that very inequality. High levels of socio-economic differentiation result in intensification of interaction within strata. Members of an elite fraternise within their own circles and reaffirm the received wisdom that globalised competition delivers prosperity, heedless of the circumstances of others. The shared assumption is that upward mobility is possible on merit, but that is only true for those who have the opportunities. Poverty and lack of opportunity are stark realities in modern Australia reflected in major national studies. This was evident in a 1998 national study published in *Australian Poverty: Then and now* (Nieuwenhuysen & Fincher 1998). It showed that there had been a substantial increase in the percentage of those living in poverty since the release of the Henderson study twenty years earlier. Whereas in 1975, 12.5 per cent of the population lived below the poverty line and 8.1 per cent lived just above the poverty line, by 1996 there were 17 per cent living just below the poverty line and 14 per cent just above. A year later, in July 1999, a United Nations Human Development Report showed that, although ranked among the top ten nations of the world on the basis of economic growth, Australia had inequality that was among the highest in the industrial world. Its richest 20 per cent earned roughly ten times more than its poorest 20 per cent. The national government response has not been to redress such inequality, but to tighten the welfare system on the assumption that welfare, rather than poverty itself, is pauperising. It is also continuing to press for further reforms to deregulate labour markets and promote freedom of individual contract that would likely depress the living wage.

Charity and philanthropy have been revived as alternative sources of welfare to take the place of governments' retreat from the field, but these are inadequate. Domestic charities report a large increase in those applying for assistance, especially on the part of the working poor. At the same time, there are diminishing amounts being donated to assist philanthropic effort. Similarly, the 1999 United Nations Report documented that Australian foreign aid levels, despite increasing levels of growth, were about half those of most other industrialised countries. In the same way that in the earlier decades of the twentieth century there was greater philanthropic concern for animal welfare than child welfare, there currently appears to be more interest in containing damage to the physical environment than in addressing domestic and global poverty. Economic globalisation and domestic deregulation have made a few Australians much richer. But others have been marginalised and made worse off without adequate government programs to protect and compensate them.

Ongoing Challenges

As Australia celebrates its centenary of federation and the beginning of a new century, it has three major items of unfinished business affecting citizenship that are legacies of nineteenth-century colonisation and twentieth-century immigration. These are multiculturalism, reconciliation with indigenous Australians and republicanising the head of state, all of which are contentious and affect the way Australia defines itself as a nation. Probably more significant, however, are the impact of global economic forces and the reduced role of the national government in mediating their influence on Australian economic and social life referred to in the previous section. This is partly due to structural changes caused by new technologies of information processing and communication that have transformed world capitalism, and partly due to government policy. While there is scope for change in the way government responds to globalisation, there is little likelihood of a return to the old political economy of protection. Australia and its people are now joined up to global affairs in ways that preclude such comprehensive government intervention. Nevertheless, the mediating role of government in managing change, ensuring some level of social justice and support for those who are less able to cope, and representing the political will of Australians in collective decision making will remain vital. Openness to a rapidly changing world entails a good deal of uncertainty. This together with lack of resolution on each of the above national issues means a public unsureness about nationhood and citizenship.

For each of these large issues that Australia currently faces, there are proponents with solutions. The National Multicultural Advisory Council in its 1999 report on *Australian Multiculturalism for a New Century* (the Roach Report) endorsed the concept of Australian multiculturalism and argued that harmony could be achieved by acknowledging a unity of diversity. This was taken up and embellished by the Australian Citizenship Council in its 2000 report, *Australian Citizenship for a New Century*, that recommended acceptance of difference as the basis of social cohesion. In contrast to this, the republican movement claimed that Australia had developed its own unique identity to the point that warranted an Australian head of state in place of the British monarchy. The reconciliation movement is premised on recognition of the special status of indigenous Australians and acknowledgment of their past dispossession by settlers and governments. Governments and their advisers have been more concerned with deregulation and with economic efficiency and growth than any of these issues. By considering them in turn we can see that all are contested and there is no overarching resolution.

Multiculturalism was adopted as official policy during the 1970s (Australian Ethnic Affairs Council, 1977, 1978, 1979). It was promoted by prominent members of disparate ethnic groups as a means of asserting cultural self-directedness and plurality. Aspects of the policy were criticised in the 1980s and the 1988 Fitzgerald Report recommended that the term be discontinued (Committee to Advise on Australian Immigration Policies 1988). There was renewed emphasis on multiculturalism in the 1990s following the launching of the National Agenda for a Multicultural Australia in 1989, but also greater contention. Some of its leading earlier proponents, such as Sir James Gobbo, suggested that the awkward term might best be abandoned because the policy was now sufficiently accepted. Prime Minister Howard was always uneasy with its implications, reluctantly coupling the term with an emphasis on Australia and national unity. Some like Jim Jupp cautioned against the promotion of national identity: 'to promote a clear identity in cultural terms would be to risk suppressing recognition of those ambiguities and diversities that have been among the greatest achievements of multiculturalism' (Jupp 1997, p. 144). In the United States Nathan Glazer confirms, albeit reluctantly, *We Are All Multiculturalists Now*, but, as he explains, the term has been captured by those promoting distinct identities and lifestyles based upon race as well as sexual practice.

In Australia, there has been a tendency to overstate and distort multi-culturalism as redefining Australian national identity and citizenship. Australian multiculturalism is best understood as it was designed: a cultural and social policy that recognises and tolerates ethnic differences and assists the social integration of migrants. Australia's national identity and civic character have been changed in the process to make it a more diverse and tolerant country. Nevertheless, compared with Canada and other genuinely multi-ethnic countries, Australia remains relatively homogeneous with ethnic groups being progressively integrated into the mainstream culture. Multi-culturalism has never played a role in migrant selection: it is a policy to facilitate the proper absorption of migrants chosen on other non-racial grounds. This point was emphasised in the important Fitzgerald Report of 1988:

> Immigration to Australia is about becoming Australian. It is not driven by multiculturalism ... Had we not allowed immigration to slip towards the margin of our concerns in the first place, had we accorded proper esteem to the cultures and languages of immi-grants and ensured that they had proper access to our systems and institutions, we might not have needed to erect structures for multicultural support ... Multiculturalism provides important support for immigrants, but as a concept it is not something which many can identify with ... (Committee to Advise on Australian Immigration Policies 1988, pp. 4–11).

The extension of multiculturalism beyond a social and cultural policy to citizenship and national identity was due to confusion and surprising ignorance about Australian civic culture and political institutions. It had the effect of devaluing Australia's traditional Anglo-Irish heritage and disquieting the large majority of Australians who knew that their identity and cohesion were not due to diversity and difference. What made good sense as a cultural policy made no sense as a civic one (Galligan 1998).

Indigenous Australians, frustrated by limited achievements in addressing historical dispossession, continue to gain inspiration from global indigenous and post-colonial movements. In 1979 an Aboriginal Information Centre was founded in London with branches in Europe to further enhance the international profile and global advocacy of Aboriginal people. The National Aboriginal Conference became a member of the World Council of Indigenous People and was host to the 1981 meeting of the Council. In the same year a delegation from the World Council of Churches investigated and made recommendations on the conditions of indigenous Australians. Of paramount importance was recognition of Aboriginal sovereignty of land. In New Zealand, the 1840 Treaty of Waitangi, whose dishonour had precipitated the Maori Wars, was given formal acknowledgment in 1985. In Australia, when the national government was presented with the Barunga Statement calling for recognition of land rights, Prime Minister Hawke's response was to suggest formation of a Treaty. In 1991, the final report of the Royal Commission into Aboriginal Deaths in Custody contained recommendations that drew inspiration from the reconciliation process in South Africa following the ending of apartheid. Subsequently a Council of Aboriginal Reconciliation was established working on a ten-year time frame to conclude its deliberations with the celebrations for the centenary of federation. Despite a global move during the 1990s towards a politics of restitution (Barkan 2000), the Howard government refused to issue a formal apology or accept the outcomes of the Reconciliation Council.

The doctrinaire pursuit of neo-liberal policies by the Commonwealth and state governments has generated its own political correctness. Formation of the One Nation party in 1996, and its subsequent success in Queensland and other states, represented a populist protest against economic restructuring and perceived preferences for ethnic groups and indigenous Australians (Abbott 1998). While crudely racist and simplistic in its policy pronouncements, One Nation has become a vehicle for angry and disadvantaged people to voice their protest. Groups marginalised by economic globalisation, especially those in the regional hinterlands and whose skills have been made obsolete by economic changes, have become politically volatile. The Kennett government in Victoria that ran an aggressive agenda of neo-liberal reform through most of the 1990s was defeated by disillusioned rural voters. Government actions as well as globalisation have been eroding the homogeneity and political inclusiveness nurtured in the formation of the Australian nation and celebrated at the jubilee of federation. The renaissance of national pride in the 1960s and 1970s has soured as economic globalisation produces greater differentiation and structural inequality that make political community more problematic.

During the 1990s critics like Hugh Stretton launched a counter attack on the neo-liberal economic agenda and its attack on the public sector (Stretton 1994). In 1997 the Canadian political critic, John Ralston Saul, and the British political reformer, Will Hutton, toured Australia promoting their respective analyses. In *The Unconscious Civilisation* (1997), Saul argued that democratic process had been deformed by a political culture of corporatism in which governments made deals with organised big business at the expense of listening to the concerns of ordinary men and women. Will Hutton argued that governments needed to pursue 'stakeholder capitalism' by fostering intermediate institutions that operated on principles of fairness in ensuring capitalism was responsive to their needs (Hutton 1996, 1998). Fred Argy, a former senior public servant who helped design and implement Australia's financial deregulation in the 1980s, published *Australia at the Cross-roads* (Argy 1998). He advocated pursuing progressive liberalism rather than the 'hard liberalism' that had gained ascendancy. By the end of the 1990s, the tide of deregulation and privatisation had peaked due to voter backlash. The pendulum is likely to swing back towards a more positive view of government both in Australia and abroad.

The republican movement of the 1990s foundered when the 1999 referendum proposal for republicanising the head of state was resound-ingly defeated. Some republican leaders attributed this to voter ignorance (Turnbull 1999) but the Australian people knew better. Those favouring a republican head of state now clearly outnumber those in favour of retaining the constitutional monarchy. Incidentally, the number of sentimental loyalists is even smaller with many constitutional monarchists favouring the system rather than being personally attached to the royal family. The referendum failed for political reasons: republicans were split with some supporting the minimalist model that was put to the vote and others opposing it who favoured an elected head of state (Galligan 1999). Leaders of both the republican and monarchist cases overstated the significance of the change that was proposed, leaving people unmoved by exaggerated claims. As has been argued elsewhere (Galligan 1995) and shown throughout the earlier chapters, Australia has been substantially a federal republic from the begin-ning of nationhood with Australians choosing to retain vestiges of British formality for their purposes. While symbolically significant, republicanising the head of state is technically difficult and of limited practical importance. While it seems inevitable and timely, bringing it about will require consensus and political skill in negotiating the change.

While there has been sustained rhetoric around unity and harmony in official discourse, there is a lack of insight and vibrancy. Grand public celebrations for the Bicentenary and the Sydney Olympics heralded a new public confidence in contemporary Australia and its heritage, but this belies a muddle and apathy about Australian citizenship. Priority has been given to education in civics in schools as a means of redressing ignorance among the young (Civics Expert Group 1994). The Centenary of Federation Advisory Committee (1994) recommended that the celebration of Australian nation-hood was to be built on recognition of 'many cultures, one nation'. Bipartisan support was given for the establishment of an Australian Citizenship Council in 1998 and a consultation process inaugurated as to the future directions of Australian citizenship. Unfortunately, release of the Australian Citizenship Council's discussion document, *Contemporary Australian Citizenship* (1999), in the jubilee year of Australian citizenship added little that was positive to the debate. The focus, corroborated by the release of its final report, emphasised the virtue of celebrating a common civic culture but could only point to some abstract values and shared differences (Australian Citizenship Council 2000). The Australian people need better public articulation of their citizenship and civic life.

There is also need for a new conceptualisation of the role of government in fostering civil society and mediating capitalist forces. The 'Third Way' has been offered by contemporary social democrats as the solution. Anthony Giddens has extolled the virtue of the third way that has become the byword and lodestar of the current British Government (Giddens 1998). In Australia, Mark Latham (Latham 1998) and Lindsay Tanner (Tanner 1999) have emphasised Amatya Sen's notion of 'social capability' (Sen 1992) in civilising global capital. American scholars, Robert Putnam (Putnam 1993) and Francis Fukuyama (Fukuyama 1995) have argued the importance of 'social capital' for the proper workings of the civic society and the market. But civil society is hardly a panacea. Social connections are certainly the very fabric of community, but such connections mirror the associations of the broader political economy and are not formed independently (Roberts 1999). To the extent that the political economy embraces neo-liberalism, the socio-economic inequality wrought by the ascendancy of the market will also skew the distribution of social capital. An understanding of the dynamic of the social advantage accruing to the possession of material and cultural property is important in understanding the current fissures in political community, not its resolution. The health of civil society depends on a more equitable distribution of material, intellectual and cultural property than the free market can provide. It requires state intervention and political will – in short the dominance of politics over markets, or at least a national policy of domestic compensation and assistance to those adversely affected by market outcomes. State intervention to redistribute resources assists the maintenance of sufficient homogeneity in civil society to support genuine republicanism and inclusive citizenship.

Back to Globalisation

Federation in 1901 created the Australian nation-state while preserving both imperial and colonial regional and municipal spheres of governance. The imperial and colonial polities were both important in shaping Australian colonial citizenship and mediating the impact of global market forces. The legacy of this era was a commitment to preserving homogeneity of ethnicity and moderating structural inequality. Construction of the nation-state produced a larger Australian polity better able to secure its place in the world and build a unique way of life within its continental boundaries. In its protective state policies and government regulation of the domestic economy, Australia anticipated the world trend towards trade protectionism that took root from the 1930s and the Keynesian revolution in managing capitalism that was embraced from the 1940s. Australia secured its survival in the world through close alliance with leading global powers, Great Britain until the 1940s and subsequently the United States. It paid an enormous price in two world wars, narrowly escaping Japanese invasion in the early 1940s, and lesser premiums through involvement in Asian wars in Korea, Malaya and Vietnam during the 1950s and 1960s.

Australia's overseas military involvement preserved insularity at home. Restrictive, and mainly British immigration, combined with protective state policies to produce a relatively closed society that bred parochialism and complacency. This was challenged after the Second World War by a multicultural immigration policy, diversifying trade to Asia, especially Japan, and by the increasing American influence. As a global superpower, the United States influenced a return to freer global markets and the establishment of the United Nations. American social and civil rights movements inspired the growth of non-government organisations that circled the globe. The Cold War constrained the growth of global civil society and governance organisation, but accelerated American influence on countries like Australia. The end of the Cold War has left Australia more independent in a more pluralist world. Australia's adoption of neo-liberal economic policies and multiculturalism undermined the old monocultural nationalism that had been dominant through the middle decades of the twentieth century.

At the beginning of the twenty-first century, Australia and its citizens are more open to the influences of globalisation than ever before, at a time when globalisation has never been more intense and intrusive. As globalisation theory reviewed in Chapter 1 predicts, this entails a reduced role for the national government and a concomitant lessening of the significance of national citizenship. The nation-state remains of primary significance but lacks sovereignty. At least for middle-sized federal countries like Australia, the national government has to negotiate with, rather than rule over, the supranational and sub-national spheres of government. As we have shown, however, this is not new since Australia was formed as a federal nation within the British Empire. Its national government has never been sovereign and independent in its rule either in international or domestic politics. Moreover, Australian citizenship has always been multi-layered with membership in global, regional and local political associations as well as the nation-state.

The Australian polity is constituted by multiple political communities so that Australian citizens have multiple memberships. A nation built upon such a matrix of governance and citizenship is well suited to the modern era of globalisation.

Globalisation brings opportunities and challenges to Australian citizens by way of self-improvement and self-advancement through exposure to diversity and opportunity. Cosmopolitanism and economic gain benefit those who can take advantage. This is usually the more privileged but special interest groups can benefit from international standards and the leveraging of international associations. The downside, however, is likely to be structural inequality. Given the reduced scope for national government mediation, especially with respect to modern information technologies and global market forces, globalisation can have a more disruptive impact on domestic economies and societies. As we have pointed out above, there are worrying aspects of this in Australia today, although it has been exacerbated by government policy that is overly doctrinaire and rigid in its pursuit of a domestic neo-liberal agenda.

Australian citizenship and government with its layering of multiple affiliations and spheres of national and sub-national polities is appropriate for a modern global nation. Such a system allows flexibility and multiple adjustments to be negotiated in ways that can deal with complexity while accommodating diversity. The modern global nation adds another sphere of governance and citizenship just as the British Empire and being British subjects did for early Australians. Australians have a long history of robust government through multiple polities. That political heritage of complexity that Australians have enjoyed, domestically through federalism and internationally through membership in global governance associations, is now being emulated by Britain and the other nations of Europe. Australia's return to globalisation at the beginning of a new century has all sorts of challenges and opportunities that the nation and its citizens should be well prepared to meet because of their rich political heritage and established institutions.

Notes

Introduction The Challenge of Globalisation

1 The term 'glocalisation' was coined by Tom Courchene, 'Glocalisation, institutional evolution and the Australian federation' in Galligan (1993).

2 See Australian Citizenship Council 2000, p. 12, where 'public acceptance of diversity' is proffered as a basis for social harmony.

3 Recent books include R. Catley, *Globalising Australian Capitalism*, Cambridge University Press, 1996 and L. Weiss, *The Myth of the Powerless State: Governing the economy in a global era*, Polity Press, 1998. Political issues are more prominent in A. Capling, M. Considine & M. Crozier, *Australian Politics in a Global Era*, Addison Wesley Longman, 1998 and J. Wiseman, *Global Nation? Australia and the politics of globalisation*, Cambridge University Press, 1998. Quentin Beresford uses globalisation to frame the study of Australian public policy in *Government, Markets and Globalisation*, Allen & Unwin, 2000.

4 An exception who adopts an historical approach is Ann Capling (2001).

1 Globalisation, Sovereignty and Citizenship

1 R. Higgott & S. Reich, 'Globalisation and sites of conflict: Towards definition and taxonomy', Centre for the Study of Globalisation and Regionalisation, Working Paper No. 01/98, University of Warwick, February 1998, p. 2, cited in S. Reich, Review of *The Myth of the Powerless State* by L. Weiss, Polity Press, 1998, in *New Political Economy* 4 (2) July 1999, p. 305.

2 Examples are M. Latham, *Civilising Global Capital: New thinking for Australian Labor*, Allen & Unwin, St Leonards, 1998; P. Alston and M. Chaim (eds) *Treaty-making and Australia: Globalisation versus sovereignty?*, Federation Press, Sydney, 1995; A. Davidson & K. Weekley (eds) *Globalisation and Citizenship in the Asia-Pacific*, Macmillan, London, 1999.

3 Western Australia was omitted because of its late decision to join federation.
4 This simple but eloquent pledge was adopted by amendment to the *Australian Citizenship Act* (Cth) 1948 in 1994. A person may choose to make the pledge as an oath under God, or as an affirmation without reference to God.

2 Citizenship without Nationhood

1 For a full account of this in one municipality in Victoria, see W. Roberts, *Getting On and Getting By: Social supports in the Australian urban community of Hotham, 1860–1890*, PhD thesis, University of Melbourne, 1999.
2 *Getting On and Getting By*, 'slum dwellings' condemned under the Public Health Act were retained for the benefit of local landlords, while reforms intended by the Shops and Factories Act of 1885 were disregarded in the interests of local proprietors.

3 Nation-state and Citizenship

1 Quoted in *Chronicle of Australia*, Penguin Books, 1993, p. 393.
2 Quoted in *Australia Through Time: 127 years of Australian history*, Mynah Press, Random House, 1993, p. 24.
3 For example, Manning Clark, *A History of Australia*. Vol. 5, Melbourne University Press, 1981, in a chapter entitled 'Federation or revolution?', p. 139, wrote: 'Federation was one of those constitutional devices recommended by apologists for bourgeois democracy for containing political equality, and stigmatising all radical change as something outside the constitutional powers of both parties to the federal compact'.

4 Imperial Dominion to Pacific Nation

1 Joseph Chamberlain's speech at the first meeting of the Colonial Conference of 1897, in A. B. Keith, *Selected Speeches and Documents on British Colonial Policy 1763–1917*, vol. II, Oxford University Press, 1918, p. 219.
2 'Clark's draft, 1891: Powers of federal parliament', appendix to J. Reynolds, 'A. I. Clark's American sympathies and his influence on the Australian federation', *Australian Law Journal* 32, 1958, pp. 67–74.
3 See opinion of Attorney-General Isaac Isaacs (5 May, 1906) in P. Brazil (ed.) *Opinions of Attorneys-General of the Commonwealth of Australia*, Australian Government Publishing Service, 1981, no. 244, p. 292.
4 *The Australian Law Journal* 10 (Supplement) October 15, 1936. Evatt and Menzies were responding to a paper on the Statute which had been written by Justice Owen Dixon of the High Court. See *ALJ* pp. 96–106 for Dixon's paper; pp. 107 ff. for the comments of Evatt and Menzies.
5 *R v Bevan; ex parte Elias and Gordon* (1942) 66 CLR 452.

5 Australian Citizen Subjects

1 *Commonwealth Parliamentary Debates*, Senate, vol. 14, 9 July 1903, p. 1933.

2 *Commonwealth Parliamentary Debates*, Senate, vol. 14, 9 July 1903, pp. 1937–8, 1941, 1943.
3 *Commonwealth Parliamentary Debates*, Senate, vol. 14, 9 July 1903, pp. 1937–8, 1941, 1943.
4 A. Gill. *Orphans of the Empire: The shocking story of child migration to Australia*, Millennium Books, 1997, p. 99, notes that between 1921 and 1967 (when the scheme ended) Barnardo sponsored roughly 3,000 child migrants to Australia.
5 Between 1925 and 1982 more than 10,000 'little brothers' arrived in Australia.
6 In 1913 Prime Minister Joseph Cook announced a comprehensive national insurance scheme that included sickness, accident, maternity, widowhood and unemployment benefits; in 1923 a Royal Commission on National Insurance was established which, in 1927, endorsed a national insurance scheme and recommended a system of compulsory contributions from employers and employees but legislation introduced by the Bruce-Page government in 1928 was opposed and the National Insurance Bill was abandoned. Although the Commonwealth Health Insurance legislation was passed in 1938, opposition and the outbreak of the Second World War prevented its implementation.
7 *Commonwealth Parliamentary Debates*, Representatives, vol. 198, 30 September 1948, p. 1060.
8 *Commonwealth Parliamentary Debates*, Representatives, vol. 198, 30 September 1948, p. 1062.
9 *Commonwealth Parliamentary Debates*, Representatives, vol. 198, 23 November 1948, pp. 3300–1.

6 New World Orders

1 Correspondence with Federal Treasury official (29 May 2000) indicates that negotiations broke down at the OECD level in October 1998, following France's withdrawal from the process.
2 The Uruguay Round of GATT (1986–1994) eventually foundered, but spawned the new global free trade promoting body, the WTO in 1995.
3 A notable exception was the Hawke government's acceptance of Chinese political refugees following the Tiananmen Square massacre in 1989.
4 See *Advisory Opinion on Namibia* (1971) ICJ Rep 16, p. 5.
5 Dates in parentheses are year of adoption of the treaty by the UN.
6 *R v Burgess; ex parte Henry* (1936) 55 CLR 608.
7 *Airlines of NSW v NSW* (No. 2) (1964–65) 113 CLR 54.
8 *NSW v Commonwealth* (1975) 135 CLR 337.
9 *Victoria v Commonwealth* (1971) 122 CLR 353.
10 *Koowarta v Bjelke-Petersen* (1982) 153 CLR 168.
11 *Commonwealth v Tasmania* (1983) 158 CLR 1.
12 For example, *Richardson v Forestry Commission* (1988), 164 CLR 261; *Queensland v Commonwealth* (1989), 167 CLR 232.
13 For example, *Polyukhovich v Commonwealth* (1991), 175 CLR 501; *Horta v Commonwealth* (1994), 123 ALR 1.

14 *Human Rights (Sexual Conduct) Act* (Cth) 1994. *Nicholas Toonen and Australia* (1994): United Nations Human Rights Committee, Communication No. 688/1992, Doc. CCPR/C/50/D/488/1992.

15 *Mabo v Queensland* (No. 2) (1992), 175 CLR 42. M. Kirby, 'The role of international standards in Australian courts', pp. 83–84, in P. Alston and M. Chiam (eds) *Treaty-Making and Australia: Globalisation versus sovereignty?*, Federation Press, 1995; H. Patapan, 'Rewriting Australian liberalism: The High Court's jurisprudence of rights', *Australian Journal of Political Science* 31 (2), pp. 225–42.

16 *Minister of State for Immigration and Ethnic Affairs v Teoh* (1995), 183 CLR 273.

17 Joint Statement by the Minister for Foreign Affairs, Senator Gareth Evans and the Attorney-General, Michael Lavarch, 10 May 1995.

18 United Nations Press Release, 28 July, 2000.

7 Citizenship in a Global Nation

1 The debate between Professors Robert Manne, Raymond Gaita, Colin Tatz and others has proceeded in the *Sydney Morning Herald, The Age* and *Quadrant* from 1997 onwards.

2 *SA Prohibition of Discrimination Act*, 1966; *SA Aboriginal Lands Trust Act*, 1966.

Bibliography

Abbott, T. (ed.) (1998). *Two Nations: The causes and effects of the One Nation party in Australia*. Melbourne: Bookman Press.

ACC *see* Australian Citizenship Council.

Adam, F. (1886). *Australian Essays*. Melbourne: W. Inglis.

Agar, M. (1996). *The Professional Stranger: An informal introduction to ethnography*. San Diego: Academic Press. First published in 1980.

Aitken, H. G. J. (ed.) (1959). *The State and Economic Growth: Papers of a conference held on October 11–13, 1956, under the auspices of the Committee on Economic Growth*. New York: Social Science Research Council.

Alafaci, M. (1999). *Savage Cows and Cabbage Leaves: An Italian life*. Sydney: Hale & Iremonger.

Alford, J. & O'Neill, D. (eds) (1994). *The Contract State: Public management and the Kennett government*. Geelong: Centre for Applied Social Research, Deakin University.

Alston, P. (ed.) (1992). *The United Nations and Human Rights: A critical appraisal*. Oxford: Clarendon Press.

Alston, P. (ed.) (1994). *Towards an Australian Bill of Rights*. Canberra and Sydney: Centre for International and Public Law, Australian National University, and Human Rights and Equal Opportunity Commission.

Alston, P. (1997). 'The myopia of the handmaidens: International lawyers and globalization'. *European Journal of International Law* 3, pp. 435–48.

Alston, P. & Chaim, M. (eds) (1995). *Treaty-making and Australia: Globalisation versus sovereignty?* Leichhardt, NSW: Federation Press in association with the Centre for International and Public Law, Australian National University.

Anderson, B. (1983). *Imagined Communities: Reflections on the origins and spread of nationalism*. London: Verso.

Archibugi, D. & Held, D. (eds) (1995). *Cosmopolitan Democracy: An agenda for a new world order*. Cambridge, Mass: Polity Press.

Archibugi, D., Held, D. & Kohler, M. (eds) (1998). *Re-imagining Political Community: Studies in cosmopolitan democracy.* Stanford: Stanford University Press.

Argy, F. (1998). *Australia at the Cross-roads: Radical free market or a progressive liberalism.* Sydney: Allen & Unwin.

Atkinson, A. (1997). *The Europeans in Australia. A history.* Vol. 1. *The Beginning.* Melbourne: Oxford University Press.

The Australasian Sketcher (1873–89), published monthly. Melbourne.

Australian Citizenship Council (1999). *Contemporary Australian Citizenship.* Discussion document (Chair: Sir Ninian Stephen). Canberra: Ausinfo.

Australian Citizenship Council (2000). *Australian Citizenship for a New Century.* Canberra: Ausinfo.

Australian Ethnic Affairs Council (1977). *Australia as a Multicultural Society* (Chairman: J. Zubrzycki). Canberra: Australian Government Publishing Service.

Australian Ethnic Affairs Council (1978). *Review of Post-Arrival Programs and Services to Migrants* (Chairman: F. Galbally). Canberra: Australian Government Publishing Service.

Australian Ethnic Affairs Council (1979). *Multiculturalism and its Implications for Immigration Policy* (Chairman: J. Zubrzycki). Joint Report with the Australian Population Council (Chairman: W. D. Borrie). Canberra: Australian Government Publishing Service.

Bagehot, W. (1963). *The English Constitution.* London: Fontana. First published in 1867.

Bailey, P. (1990). *Human Rights: Australia in an international context.* North Ryde: Butterworths.

Baker, P. J. N. (1929). *The Present Juridical Status of the British Dominions in International Law.* London: Longman, Green and Co.

Barkan, E. (2000). *The Guilt of Nations: Restitution and negotiating historical injustices.* New York: W. W. Norton.

Barrett, B. (1971). *The Inner Suburbs: The evolution of an industrial area.* Melbourne: Melbourne University Press.

Beer, S. (1993). *To Make a Nation: The rediscovery of American federalism.* Cambridge, Mass: Harvard University Press.

Beiner, R. (ed.) (1995). *Theorizing Citizenship.* Albany: State University of New York Press.

Bell, S. (1997). 'Globalisation, neo-liberalism and the transformation of the Australian state'. *Australian Journal of Political Science* 32 (3), pp. 345–67.

Bell, S. & Head, B. (eds) (1994). *State, Economy and Public Policy.* Melbourne: Oxford University Press.

Beresford, Q. (2000). *Government, Money and Globalisation: Public policy in context.* Sydney: Allen & Unwin.

Berger, S. & Dore, R. (eds) (1996). *National Diversity and Global Capitalism.* Ithaca: Cornell University Press.

Betts, K. (1999). *The Great Divide: Immigration politics in Australia.* Sydney: Duffy & Snellgrove. First published 1988 by Melbourne University Press as *Ideology and Immigration.*

Birrell, R. (1995). *A Nation of Our Own: Citizenship and nation-building in Federation Australia.* Melbourne: Longman.

Birrell, R. (2001). *Federation: The secret story.* Sydney: Duffy & Snellgrove. An earlier version of this book was published in 1995 by Longman as *A Nation of Our Own.*

Blainey, G. (1982). *The Tyranny of Distance: How distance shaped Australia's history.* Melbourne: Macmillan. First published 1968.

Botsman, P. (2000). *The Great Constitutional Swindle: A citizens' view of the Australian Constitution.* Sydney: Pluto Press.

Braudel, F. (1981). *Civilisation and Capitalism, 15th–18th Centuries.* Vol. 1. *The Structures of Everyday Life: The Limits of the Possible.* Tr. Sian Reynolds. New York: Harper and Row.

Braudel, F. (1982). *Civilisation and Capitalism, 15th–18th Centuries.* Vol. 2. *The Wheels of Commerce.* Tr. Sian Reynolds. New York: Harper and Row.

Braudel, F. (1984). *Civilisation and Capitalism, 15th–18th Centuries.* Vol. 3. *The Perspective of the World.* Tr. Sian Reynolds. London: Collins.

Brazil, P. (ed.) (1981). *Opinions of Attorneys-General of the Commonwealth of Australia.* Canberra: Australian Government Publishing Service.

Brett, J. (1998). 'Representing the unrepresented: One Nation and the formation of the Labor party'. In T. Abbott (ed.) *Two Nations: The causes and effects of the rise of the One Nation party in Australia.* Melbourne: Bookman Press, pp. 26–37.

Brigden, J. B., Copland, D. B., Dyason, E. C., Giblin, L. F. and Wickens, K. (1929). *The Australian Tariff: An economic enquiry.* Melbourne: Melbourne University Press.

Bryce, J. (1888). *The American Commonwealth.* Vols 1–3. London: Macmillan.

Buergenthal, T. (1997). 'The normative and institutional evolution of international human rights'. *Human Rights Quarterly* 19 (4), pp. 703–23.

Bull, H. (1997). *The Anarchical Society: A study of order in world politics.* London: Macmillan.

Burchill, S. & Linklater, A. (1996). *Theories of International Relations.* London: Macmillan.

Burgmann, M. & Burgmann, V. (1995). *Green Ban, Red Union: Environmental activism and the New South Wales Builders' Labourer's Federation.* Sydney: University of New South Wales Press.

Burgmann, V. (1993). *Power and Protest: Movements for change in Australian society.* Sydney: Allen & Unwin.

Burgmann, V. (1995). *Revolutionary Industrial Unionism: The Industrial Workers of the World in Australia.* Cambridge: Cambridge University Press.

Butlin, N. (1959). 'Colonial socialism in Australia 1860–1900'. In H. G. J. Aitken (ed.) *The State and Economic Growth.* New York: Social Science Research Council, pp. 26–78.

Camilleri, J. A. & Falk, J. (1992). *The End of Sovereignty?: The politics of a shrinking and fragmenting world.* Aldershot: Edward Elgar.

Capling, A. (2001). *Australia and the Global Trade System: From Havana to Seattle.* Cambridge: Cambridge University Press.

Capling, A. & Galligan, B. (1992). *Beyond the Protective State.* Cambridge: Cambridge University Press.

Capling, A., Considine, M. & Crozier, M. (1998). *Australian Politics in a Global Era.* Melbourne: Addison Wesley Longman.

Carens, J. (2000). *Culture, Citizenship and Community: A contextual exploration of justice as even handedness.* New York: Oxford University Press.

Cassese, A. (1992). 'The General Assembly: Historical perspective 1945–1989'. In P. Alston (ed.) *The United Nations and Human Rights: A critical appraisal.* Oxford: Clarendon Press.

Castells, M. (1996). *The Information Age: Economy, society and culture*. Vol. 1. *The Rise of the Network Society*. Cambridge, Mass: Blackwell Publishers.

Castells, M. (1997). *The Information Age: Economy, society and culture*. Vol. 2. *The Power of Identity*. Cambridge, Mass: Blackwell Publishers.

Castells, M. (1998). *The Information Age: Economy, society and culture*. Vol. 3. *End of Millennium*. Cambridge, Mass: Blackwell Publishers.

Castells, M. (2000). 'Information technology and global capitalism'. In Hutton and Giddens (2000).

Castles, F. (1996). 'On the credulity of capital: or why globalisation does not prevent variation in domestic policy making'. *Australian Quarterly* 68 (2), pp. 65–74.

Castles, S. (2000). 'The future of Australian citizenship in a globalising world'. In K. Rubenstein (ed.) *Individual, Community, Nation: 50 years of Australian citizenship*. Melbourne: Australian Scholarly Publishing, pp. 119–134.

Cathcart, M. (1988). *Defending the National Tuckshop: Australia's secret army intrigue of 1931*. Melbourne: McPhee Gribble/Penguin.

Catley, R. (1996). *Globalising Australian Capitalism*. Cambridge: Cambridge University Press.

Centenary of Federation Advisory Committee (1994). *2001: A report from Australia* (Chair: J. Kirner). Canberra: Australian Government Publishing Service.

Charlesworth, H. (1994). 'The Australian reluctance about rights'. In Alston, P. (ed.) *Towards an Australian Bill of Rights*. Canberra and Sydney: Centre for International and Public Law, Australian National University, and Human Rights and Equal Opportunity Commission, pp. 21–53.

Charlesworth, H. (1995). 'Australia's split personality: implementation of human rights treaty obligations in Australia'. In P. Alston & M. Chiam (eds) *Treaty-making and Australia: Globalisation versus sovereignty?* Sydney: Federation Press in association with the Centre for International and Public Law, Australian National University, pp. 129–40.

Charlesworth, H. (1997), 'International human rights law and Australian federalism'. In B. R. Opeskin & D. R. Rothwell (eds) *International Law and Australian Federalism*. Melbourne: Melbourne University Press, pp. 280–305.

Charlesworth, H. (1998). 'Dangerous liaisons: Globalisation and Australian public law'. *Adelaide Law Review* 20, pp. 57–72.

Chesterman, J. & Galligan, B. (1997). *Citizens without Rights: Aborigines and Australian citizenship*. Cambridge: Cambridge University Press.

Chesterman, J. & Galligan, B. (eds) (1999). *Defining Australian Citizenship: Selected documents*. Melbourne: Melbourne University Press.

Civics Expert Group (1994). *Whereas the People: Civic and citizenship education*. (Chair: S. McIntyre). Canberra: Australian Government Publishing Service.

Clark, C. M. H. (1981). *A History of Australia*. Vol. 5. *The People Make Laws, 1888–1915*, Melbourne: Melbourne University Press.

Collins, H. (1985). 'Political ideology in Australia: The distinctiveness of a Benthamite society'. *Daedalus* 114 (1), pp. 147–169.

Commission on Global Governance (1995). *Our Global Neighborhood: The report of the Commission on Global Governance*. Oxford and New York: Oxford University Press.

Committee to Advise on Australian Immigration Policies (1988). *Immigration: A commitment to Australia* (Chairman: S. Fitzgerald). Canberra: AGPS.

Commonwealth Parliament, Australia, Joint Standing Committee on Migration (1994). *Australians All: Enhancing Australian citizenship*. Canberra: Australian Government Publishing Service.

Commonwealth Parliament, Australia, Joint Standing Committee on Treaties (1999). Report 18, *Multilateral Agreement on Investment: Final report*. Canberra: The Committee.

Commonwealth Parliament, Australia, Senate Legal and Constitutional References Committee (1995). *Trick or Treaty?: Commonwealth power to make and implement treaties*. Canberra: The Parliament of the Commonwealth of Australia.

Cooper, A., Higgott, R. & Nossal, K. (1993). *Relocating Middle Powers: Australia and Canada in a changing world order*. Melbourne: Melbourne University Press.

Corrigan, P. & Sayer, D. (1985). *The Great Arch: State formation as cultural revolution*. Oxford: Basil Blackwell.

Courchene, T. (1993). 'Glocalisation, institutional evolution and the Australian federation'. In B. Galligan (ed.) *Federalism and the Economy: International, national and state issues*. Canberra: Federalism Research Centre, Australian National University, pp. 64–117.

Courchene, T. (ed.) (1997). *The Nation State in a Global/Information Era: Policy challenges*. The Bell Canada Papers on Economic and Public Policy. Kingston, Ontario: John Deutsch Institute for the Study of Economic Policy.

Cox, R. W. (1992). 'Multilateralism and world order'. *Review of International Studies* 18, pp. 161–180.

Crisp, L. F. (1990). *Federation Fathers*. Ed. J. Hart. Melbourne: Melbourne University Press.

Cuffley, P. (1983). *Cottage Gardens in Australia*. Canterbury, Victoria: Five Mile Press.

Curtin, J. (1945). Broadcast to the United States, 14 March 1942 in H. V. Evatt *Foreign Policy of Australia*. Sydney: Angus & Robertson, pp. 42–46.

Davidson, A. (1991). *The Invisible State: The Formation of the Australian State 1788–1901*. Cambridge: Cambridge University Press.

Davidson, A. (1997). *From Subject to Citizen: Australian citizenship in the twentieth century*. Cambridge: Cambridge University Press.

Davidson, A. & Weekley, K. (eds) (1999). *Globalization and Citizenship in the Asia-Pacific*. London: Macmillan.

Davis, G. & Keating, M. (eds) (2000). *The Future of Governance: Policy choices*. St. Leonards, NSW: Allen & Unwin.

de Garis, B. K. (1969). 'The Colonial Office and the Commonwealth Constitution Bill'. In A. W. Martin (ed.) *Essays in Federation*. Melbourne: Melbourne University Press, pp. 94–121.

de Serville, P. (1980). *Port Phillip Gentlemen and Good Society before the Gold Rushes*. Melbourne: Oxford University Press.

Deakin, A. (1968). *Federated Australia: Selections from letters to the Morning Post 1900–1910*. Ed. J. A. La Nauze. Melbourne: Melbourne University Press.

Department of Foreign Affairs and Trade, Australia (1997). *In the National Interest: Australia's foreign and trade policy White Paper*. Canberra: Department of Foreign Affairs and Trade.

Department of Foreign Affairs and Trade, Australia (1999). *Composition of Australian Trade, 1998–1999*. Canberra: Department of Foreign Affairs and Trade.

DFAT *see* Department of Foreign Affairs and Trade, Australia.

Dicey, A. V. (1982). *Introduction to the Study of the Law of the Constitution.* Indianapolis: Liberty Fund. First published in 1885.

Doeker, G. (1966). *The Treaty-Making Power in the Commonwealth of Australia.* The Hague: Martinus Nijhoff.

Dow, G. (1974). *Samuel Terry: The Botany Bay Rothschild.* Sydney: Sydney University Press.

Downer, A. (1999). Statement to UN General Assembly. New York.

Downer, A. (2000). 'Upholding the "sword of justice": International law and the maintenance of international peace and security'. Speech to Joint Meeting of the Australian and New Zealand Society of International Law (ANZSIL) and the American Society of International Law (ASIL), Canberra, 28 June.

Dozier, R. R. (1983). *For King, Constitution and Country: The English Loyalists and the French Revolution.* Lexington: University of Kentucky Press.

Edwards, M. (2001). *Social Policy, Public Policy: From problem to practice.* Sydney: Allen & Unwin.

Eggleston, F. W. (1932). *State Socialism in Victoria.* London: P. S. King & Son.

Eggleston, F. W. (1933). 'Australia and the Empire'. In J. Holland Rose, A. P. Newton, E. A. Benians (eds) *The Cambridge History of the British Empire.* Vol. 7, Part 1, Chapter XVIII. Cambridge: Cambridge University Press.

Eggleston, F. W. (1946). Foreword in H. V. Evatt, *Australia in World Affairs.* Sydney: Angus & Robertson.

Eggleston, F. W. (1957). *Reflections on Australian Foreign Policy.* Melbourne: F. W. Cheshire.

Ehrenberg, J. (1999). *Civil Society: The critical history of an idea.* New York: New York University Press.

Evans, G. & Grant, B. (1993). *Australia's Foreign Relations: in the world of the 1990s,* 2nd edn. Melbourne: Melbourne University Press. First published 1991.

Evans, P. B., Jacobson, H. K. & Putnam, R. D. (eds) (1993). *Doubled-edged Diplomacy: International bargaining and domestic politics.* Berkeley: University of California Press.

Evatt, H. V. (1945). *Foreign Policy of Australia: Speeches by the Rt. Hon. H. V. Evatt.* Sydney: Angus & Robertson.

Evatt, H. V. (1946). *Australia in World Affairs.* Sydney: Angus & Robertson.

Federation Debates, Sydney (1891). *Official Report of the National Australasian Convention Debates.* Sydney: G. S. Chapman, Acting Government Printer.

Federation Debates, Adelaide (1897). *Official Report of the National Australasian Convention Debates.* Adelaide: C. E. Bristow, Government Printer.

Federation Debates, Sydney (1897). *Official Record of the Debates of the Australasian Federal Convention.* Sydney: W. A. Gullick, Government Printer.

Federation Debates, Melbourne (1898). *Official Record of the Debates of the Australasian Federal Convention.* 2 vols. Melbourne: Government Printer.

Fischer, G. (1989). *Enemy Aliens: Internment and the homefront experience in Australia, 1914–20.* St Lucia: University of Queensland Press.

Fukuyama, F. (1991). *The End of History and the Last Man.* New York: Free Press.

Fukuyama, F. (1995). *Trust: The social virtues and the creation of prosperity.* Ringwood: Penguin Books.

Galligan, B. (1989). *Utah and Queensland Coal.* St Lucia: University of Queensland Press.

Galligan, B. (ed.) (1993). *Federalism and the Economy: International, national and state Issues*. Canberra: Federalism Research Centre, Australian National University.

Galligan, B. (1995). *A Federal Republic: Australia's constitutional system of government*. Cambridge: Cambridge University Press.

Galligan, B. (1998). 'Reconstructing Australian citizenship'. *Quadrant* 42 (11), pp. 11–18.

Galligan, B. (1999). 'Let the people vote'. *Quadrant* 43 (10), pp. 46–52.

Galligan, B. & Rimmer, B. (1997). 'The political dimensions of international law in Australia'. In B. R. Opeskin & D. R. Rothwell (eds) *International Law and Australian Federalism*. Melbourne: Melbourne University Press, pp. 316–321.

Galligan, B. & Roberts, W. (2000). 'By the People for the People: The role of Mechanics' Institutes in local civics from Colonialism to Federation'. In *Rediscovering Mechanics' Institutes*. Melbourne: Local Government Division, Department of Infrastructure, pp. 67–78.

Geertz, C. (1995). *After the Fact: Two countries, four decades, one anthropologist*. Cambridge, Mass: Harvard University Press

Giddens, A. (1990). *The Consequences of Modernity*. Cambridge, Mass: Polity Press.

Giddens, A. (1998). *The Third Way: The renewal of social democracy*. Malden, Mass: Polity Press.

Giddens, A. (2000). *The Third Way and Its Critics*. Malden, Mass: Polity Press.

Gill, A. (1997). *Orphans of the Empire: The shocking story of child migration to Australia*. Sydney: Millennium Books.

Glazer, N. (1997). *We Are All Multiculturalists Now*. Cambridge, Mass: Harvard University Press.

Goldfinch, S. (2000). *Remaking New Zealand and Australian Economic Policy*. Wellington: Victoria University Press.

Goldman, K. (1996). 'International relations: An overview'. In R. E. Goodin & H. Klingemann (eds) *A New Handbook of Political Science*. Oxford: Oxford University Press, pp. 401–27.

Goodin, R. E. & Klingemann, H. (eds) (1996). *A New Handbook of Political Science*. Oxford: Oxford University Press.

Greenwood, G. & Grimshaw, C. (1977). *Documents on Australian International Affairs 1901–1918*. Melbourne: Thomas Nelson.

Gregory, R. G. (1995). *The Macro Economy and the Growth of Ghettos and Urban Poverty of Australia*. Canberra: Centre for Economic Policy Research, Australian National University.

Gullett, H. S. (1993). 'Australia in the World War: Military'. In *The Cambridge History of the British Empire*. Vol. 7, Part 1, 1933, pp. 546–66.

Gyngell, A. & Wesley, M. (2000). 'Interweaving of foreign and domestic policy: International policy'. In G. Davis & M. Keating (eds) *The Future of Governance: Policy choices*. St. Leonards, NSW: Allen & Unwin.

Habermas, J. (1995). 'Citizenship and National Identity: Some reflections on the future of Europe'. In R. Beiner (ed.) *Theorizing Citizenship*. Albany: State University of New York Press, pp. 255–81.

Hainsworth, D. (ed.) (1968). *Builders and Adventurers: The traders and the emergence of the colony, 1788–1821*. Melbourne: Cassell Australia.

Hainsworth, D. (1971). *The Sydney Traders: Simeon Lord and his contemporaries 1788–1821*. Melbourne: Cassell Australia.

Hancock, W. K. (1961). *Australia*. Brisbane: Jacaranda Press. First published 1930.

Hasluck, N. (1998). 'Deconstructing the High Court'. *Quadrant* 42 (7&8), pp. 12–20.

Hasluck, N. (1999). *Our Man*. Ringwood: Penguin.

Hayden, W. (1986). 'Human rights: Vision and reality'. Address to the Catholic Commission for Justice and Peace, Canberra, 2 May.

Hazareesingh, S. (1998). *From Subject to Citizen: The Second Empire and the emergence of modern French democracy*. Princeton: Princeton University Press.

Held, D. (1995). *Democracy and the Global Order: From the modern state to cosmopolitan governance*. Cambridge: Polity Press.

Held, D. (1998). 'Democracy and Globalisation'. In Archibugi 1998.

Higgott, R. (1989). 'The ascendancy of the economic dimension in Australian-American relations'. In J. Ravenhill (ed.) *No Longer an American Lake?* St. Leonards, NSW: Allen & Unwin, pp. 132–68.

Higgott, R. (1991). 'The politics of Australia's international economic relations: Adjustment and two-level games'. *Australian Journal of Political Science* 26, pp. 2–28.

Hirst, J. (1973). *Adelaide and the Country 1870–1917: Their social and political relationship*. Melbourne: Melbourne University Press.

Hirst, J. (1988). *The Strange Birth of Colonial Democracy: New South Wales, 1848–1884*. Sydney: Allen & Unwin.

Hirst, J. (2000). *The Sentimental Nation: The making of the Australian Commonwealth*. Melbourne: Oxford University Press.

Hirst, P. & Thompson, G. (1996). *Globalization in Question: The international economy and the possibilities of governance*. London: Polity Press.

Hobsbawm, E. (1962). *The Age of Revolution: Europe 1789–1848*. London: Weidenfeld & Nicolson.

Holland, K., Morton, F. & Galligan, B. (eds) (1996). *Federalism and the Environment: Environmental policymaking in Australia, Canada and the United States*. Westport, Conn.: Greenwood Press.

Holmes, S. (1998). 'What Russia teaches us now'. *The American Prospect* 33, July–August, 1997, pp. 30–39.

Holton, R. (1998). *Globalisation and the Nation State*. London: Macmillan.

Hudson, W. (2000). 'Differential citizenship'. In W. Hudson and J. Kane (eds) *Rethinking Australian Citizenship*. Cambridge: Cambridge University Press, pp. 15–25.

Hudson, W. J. (1993). *Australia and the New World Order: Evatt at San Francisco 1945*. Canberra: Australian Foreign Policy Publications Program, Australian National University.

Hudson, W. & Bolton, G. (eds) (1997). *Creating Australia: Changing Australian history*. Sydney: Allen & Unwin.

Hudson, W. & Kane, J. (eds) (2000). *Rethinking Australian Citizenship*. Cambridge: Cambridge University Press.

Huntington, S. P. (1997). *The Clash of Civilisations: Remaking of World Order*. New York: Simon & Schuster.

Hutchings, K. (1999). 'Political theory and cosmopolitan citizenship'. In K. Hutchings & R. Danreuther (eds) *Cosmopolitan Citizenship*. London: Macmillan Press, pp. 3–32.

Hutchings, K. & Danreuther, R. (eds) (1999). *Cosmopolitan Citizenship*. London: Macmillan.

Hutton, W. (1996). *The State We're In*. London: Vintage.

Hutton, W. (1998). *The Stakeholding Society: Writings on politics and economics*. Ed. D. Goldblatt. Malden, Mass: Polity Press.

Hutton, W. & Giddens, A. (eds) (2000). *On the Edge: Living with Global Capitalism*. London: Jonathan Cape.

Inglis, K. (1981). 'Young Australia 1870–1900: The idea and the reality'. In G. Featherstone (ed.) *The Colonial Child*. Melbourne: Royal Historical Society of Victoria, pp. 1–23.

Inglis, K. (1998). *Sacred Places: War memorials on the Australian landscape*. Melbourne: Miegunyah Press at Melbourne University Press.

Irving, H. (1997). *To Constitute a Nation: A cultural history of Australia's Constitution*. Cambridge: Cambridge University Press.

Irving, H. (ed.) (1999). *The Centenary Companion to Australian Federation*. Cambridge: Cambridge University Press.

Janoski, T. (1998). *Citizenship and Civil Society: A framework of rights and obligations in liberal, traditional and social democratic regimes*. Cambridge: Cambridge University Press.

Joyce, R. B. (1984). *Samuel Walker Griffith*. St Lucia: University of Queensland Press.

Jupp J. (1997) 'Immigration and national identity'. In G. Stokes (ed.) *The Politics of Identity in Australia*. Melbourne: Cambridge University Press.

Kalantzis, M. (2000). 'Multicultural citizenship'. In W. Hudson & J. Kane (eds) *Rethinking Australian Citizenship*. Cambridge: Cambridge University Press, pp. 99–110.

Kaplan, G. (1996). *The Meagre Harvest: The Australian Women's Movement 1950s–1990s*. Sydney: Allen & Unwin.

Keating, P. (2000). *Awakening: Australia faces the Asia Pacific*. Melbourne: Macmillan.

Keith, A. B. (ed.) (1918). *Selected Speeches and Documents on British Colonial Policy 1763–1917*. Vols I & II. London: Oxford University Press.

Keith, A. B. (1933). *The Constitutional Law of the British Dominions*. London: Macmillan.

Keith, A. B. (1961). *Speeches and Documents on the British Dominions 1918–1931: From self-government to national sovereignty*. Oxford: Oxford University Press. First published 1932.

Kelly, P. (1994). *The End of Certainty: Power, politics and business in Australia*. Sydney: Allen & Unwin. First published 1992.

Keohane, R. & Nye, J. S. (1977). *Power and Interdependence: World politics in transition*. Boston: Little, Brown.

Keohane, R. (1996). 'International relations, old and new'. In R. E. Goodin and H. Klingemann (eds) *A New Handbook of Political Science*. Oxford: Oxford University Press, pp. 462–76.

Kewley, T. H. (1980). *Australian Social Security Today: Major developments from 1900 to 1978*. Sydney: Sydney University Press.

King, J. (1989). *The Battle for the Bicentenary*. Sydney: Hutchinson Australia.

Kirby, M. (1995). 'The role of international standards in Australian courts'. In P. Alston & M. Chiam (eds) *Treaty-Making and Australia: Globalisation versus sovereignty?*. Sydney: Federation Press in association with the Centre for International and Public Law, Australian National University, pp. 83–84.

Kirby, M. (2000). 'International law – Down in the engine room'. Paper presented to the ANZSIL and ASIL joint conference, Sydney.

Knightley, P. (2000). *Australia: A biography of a nation*. London: Jonathan Cape.

Kobal, I. (1999). *The Snowy: Cradle of New Australia*. Rydalmere, NSW: I. Kobal.

Krasner, S. (1999). *Sovereignty: Organised hypocrisy*. Princeton: Princeton University Press.

Kunz, E. (1988). *Displaced Persons: Calwell's New Australians*. Sydney: Australian National University Press.

Kymlicka, W. & Norman, W. (1995). 'Return of the citizen: A survey of recent work on citizenship'. In R. Beiner (ed.) *Theorizing Citizenship*. Albany: State University of New York Press, pp. 283–322.

La Nauze, J. A. (1972). *The Making of the Australian Constitution*. Melbourne: Melbourne University Press.

Latham, J. G. (1929). *Australia and the British Commonwealth*. London: Macmillan.

Latham, M. (1998). *Civilising Global Capital: New thinking for Australian Labor*. Sydney: Allen & Unwin.

Lillich, R. B. & Hannum, H. (1995). *International Human Rights: Documentary supplement*. Boston: Little, Brown.

Linklater, A. (1998). 'Citizenship and sovereignty in the post-Westphalian state'. In D. Archibugi et. al. (eds) *Re-imagining Political Community: Studies in cosmopolitan democracy*, pp. 113–37.

Linklater, A. (1999). 'Cosmopolitan citizenship'. In K. Hutchings & R. Danreuther (eds) *Cosmopolitan Citizenship*. London: Macmillan Press, pp. 35–59.

Livingston, K. (1996). *The Wired Nation Continent: The communication revolution and federating Australia*. Melbourne: Oxford University Press.

Loveday, P, Martin, A. W. & Parker, R. S. (1977). *The Emergence of the Australian Party System*. Sydney: Hale & Iremonger.

Lynch, G. & Galligan, B. (1996). 'Environmental policymaking in Australia: The role of the courts'. In K. Holland, F. Morton & B. Galligan (eds) *Federalism and the Environment*. Westport, Conn.: Greenwood Press, pp. 205–25.

MacCormick, N. (1993). 'Beyond the Sovereign State'. *Modern Law Review* 56, pp. 1–18.

Macintyre, S. (1990). *The Oxford History of Australia, Volume 4, 1901–1942, The Succeeding Age*. Melbourne: Oxford University Press.

Macintyre, S. (1999). *Reds: The Communist Party of Australia from origins to illegality*. Sydney: Allen & Unwin.

Macintyre, S. (2000). 'The fortunes of Federation'. In D. Headon and J. Williams (eds) *Makers of Miracles: The cast of the Federation story*. Melbourne: Melbourne University Press, pp. 3–20.

Macmahon Ball, W. (1945). Introduction to H. V. Evatt, *Foreign Policy of Australia: Speeches by the Rt. Hon. H. V. Evatt*. Sydney: Angus & Robertson.

Marshall, T. H. (1992). 'Citizenship and social class'. In T. H. Marshall and T. Bottomore (eds) *Citizenship and Social Class*. London & Concord, Mass: Pluto Press.

Martin, A. W. (ed.) (1969). *Essays in Federation*. Melbourne: Melbourne University Press.

Martin, G. (1986). *Bunyip Aristocracy: The New South Wales constitution debate of 1853 and hereditary institutions in the British colonies*. Sydney: Croom Helm.

Mason, A. (1988). 'The Australian Constitution 1901–1988'. *Australian Law Journal* 62, pp. 752–760.

McDermott, P. (1990). 'External affairs and treaties – the founding fathers' perspective'. *University of Queensland Law Journal* 16 (1), pp. 123–36.

McDougall, D. (1998). *Australian Foreign Relations: Contemporary perspectives.* South Melbourne: Longman.

McKinlay, B. (1970). *The First Royal Tour, 1867–1868.* Adelaide: Rigby.

McMinn W. G. (1994). *Nationalism and Federalism in Australia.* Melbourne: Oxford University Press.

Meaney, N. (1985). *Australia and the World: A documentary history from the 1870s to the 1970s.* Melbourne: Longman Cheshire.

Menzies, R. (1936). Response to Owen Dixon, 'The Statute of Westminster 1931'. *Australian Law Journal* 10 Supplement, pp. 96–112.

Menzies, R. (1967). *Central Power in the Australian Commonwealth: An examination of the growth of Commonwealth power in the Australian Federation.* Charlottesville: University Press of Virginia.

Merriam, C. E. (1931). *The Making of Citizens: A comparative study of methods of civic training.* Chicago: University of Chicago Press.

Metin, A. (1977). *Socialism without Doctrine.* Tr. Russell Ward. Chippendale, NSW: Alternative Publishing Service Cooperative. First published 1901.

Mill, J. S. (1972). *Representative Government.* London: Dent & Sons. First published 1861.

Millar, T. B. (1978). *Australia in Peace and War: External relations, 1788–1977.* Canberra: Australian National University Press.

Miller, D. (1999). 'Bounded citizenship'. In K. Hutchings & R. Danreuther (eds) *Cosmopolitan Citizenship.* London: Macmillan Press, pp. 60–79.

Moore, W. Harrison (1900). 'The Commonwealth of Australia Bill'. *Law Quarterly Review* 16, pp. 35–43.

Moore, W. Harrison (1926). 'The Dominions and Treaties'. *Journal of Comparative Legislation and International Law* 8, pp. 21–37.

Morris, J. (1968). *Pax Britannica: The climax of an empire.* London: Faber.

Murdoch, W. (1911). *The Struggle for Freedom* 6th edn. Melbourne: Whitcombe and Tombs.

Nadel, G. (1957). *Australia's Colonial Culture: Ideas, men and institutions in mid-nineteenth century eastern Australia.* Melbourne: Cheshire.

Nash, S. (2000). 'Human Rights Law Update'. *New Law Journal* 150, No. 6939, June 2000, pp. 859–60.

National Multicultural Advisory Council (1999). *Australian Multiculturalism for a New Century: Towards inclusiveness* (Chairman: N. Roach). Canberra: National Multicultural Advisory Council.

Nieuwenhuysen, J. & Fincher, R. (eds) (1998). *Australian Poverty: Then and now.* Melbourne: Melbourne University Press.

Nord, P. (1995). *The Republican Moment: Struggles for democracy in nineteenth century France.* Cambridge, Mass: Harvard University Press.

O'Brien, R., Goetz, A., Scholte, J. & Williams, M. (eds) (2000). *Contesting Global Governance: Multilateral economic institutions and global social movements.* Cambridge: Cambridge University Press.

O'Farrell, P. (1986). *The Irish in Australia.* Sydney: University of New South Wales Press.

Oldfield, A. (1992). *Woman Suffrage in Australia: A gift or a struggle?* Cambridge: Cambridge University Press.

Olds, M. (ed.) (1995). *Australia Through Time: 127 years of Australian history*. Sydney: Mynah Press.

Opeskin, B. R. & Rothwell, D. R. (eds) (1997). *International Law and Australian Federalism*. Melbourne: Melbourne University Press.

Osborne, D. & Gaebler, T. (1992). *Reinventing Government: How the entrepreneurial spirit is transforming the public sector*. Reading, Mass: Addison-Wesley.

Panich, C. (1988). *Sanctuary?: Remembering post-war immigration*. Sydney: Allen & Unwin.

Patapan, H. (1996). 'Rewriting Australian liberalism: The High Court's jurisprudence of rights'. *Australian Journal of Political Science* 31 (2), pp. 225–242.

Paterson, M. (1999). 'Globalisation, ecology and resistance'. *New Political Economy* 4 (1), pp. 129–45.

Polanyi, K. (1985). *The Great Transformation*. Boston: Beacon Press. First published in 1944.

Putnam, R. (1993). *Making Democracy Work: Civic traditions in modern Italy*. Princeton: Princeton University Press.

Putnam, R. (2000). *Bowling Alone: The collapse and revival of American community*. New York: Simon & Schuster.

Quick, J. & Garran, R. (1976). *The Annotated Constitution of the Australian Commonwealth*. Sydney: Legal Books. First published 1901.

Randall, S. & Gibbins, R. (eds) (1994). *Federalism and the New World Order*. Calgary: University of Calgary Press.

Ravenhill, J. (1989). 'Political turbulence in the South Pacific'. In J. Ravenhill (ed.) *No Longer an American Lake?*. Sydney: Allen & Unwin, pp. 1–40.

Ravenhill, J. (1994). 'Australia and the global economy'. In S. Bell & B. Head (eds) *State, Economy and Public Policy in Australia*. Melbourne: Oxford University Press.

Reeves, W. P. (1969). *State Experiments in Australia and New Zealand*. South Melbourne: Macmillan. First published Grant Richards, London, 1902.

Reich, S. (1999). Review of *The Myth of the Powerless State* by Linda Weiss, Polity Press, 1998. In *New Political Economy* 4 (2), pp. 305–10.

Renouf, A. (1979). *The Frightened Country*. South Melbourne: Macmillan.

Reynolds, H. (1982). *The Other Side of the Frontier: Aboriginal resistance to the European invasion of Australia*. Ringwood: Penguin.

Reynolds, H. (1996). *Frontiers: Aborigines, settlers and land*. Sydney: Allen & Unwin. First published 1987.

Reynolds, H. (1998). *The Whispering in Our Hearts*. Sydney: Allen & Unwin.

Reynolds, J. (1958). 'A. I. Clark's American sympathies and his influence on the Australian federation'. *Australian Law Journal*, Vol. 32, pp. 67–74.

Roberts, W. (1999). *Getting on and Getting By: Social supports in the Australian urban community of Hotham, 1860–1890*. PhD Thesis, University of Melbourne.

Roberts, W. (1999). 'Doing one's duty: Voluntary governance in nineteenth-century Australia'. In *Proceedings of the 1999 Conference of the Australasian Political Studies Association*, Department of Government, University of Sydney, 1999, vol. 3, pp. 683–94.

Roberts, W. (2001). 'The politics of Federation', *Melbourne Journal of Politics*, 27 (forthcoming).

Roe, M. (1965). *Quest for Authority in Eastern Australia, 1835–1851*. Melbourne: Melbourne University Press in association with the Australian National University.

Roe, M. (1995). *Australia, Britain and Migration 1915–1940: A study of dark hope*. Cambridge: Cambridge University Press.

Rousseau, J-J. (1968). *The Social Contract*. Tr. M. Cranston. Harmondsworth: Penguin. First published 1762.

Royal Commission on the Constitution, Commonwealth of Australia (1929). *Report of the Royal Commission on the Constitution*. Canberra: Government Printer.

Royal Institute of International Affairs (1937). *The British Empire: A report on its structure and problems*. Oxford: Oxford University Press.

Rubenstein, K. (2000). 'The High Court of Australia and the legal dimensions of Australian citizenship'. In K. Rubenstein (ed.) *Individual, Community, Nation: Fifty years of Australian citizenship*. Melbourne: Australian Scholarly Publishing, pp. 21–32.

Rubenstein, K. (ed.) (2000). *Individual, Community, Nation: Fifty years of Australian citizenship*. Melbourne: Australian Scholarly Publishing.

Russell, I. (1992). 'Australia's Human Rights Policy: From Evatt to Evans'. In I. Russell, P. Van Ness & B. Chua, *Australia's Human Rights Diplomacy*. Canberra: Australian Foreign Policy Publications Program, Australian National University, pp. 3–48.

Russell, I., Van Ness, P. & Chua, B. (1992). *Australia's Human Rights Diplomacy*. Canberra: Australian Foreign Policy Publications Program, Australian National University.

Russell, P. (1993). *Constitutional Odyssey: Can Canadians become a sovereign people?* 2nd edn. Toronto: University of Toronto Press.

Safran, W. (1997). 'Citizenship and nationality in democratic systems: Approaches to defining and acquiring membership in the political community'. *International Political Science Review* 18 (3), pp. 313–335.

Sassens, S. (1999). *Guests and Aliens*. New York: Norton.

Saul, J. R. (1997). *The Unconscious Civilisation*. Ringwood: Penguin.

Saunders, C. (1995). 'Articles of faith or lucky breaks? The Constitutional Law of International Agreements in Australia'. *Sydney Law Review* 17, pp. 150–76.

Saunders, M. (1986). *The Australian Peace Movement: A short history*. Canberra: Peace Research Centre, Australian National University.

Sawer, G. (1956). *Australian Federal Politics and Law, 1901–1929*. Melbourne: Melbourne University Press.

Sawer, G. (1961). Opinion. Appendix III to the *Report from the Select Committee on Voting Rights of Aborigines*, Part 1. Canberra: Commonwealth Parliamentary Papers. Vol. 2.

Schuck, P. (2000). 'Citizenship in federal systems'. In K. Rubenstein (ed.) *Individual, Community, Nation: Fifty years of Australian citizenship*, pp. 150–69.

Schuck, P. H. (1998). *Citizens, Strangers and In-betweens: Essays on immigration and citizenship*. Boulder, Colo: Westview Press.

Scott, A. J. (1998). *Regions and the World Economy: The coming shape of global production, competition and political order*. New York: Oxford University Press.

Scott, A. J., Agnew, J., Soja, E.W. & Storper, M. (1999). 'Global city-regions'. Theme paper prepared for the conference on Global City-Regions, UCLA, 21–23 October.

Scott, E. (1933). 'Australia in the World War: Political'. In J. Holland Rose, A. P. Newton, E. A. Benians (eds) *The Cambridge History of the British Empire*. Vol. 7, Part 1. Cambridge: Cambridge University Press, pp. 566–85.

Selznick, P. (1992). *The Moral Commonwealth: Social theory and the promise of community*. Berkeley: University of California Press.

Sen, A. (1992). *Inequality Re-examined*. Cambridge, Mass: Harvard University Press.

Sennett, R. (1998). *The Corrosion of Character: The personal consequences of work in the New Capitalism*. New York: Norton.

Serle, G. (1971). *The Rush to be Rich: A history of the Colony of Victoria 1883–89*. Melbourne: Melbourne University Press.

Serle, G. (1977). *The Golden Age: A history of the Colony of Victoria 1851–1861*. Melbourne: Melbourne University Press.

Smith, G., Cox, D. & Burchill, S. (1996). *Australia in the World: An introduction to Australian foreign policy*. Melbourne: Oxford University Press.

Smyth, P. & Cass, B. (1998). *Contesting the Australian Way: States, markets and civil society*. Cambridge: Cambridge University Press.

Steven, M. (1965). *Merchant Campbell 1769–1846: A study in colony trade*. Melbourne: Oxford University Press.

Stretton, H. (1994). *Public Goods, Public Enterprise, Public Choice: Theoretical formulations of the contemporary attack on government*. London: Macmillan.

Tanner, L. (1999). *Open Australia*. Sydney: Pluto Press.

Teeple, G. (1995). *Globalization and the Decline of Social Reform*. Atlantic Highlands, NJ: Humanities Press.

Tenbensel, T. (1996). 'International human rights conventions and Australian political debates: issues raised by the Toonen Case'. *Australian Journal of Political Science* 31 (1), pp. 7–23.

Thompson, M. M. H. (1996). *The First Election: The New South Wales Legislative Council Election of 1843*. Goulburn, NSW: Alpha Desktop Publishing.

Thornton, A. P. (1963). *Doctrines of Imperialism*. New York: John Wiley.

Torpey, J. (2000). *The Invention of the Passport: Surveillance, citizenship and the state*. Cambridge: Cambridge University Press.

Triggs, G. (1982). 'Australia's ratification of the international covenant on civil and political rights: Endorsement or repudiation?'. *International and Comparative Law Quarterly* 31, pp. 278–306.

Trollope, A. (1967). *Australia*. St Lucia: University of Queensland Press. First published 1873.

Turnbull, M. (1999). *Fighting for the Republic: The ultimate insider's account*. Melbourne: Hardie Grant.

Twomey, A. (1995). 'Procedure and practice of entering and implementing treaties'. Parliamentary Research Service Background Paper No. 27, Department of Parliamentary Library.

Wade, R. (1996). 'Globalization and its limits: Reports of the death of the national economy are greatly exaggerated'. In S. Berger & R. Dore (eds) *National Diversity and Global Capitalism*. Ithaca: Cornell University Press, pp. 60–88.

Walker, D. (1997). 'Australia as Asia'. In W. Hudson & G. Bolton (eds) *Creating Australia: Changing Australian history*, pp. 131–41.

Walker E. A. (1943). *The British Empire: Its structure and spirit*. Royal Institute of Commonwealth Affairs and Oxford University Press.

Walker, R. B. (1982). 'Funds across the Sea: Philanthropic assistance from Australia to the United Kingdom in the nineteenth century'. *Journal of the Royal Australian Historical Society* 68, Part 2, pp. 107–21.

Wallerstein, I. (1974). *The Modern World System I. Capitalist Agriculture and the Origins of the European World-Economy in the Sixteenth Century*. London: Academic Press.

Wallerstein, I. (1980). *The Modern World System II. Merchantilism and the Consolidation of the European World-Economy, 1600–1750*. London: Academic Press.

Walzer, M. (1995). 'The concept of Civil Society'. In M. Walzer (ed.) *Toward a Global Civil Society*. Providence: Bergahn Books, pp. 7–28.

Walzer, M. (ed.) (1995). *Toward a Global Civil Society*. Providence: Bergahn Books.

Waters, M. (1995). 'Globalisation and the social construction of rights'. Symposium: Human Rights and the Sociological Project. *Australia and New Zealand Journal of Sociology* 31 (2), pp. 29–36.

Weiss, L. (1998). *The Myth of the Powerless State: Governing the economy in a global era*. Cambridge: Polity Press.

Wheare, K. C. (1953). *The Statute of Westminster and Dominion Status*. 5th edn. London: Oxford University Press. First published in 1938.

Whitlam, E. G. (1974). Address to UN General Assembly. In *Australian Foreign Affairs Review* 45.

Williams, D. (2000*a*). 'International Law and Responsible Engagement'. Canberra: ANZSIL-ASIL Conference Keynote Address, 29 June.

Williams, D. (2000*b*). 'Globalisation and Law Reform: Cooperation through technology'. Perth: Speech to Australasian Commonwealth Law Reform Agencies Conference.

Williams, G. (1999). *Human Rights under the Australian Constitution*. Melbourne: Oxford University Press.

Winter, G. (1993). *The Hand of Friendship: A history of the Good Neighbour Council of Tasmania, 1949–1992*. Hobart: Good Neighbour Council of Tasmania.

Wiseman, J. (1998). *Global Nation? Australia and the politics of globalisation*. Cambridge: Cambridge University Press.

Zines, L. (1992). *The High Court and the Constitution*. 3rd edn. Melbourne, Butterworths. First published 1981.

Index